PRESIDENTS WHO SHAPED THE AMERICAN WEST

PRESIDENTS WHO SHAPED THE AMERICAN WEST

GLENDA RILEY and RICHARD W. ETULAIN

UNIVERSITY OF OKLAHOMA PRESS : NORMAN

LIBRARY OF CONGRESS CATALOGING-IN-PUBLICATION DATA

Names: Riley, Glenda, 1938– author. | Etulain, Richard W., author.
  Title: Presidents who shaped the American West / Glenda Riley and Richard W. Etulain.
  Description: Norman, OK : University of Oklahoma Press, [2018] | Includes index.
  Identifiers: LCCN 2017024249 | ISBN 978-0-8061-5907-2 (pbk. : alk. paper)
  Subjects: LCSH: Presidents—United States. | West (U.S.)—History.
  Classification: LCC E176.1 .G45 2018 | DDC 978—dc23
  LC record available at https://lccn.loc.gov/2017024249

For my husband, Allan "Al" E. Yeomans, a partner of great distinction
GR

For Joyce Etulain, my mainstay for more than fifty years
RWE

CONTENTS

ILLUSTRATIONS

All images courtesy of the Library of Congress, Washington, D.C.

PRESIDENTS WHO SHAPED THE AMERICAN WEST

INTRODUCTION

Almost anyone can describe the historical American presidency and get some agreement from others, but it is unlikely that a group of folks, whether laypeople or scholars, could easily commit to a definition of the American West, past or present. The West is difficult to define because its edge, often called a frontier, moved westward with population growth. As a result, there came into being the "old" West, the frontiers of Tennessee, Kentucky, and Indiana. Added to this in 1803 was the Louisiana Territory, located west of the Appalachian Mountains and the Mississippi River. Eventually, in a less predictable fashion, came the frontier of Nebraska and the Dakotas; the far-distant frontiers of California and the Pacific Northwest; and later both Hawaii and Alaska, neither contiguous parts of the United States. For the purposes of this book, we have defined the West comprehensively as the trans-Mississippi region, reaching from the Great River to the Pacific coast, as well as to Hawaii and Alaska, and dating from the Louisiana Purchase of 1803 to the present.

Using these parameters, we have brought selected presidents together with the West in hopes of achieving two objectives: one is to show how presidential decisions shaped the West and helped make it what it is today; the second is to better understand the presidents through their interactions with the American West. Ten presidents who had a clear influence—whether positive or negative—on the region are examined in individual chapters consisting of short biographies, coverage of that president's relations with the West, and an assessment of his actions and policies affecting the West. The ten presidents so analyzed are Thomas Jefferson, Andrew Jackson, James K. Polk, Abraham Lincoln, and Theodore Roosevelt—spanning the first one hundred–plus years of presidential history—and Franklin D. Roosevelt, Dwight D. Eisenhower, Lyndon Baines Johnson, James E. "Jimmy" Carter Jr., and Ronald Reagan—taking the story through the twentieth century. Because the West has now become a constant part of a president's agenda, a final overview brings the narrative up to date with George H. W. Bush, William J. "Bill" Clinton, George W. Bush, and Barack H. Obama.

Even though the presidency itself changed during these years and western issues varied, the essays reveal an amazing similarity of themes. Not all of these are developed in every essay, but they frequently recur, weaving intricate historical threads tying together the American presidency and the American West.

GROWING THE WEST

One important idea is the physical creation of the West as a region of the United States. It is not surprising that the young United States, an ambitious nation interested in gaining influence and power, would seek opportunities to expand its western boundaries. During the early nineteenth century, President Thomas Jefferson initiated the quest for land with the Louisiana Purchase of 1803, which roughly doubled the size of the existing United States and effectively created a region called the American West. Later, as a result of the Mexican-American War, President James K. Polk signed an 1848 treaty that resulted in the country's third-largest acquisition. Twenty years later, in 1867, the United States purchased Alaska from Russia and in 1898 annexed the islands of Hawaii.

Despite the distance in time, the motives for purchasing Louisiana in 1803, taking part of Mexico in 1848, and annexing Alaska in 1867 and Hawaii in 1898 stemmed from the same concerns. These places offered huge areas of land, but their entry into the United States was also designed to remove the threat to security and trade posed by foreign powers on or near American boundaries. In the case of the Louisiana Purchase, this meant France, Spain, and England. The Mexican cession removed interference by Spain and Mexico in American holdings. In the case of Alaska and Hawaii, annexation posed barriers to possible Russian and British interruptions of American commerce.

Well into the twentieth century, President Dwight D. Eisenhower finally brought these last two acquisitions into the United States and completed the country's western boundary. In 1958, he urged Congress to admit Alaska into the Union, which it did after much discussion and an attempt to tie Alaskan statehood to that of Hawaii. With its Asian population, critics said, Hawaii would upset balances in the electoral college and in Congress. On January 3, 1959, Eisenhower signed the bill making Alaska the 49th state. On August 21, 1959, Hawaii was admitted as the 50th state, thus ending land acquisitions to the West.

NEGOTIATIONS WITH NATIVE AMERICANS

Whatever Jefferson hoped to start, he got more than he could have imagined. This was also true in negotiating with native-born peoples in the West. Because white people usually grabbed Native American lands and destroyed the Indians' livelihoods, they needed a plausible (at least to whites) rationale for government policies. Jefferson argued that because Indian societies were then at a lower level of economic, political, and sociocultural development than white society, it was logical, and probably even the Divine intention, that whites should replace Indians. Jefferson set aside reserves of western land for displaced Native Americans, and the reservation system was born. President Andrew Jackson followed up during the late 1820s and early 1830s by "removing" thousands of Native Americans from their eastern homes and resettling them on reserves of land in Oklahoma Territory.

Because attempts through the years at reforming the traditional reservation system were unsuccessful, Indian policy continued to distress presidents who had to reconcile Indian needs with those of the larger population. In 1981, for example, President Ronald Reagan called for a cut in federal funds to Native Americans, including a sizable decrease in economic development monies. Early in 1983, however, he released a statement assuring Native Americans of his administration's support in helping them gain self-determination and stable economies. Then, later that year, he announced more cuts in Indian appropriations, maintaining that federal funding made Indians "incompetent wards" of the government. Obviously, a situation that confounded Jefferson, Jackson, and their nineteenth-century successors continued to baffle modern executives as well.

WESTWARD MIGRATION

There was also the task of convincing Americans to move westward. Thousands of western acres could provide homes not only for the growing American population, but for immigrants as well. At first, it was slow business to persuade people that settlement in a largely unknown place was a viable undertaking. In 1840, only 4 percent of Americans lived in the West, but then the "great migration" began, so that by the end of the century, in 1900, 17 million did so. As a result, presidents expended tremendous amounts of federal income, as well as time and energy, in creating settler populations. President Abraham Lincoln, for instance, tried to induce people to move westward with the Homestead Act of 1862, which made land available to blacks and women as well as white men, and was enormously successful. In 1902, President Theodore Roosevelt's Reclamation Act drained or cleared unfarmed land, which the president offered to would-be settlers at home and abroad, an approach that proved second only to Lincoln's program in shifting people westward. As a result, the mean center of American population moved from Kent County, Maryland, in 1790 to Crawford County, Missouri, in 1990.

During settlement, western migrants were typically white, but increasingly Asians, blacks, and Hispanics established themselves in the West. Of Asians, the Chinese were the largest group to migrate to the West, the Japanese less numerous. Despite his own ambivalence regarding Asians, President Theodore Roosevelt moderated Chinese exclusion laws in California and stood up for Japanese people already living in the West by arguing that Japanese children should be admitted to California schools. Still, the status of people of color living in the West remained low.

By 1900, census data revealed that the West encompassed a total of more people of color than other U.S. regions. Although poor people and those of color have been notoriously undercounted and the inclusion of illegal migrants in the census is controversial, these persons were often visible, if uncounted. For example, black ghettoes and Hispanic barrios existed in such cities as El Paso and San Antonio, Texas, where people of color came to work for railroads, smelters, and other industries. On the land, the situation was too often similar; whites were owners, nonwhites were workers who lived and toiled in dismal conditions and experienced deep-seated prejudice.

Yet it was not until the mid-1960s that a president stepped in. On January 2, 1964, President Lyndon B. Johnson signed the Civil Rights Act into law, banning unequal treatment in schools, employment, elections, and public places. These provisions were difficult to enforce, yet Johnson's action heralded a new way of thinking that would also serve as a model for the women's rights campaign. Unfortunately, Johnson had far less success in attacking the poverty that especially bedeviled people of color. Despite the comprehensive reforms announced in his 1964 State of the Union speech, as well as the fabled wealth of the West, destitution remains widespread. Between 2010 and 2014, for example, in nine western states—Arizona, Arkansas, California, Missouri, Nevada, New Mexico, Oklahoma, Oregon, and Texas—20 percent or more of the children were living in poverty, as opposed to ten states in the South and five in the North, where the figure was less than 20 percent. Clearly, despite presidential intervention, poverty remains an endemic problem in parts of the West.

TRANSPORTATION AND RESOURCES

Another frequent thread in the following essays is the implementation of a transportation revolution in the West. For early presidents, this meant such public improvements as toll roads and canals and, after the invention of the steam engine, the development of rivers and ports. Soon, steam-powered railroads made such industries as ranching, farming, and mining in the West profitable and linked western suppliers with eastern manufacturers and consumers. When President Lincoln came to office, he welcomed the opportunity to help the West. Not only did he promote smaller railway companies, but he put in place the beginnings of the first transcontinental railroad in the nation, the two halves of which joined in Promontory, Utah, in 1869.

Rail shipping and travel were the norm until the coming of gas-powered vehicles early in the twentieth century. It was President Dwight D. Eisenhower who recognized the boon that a network of superhighways would be to the nation, especially the West, with its great distances. Although earlier legislation had been proposed and vetoed, plans submitted and abandoned, and possible corridors suggested by President Franklin Roosevelt, it was Eisenhower who promoted a road system that proved revolutionary not only for shipping and travel, but for military defense.

In 1954, Eisenhower championed the construction of a limited-access superhighway that would eventually form a web across the nation. Initial construction began under the Federal Aid Highway Act of 1956. Although Nebraska claimed the completion of its final section of I-80 in October of 1974, it was October of 1992 before a ceremony in Colorado declared the network complete. When the superhighway finally opened, it claimed the distinction of being the second-longest road in the world, next to one in China. The Dwight D. Eisenhower National System of State and Defense Highways also brought incalculable gains to the West in terms of trade, travel, and tourism.

POLITICAL POWER OF THE WEST

Another important theme here is the politicization of the West. As the region developed and prospered, its political importance grew until the West became a power to be reckoned with. The West had always been a distinct political region, in that early settlers had to make their own rules and establish their own institutions. One example were the gold miners in 1850s California who created regulations regarding such issues as claim sharing and claim jumping, and set up rudimentary courts to enforce policies. Divorce and desertion were also local matters handled with such liberality that today the West as a region has the most relaxed divorce and desertion provisions, as well as the highest divorce rate, in the nation. But, as settlers flowed into western areas, many called for law and order as well as participation in, and recognition from, the federal government.

Of course, political considerations were ever present under all presidents. The most significant issue in the ongoing controversies of the nineteenth century was slavery. Although Jefferson had provided a clause in the Ordinance of 1787, or the Northwest Ordinance, prohibiting slavery in northwestern territories, Presidents Andrew Jackson and James K. Polk each worked in his own way to open the West to slavery, which, if successful, would have rewritten the history of the West and the nation. When President Lincoln stood against the extension of slavery into western territories, his position created a crisis for the West, for it became a pawn between North and South in the run-up to the Civil War. During the war itself, military campaigns launched in the West aimed at tying the region to either the Confederate or Union governments. Suddenly, it seemed, presidents and their supporters recognized the value of the West.

After the Civil War, the balance of political power shifted significantly. The North and the West stood united against the defeated South, which lacked representation in Congress. In the West, new states formed one after another. Between the end of the Civil War and the end of the nineteenth century, nine western territories became states, each sending representatives to Congress to speak on behalf of western causes, act as a western faction in decisions, and demand a share of federal largesse for such projects as building western railroads and opening more western land for settlement.

At the turn of the twentieth century, the West came into its own. Theodore Roosevelt was the first successful presidential candidate to campaign in the West, thus giving the region an important nod of respect. As president, he extolled everything about the West, from western values to resources, and targeted the region for preservation and conservation programs. Subsequent presidents followed his lead for, by then, many were themselves westerners. In the seventeen elections between 1948 and 2012, fifteen of the victorious candidates had been born in the trans-Mississippi West or had spent a significant part of their lives there. Accompanying presidents with western ties were colleagues, party members, appointees, and even opponents from the West.

At the same time, western states gained power in the nation's electoral college. Because of its burgeoning population, the West went from zero electoral votes in 1800 to 222 in 2016. After 1980, the rest of the nation seemed stuck with 316 electoral votes. In roughly two centuries, the West had moved dramatically from no electoral voting power to delivering more than one-third of the total. Not only were the West's electoral votes increasing from election to election, but the rate of growth was quickening. With numerous population centers in its column, the West undoubtedly will continue increasing its numbers of electoral votes.

CONSERVING THE WEST

The last motif to be examined in each of these chapters is the saving of western environments. Although the West developed socially, economically, and politically, the East continued to look on the West as primarily a supplier having inexhaustible caches of everything from timber and animals to water and mineral resources. The West happily accepted this profitable position, even though such trade destroyed massive amounts of timber and other resources. This carnage led to outrage on the part of people who were able to think beyond immediate profits. During the early 1900s, President Theodore Roosevelt and his close associate, Gifford Pinchot, harangued the American people, maintaining that there was no such thing as an inexhaustible resource, only eventual and tragic depletion.

Roosevelt soon became known as the "conservationist" president, yet his view was not a new one. Jefferson had envisioned farmers living in harmony with nature, and well-planned cities surrounded by beauty. Later, in 1862, Lincoln set aside Yosemite in California, which became a national park in 1890. In 1906, Theodore Roosevelt increased a president's power to protect the environment by supporting and signing the Antiquities Act of 1906. He also set a precedent for later presidents who accepted the need to save the nation's natural and built environment, especially in the vast West. For example, in 1965, President Johnson called for the conservation and restoration of "natural beauty," and proposed twelve new parks, six of which would be located in the West. Later, in 1980, President Carter promoted the Alaska National Interest Lands Conservation Act, which set aside an area larger than California. By 2000, attention had shifted to wise use of such western resources as water, natural gas, and especially oil.

As a result of this complex perspective, the following examination of the cross-country connections between U.S. presidents and the American West provides enlarged understandings of occupants of the White House in relation to people residing west of the Mississippi River. These presidential-regional relationships also cast new light on two overarching themes of western history: continuity and change. From Thomas Jefferson to chief executives in the twentieth-first century, all have dealt with a region ever-shifting in identity and needs. These shifts have added social, economic, political, and environmental complexities to the American West, making it a region that is increasingly difficult to fathom and manage. By examining the presidential-regional linkages, we have come to greater comprehension of presidents and the American West. We hope readers benefit from our insights and are challenged to pursue thoughts of their own.

THOMAS JEFFERSON, 1801–1809

Chapter 1

THOMAS JEFFERSON
CREATING THE AMERICAN WEST

A grand vision of the American West as a productive, even paradisiacal, region developed in the mind of Thomas Jefferson long before the place itself became a reality for explorers, mapmakers, traders, and immigrants. The man famous for writing the Declaration of Independence, who later became the third president of the new United States, moved quickly when the opportunity arose to expand American power and protect the nation's borders by annexing the Louisiana Territory. As president, he would initiate the Louisiana Purchase in 1803 and send out the Corps of Discovery to determine just what America had bought. In so doing, Jefferson created the American West and started the legendary western odyssey on its way.

One might ask why an eastern statesman, political philosopher, and southern planter would get so involved with the American West. Certainly, Jefferson never saw the West himself; the Appalachian Mountains and the difficulties of travel kept him from ever crossing the high divide. Yet he had frontier origins, growing up in a backcountry Virginia family. As a boy, he observed firsthand the importance to his family of migration, settlement, harmonic relations with indigenous people, and secure borders. Later, as a college student, he devoted a portion of his studies to Native Americans and read widely in the history of exploration, economic development, and empire building in all parts of the world. This habit of reading widely continued through his life.

Jefferson, however, was more than a knowledgeable planter and a curious scholar. His searching and highly romantic mind supplied a rich imagery to accompany his dreams. At one time or another, he romanticized everything from western lands to western peoples. In 1781, for example, Jefferson, then in his late twenties, met with the Kaskaskia chief Jean Baptiste du Coigne, who had named his son Jefferson. After the men exchanged gifts, Jefferson assured du Coigne that both their peoples "are Americans, born in the same land, and having the same interests," and thus able to enjoy a long "friendship." Years later, in Jefferson's 1785 *Notes on the State of Virginia*, he endorsed another Native American, John Logan, the Mingo leader struck down in 1774 at the beginning of Lord Dunmore's War. Jefferson defended Logan and eulogized him as a great chief, a "noble savage," who tragically but inevitably fell victim to the forces of British invasion and American avarice. He concluded that Indians only needed to learn white-style agriculture and lifestyles to progress from "savagery" to "civilization." Unfortunately, history proved both scenarios wrong.

The tragedy of Thomas Jefferson's career would be that his rich inner life clashed with the harsh facts of public and political life. Time and again, his imaginings of the western landscape—and of its indigenous peoples—crumpled in the face of reality, leaving Jefferson confused and even saddened. His ultimate triumph would be that he often overcame his disappointments, bowed up, and created a phenomenon, the American West, which captured the world's imagination, in his own time and for long after.

A SON OF THE FRONTIER

The exemplar frontiersman in Jefferson's life was his father, Peter Jefferson. During the 1730s and 1740s, Peter helped open Virginia for the expansion of white settlement. As a surveyor and noted cartographer, Peter laid out many metes and bounds, including those for his own home, Shadwell, which he helped build. It was here that Thomas was born in 1743. Peter Jefferson, who now also raised tobacco and served in the House of Burgesses, taught his son to love the land and nature, while his mother, Jane Randolph Jefferson, one of Virginia's well-known Randolphs, steered Thomas toward books, art, and music.

Life outside his family was less pleasant. Although the Jeffersons lived in a transition zone, where violent contact between Native Americans and white settlers had significantly declined, many displaced Indians remained, along with stories of their cruelty and rapaciousness. Rather than coming to view Native Americans as natural enemies, however, Jefferson developed an ambivalence toward them, which often leaned more toward the positive than the negative. In 1760, when young Jefferson matriculated at Williamsburg's College of William and Mary for a two-year program of reading law with noted attorney George Mason, he also chose to study Native languages and cultures, a pursuit that he continued throughout his life. At the same time, Jefferson followed his father's acquisitive model by accumulating Indians' hereditary lands. Eschewing his own scruples, Jefferson dabbled in western land speculation, often buying areas that had been taken by forceful persuasion from Indians. As early as 1757, he had inherited five thousand acres of Virginia land, plus an unknown number of slaves, from his deceased father, but it was not until 1769, the year he began building his plantation, Monticello, that he purchased his own land, which eventually ran into thousands of acres.

JEFFERSON'S EARLY IDEAS

Well before 1800, when Jefferson gained international recognition as president of the fledgling United States, he began to develop staunch principles regarding U.S. ownership and operation of land. An early tenet concerned western areas, which he believed must be in American hands for national security reasons. After the end of the American Revolution in 1783, he objected to a British presence in the Ohio Valley. Rather than withdrawing from U.S. borders, as had been stipulated by treaty, some British troops had remained—and had incited anti-American outbreaks by such groups as the Shawnee, Mingo, and Cherokee peoples, who covered much of the Ohio River valley and southward. It not only appeared to Jefferson that the British had designs on the American-held area, but he faulted the Shawnees for using the situation to keep white people off their traditional lands.

At the same time, Jefferson came to suspect France of plans that could greatly imperil the U.S. backcountry. When he looked west to the Mississippi River, which was at that time the nation's western boundary and a major trade tributary, he recognized that the closure of the port of Spanish-controlled New Orleans could choke off American trade. Jefferson especially feared a land grab of the Mississippi River and its environs from Spain by France, who would be a fearsome neighbor for the United States. Between 1790 and 1793, when Jefferson served as the country's first secretary of state under President George Washington, he heard dark rumors regarding a possible French conspiracy to seize the New Orleans area. Jefferson gradually concluded that he had no choice but to advocate expansionism, especially aimed at the Mississippi River and perhaps its surroundings.

Jefferson was an expansionist in other ways as well. He urged the infant nation to enlarge its holdings to accommodate America's growing population, especially farmers, which he underestimated as doubling during the next century. Because Jefferson envisioned America as primarily a nation of yeoman farmers, he believed that the country must add huge numbers of acres to support thousands, and perhaps more, of farm families. Jefferson argued that American farmers needed access to productive soil and spatial freedom to create an agricultural wonderland and an "empire of liberty," a democratic society of free men and women dedicated to republican principles. In 1781, he wrote, "Those who labor in the earth are the chosen people of God . . . whose breasts he has made his peculiar deposit for substantial and genuine virtue."

During this period, Jefferson also paid attention to the more practical aspects of land administration. As Virginia's delegate to the Confederation Congress, Jefferson initiated the Land Ordinance of 1784 by putting forth a resolution to sell public lands for revenue to relieve that government's war debts, and to grant new states equality with existing states. He also suggested a provision giving white farmers inexpensive or free land. The latter provision failed to pass, as did his suggestion that slavery be prohibited in western acquisitions. Later, Jefferson helped shape the Ordinance of 1785, establishing the township method of surveying, and the Ordinance of 1787, or the Northwest Ordinance, which included the prohibition of slavery in western territories. The provisions that public lands could be sold by the U.S. government for income and would be surveyed in a grid pattern, with a section devoted to education, lent stability and order to the West, while the provision that new western territories be free of slavery would cause the West to become a bone of contention between North and South before the Civil War.

Because Jefferson envisioned American farmers as white men, he also maintained that the indigenous population, Native Americans, would have to be controlled and contained. Jefferson believed that four stages of human development existed: hunter, herder, farmer, and urban dweller. He judged Natives to be in the first stages, in which group sustenance depended upon a huge tract of land, whereas white Americans, who had achieved the more advanced stages, could use the same amount of land to support far greater numbers. Although Jefferson thought it inevitable that white Americans would elbow Indians aside, he believed that the invaders had a humane responsibility to provide the lesser beings with individual grants of farm acreage and some stewardship. The latter would include protection from land-hungry whites and a "civilizing" program that would help Indians adjust to life in a white West. Concomitant assumptions were that Christianity and white moral values would prevail.

During this period, several difficult situations honed Jefferson's thinking, toning down or even eradicating some of his earlier romanticism. Between 1779 and 1781, his wartime service as the second governor of Virginia involved him in Indian controversies, forcing him to realize that "antagonistic" and "belligerent" Native Americans wanted little to do with whites, while "friendly" Indians were amenable to the whites' plans for them. In the first category fell the Shawnees, whom Jefferson, acting through longtime Indian-fighter George Rogers Clark, decimated by means of a murderous campaign in the Ohio Valley. In 1777, Clark had volunteered to lead Kentucky men to resolve the situation in the upper Ohio area. Clark's sentiments were clear. He would, of course, expel the British, but would also subdue the Indians.

By then, political pressures and incendiary incidents had made Jefferson feel almost as strongly as Clark did about the Shawnees, so that he supported "the total suppression" of what he saw as "savage insolence and cruelties" and perhaps the elimination of Shawnees altogether. As Virginia's governor, Jefferson's near-obsession with the Shawnees caused him to slight Virginia's defense against the British, especially the invasion led by General Benedict Arnold during the winter of 1780–81. Jefferson narrowly escaped official censure by the Virginia Assembly, which agreed with Continental general Nathanael Greene's damning statement that Jefferson was engaged in "conquest abroad" at a time when Virginia's "powers were necessary to secure herself from ruin at home."

Jefferson salvaged his rather bedraggled view of Native Americans by defining two types. He concluded that "resistant" Indians were at the root of uprisings. He argued that they could be brought around through "instruction" and that a "civilization plan" could resolve the issue of resistant Indians. As Washington's secretary of state, Jefferson had agreed with the president that persuadable Indians such as Jean Baptiste du Coigne could indeed be "civilized," thus making them into the second type, cooperative Indians. Jefferson thus supported Washington's civilization policy, which sent teachers and missionaries to "peaceful" Indians and granted them small farms, implements, domestic animals, and supplies. An important difference between this approach and such earlier Indian schools as Brafferton Institution, founded in the 1690s at the College of William and Mary, was that Brafferton took Indian lads from their homes to educate them, often returning them as men who had difficulty adapting to their former way of life. The later program sent people to Native Americans living in their home areas, teaching them the rudiments of English, white-style farming, and Christianity (if the individual so desired.)

In addition to land and Native Americans, another strong current of Jefferson's thinking during these years stemmed from his love of natural science. Jefferson was unstoppable in his quest to understand the physical universe and, early in his political career, he showed interest in gathering data regarding the potential of western areas, many of which the United States did not own. In 1786, Jefferson found a man of "ingenuity" named John Ledyard, who had plans of eventually walking across North America to the Pacific Ocean. Although Jefferson supported Ledyard's immediate schemes through letters and cash contributions from his own pocket, nothing useful to Jefferson materialized. Other explorers who attracted Jefferson's attention, to little or no avail, included frontier fighter George Rogers Clark; André Michaux, agent to the French counsel to the United States; and wild-horse hunter Philip Nolan.

Jefferson further evinced his enthusiasm for western exploration by buying and reading a veritable library of books and articles concerning geography, flora and fauna, indigenous peoples, explorers, and related topics. He also collected maps, letters of instruction, journals, and ships' logs of expeditions as far away as Russia. And he developed his own utopian image of western lands. As an Enlightenment thinker who believed in order, balance, and stability, Jefferson envisioned a wilderness that would in many ways replicate the American East, with miles of fertile soil, soft rolling hills, and navigable waterways that could be joined by canals to provide access to ports on the western coast. In other words, Jefferson dreamed of the chimerical Northwest Passage. These unfounded assumptions underwrote his vision of exploring and developing a virtually unlimited western garden for his farmers.

JEFFERSON AS PRESIDENT

On March 4, 1801, when Chief Justice John Marshall swore in Thomas Jefferson as America's third president and first from the Democratic-Republican Party, the new chief executive brought well-formed ideas with him to Washington. At the time, Jefferson was internationally known as the author of the Declaration of Independence, an influential American leader who had served in many capacities, the scion of Monticello, and a leading member of the coastal elite. For most people, however, Jefferson's plans for the trans-Appalachian West, as well as for trans-Mississippi areas that had barely been probed by European explorers and traders, were largely unknown and even unanticipated. Soon, however, President Jefferson established himself as the primary and most powerful advocate of colonizing western lands and indigenous peoples—as well as of exploiting the region through scientific discovery. These concerns drove the new president; they threaded their way through virtually everything he said and did concerning the trans-Appalachian and trans-Mississippi Wests. And he was frequently moved to use a variety of means, some questionable, to deal with these concerns.

As president, Jefferson began in a conciliatory manner, paying respect to former President Washington and to Native Americans by continuing Washington's civilization policy. In December 1801, Jefferson commended the idea of civilizing indigenous tribes in his annual address to Congress, submitted a report showing progress among Creek Indians, and indicated his willingness to continue the program. Because Jefferson had learned from Washington the possible value of missionaries in teaching aspects of white civilization, he agreed to accept assistance from missionaries, a significant concession for him as he personally questioned the value of organized religion.

In January 1802, Jefferson showed further concern for Native Americans by asking Congress to pass a regulatory act that resembled Washington's Indian Trade and Intercourse Act. The legislation that Jefferson proposed would forbid any entity but the federal government to purchase Indian lands, levy punishments on non-Indians who committed crimes in Indian jurisdictions, or issue licenses for vendors trading with Indians. Jefferson's Congress responded on March 30, 1802, by approving "An Act to Regulate Trade and Intercourse with the Indian Tribes, and to Preserve Peace on the Frontiers." In addition to the above provisions, Section 13 allotted a pittance of ten thousand dollars annually for the furtherance of Indian civilization, including giving Native Americans farm animals, tools, goods, and cash. Other sections provided for a boundary line between Americans and Indians, controls on the distribution of alcohol, and punitive actions toward encroaching or dishonest whites. Every subsequent year until 1807, Jefferson reported progress. In that year, the president admitted to "some fermentation" among Indians, but in 1808, he resumed his positive tone.

In reality, difficulties were rife. The Act to Regulate Trade proved almost impossible to enforce, partly because of Jefferson's military cutbacks and partly because of the paucity of troops assigned to protect Native Americans. Moreover, the civilization program largely reached only such advanced groups as the Cherokees in Georgia and Tennessee. Farther west, greedy white men crossed boundary lines with impunity, smuggled exorbitantly priced alcohol to Indians, or ignored the regulations outright and cheated Indians however they could. The huge amounts of liquor going to Indians, much of it adulterated with such ingredients as pungent spices or urine, resulted in addiction by Native men and women. Because drunken Indians could not manage even meager resources, poverty followed. As early as July

1801, William Henry Harrison, governor of the combined territories of Louisiana and Indiana, complained bitterly that illegal traders furnished "six thousand Gallons" of alcohol annually to only six hundred "Warriors" living along the Wabash River. He added that these people were "half naked, filthy and enfeebled with Intoxication" and quite willing to murder anyone so that even chiefs and close relatives routinely fell "under the strokes of their tomahawks & Knives." Although Harrison and others tried to enforce rules, they faced scant or zero budgets, the policing of incredibly long borders, and harassment from imprudent whites who called them unpatriotic for "siding" with the Indians.

At the root of these disputes was whites' desire to relieve Indians of their western lands. Even Jefferson, from his first days in office, set as a high priority the obtaining of Indian lands. Jefferson spoke and wrote of an empire for liberty; bustling commerce on western waterways and in major ports; white Americans enjoying freedom of speech and livelihood; and Native Americans peacefully living white-style lives. For this to happen, someone had to live at the bottom of the scale. Jefferson had the answer. He wrote in his *Notes* that, because of their racial background and physical and mental limitations, black people would be among those perennially on the lower rungs of the ladder of success. This is not meant to suggest that Jefferson approved of slavery. Although mired economically and politically in slavery himself, Jefferson had long opposed the institution that defined black people as property. In 1778, as a member of the Virginia legislature, he had called for the abolition of slavery, and he later proposed that a similar provision be included in the land ordinances of the 1780s. Although he would later ignore slavery in the Louisiana Purchase lands so the French could not claim interference with their "interests" and cancel the sale, he continued to seek a solution to what he judged as the anathema of slavery. For a while, Jefferson argued for gradual emancipation coupled with returning former slaves to their homeland in Africa, where they could establish a black-ruled nation. Even though African colonization proved too difficult and expensive, as well as unappealing to many black women and men who thought of themselves as Americans, Jefferson did not give up his attack on slavery in general.

In his annual message to Congress in 1806, the president spoke against the transatlantic slave trade, asking that the United States withdraw "from all further participation in those violations of human rights . . . which the morality, the reputation, and the best of our country have long been eager to proscribe." On March 2, 1807, Jefferson triumphantly signed into law an Act Prohibiting Importation of Slaves, which he described as ending a "great moral and political error." After the provision went into effect on January 1, 1808, the response was mixed, with some slave owners buying smuggled or domestic slaves, while others encouraged increased "breeding" among slaves they already owned. Still, the legislation marked a major turning point in American slaveholding in that it affected western thinking and policies to the point that in much of the West slavery was thereafter an open question rather than a given.

Oddly enough, although Jefferson argued against slavery, especially in western areas where thinking and modes of production did not support slavery, his Indian policies impoverished and made dependent Native Americans, causing them, rather than blacks, to sink to the lowest rungs on the ladder. Yet, the demeaning of Indians does not appear to have been Jefferson's goal. In fact, in his mind, American Indians, who were slightly more "able" than blacks, had a choice. They could decide to copy white Americans (which he favored), or choose a dead-end life on western reserves (which he was beginning to see as the alternative).

By February 1803, Jefferson admitted that very few Native Americans wished to become pseudowhites. He became disillusioned with the civilization program and decided to give it up, along with Washington's idea that all Indian negotiations should require the consent of Indian leaders. In no uncertain terms, Jefferson set out his new Native American policy. First, he supplied motivation for Indians to sell and relocate. Although he said he wanted "perpetual peace" with Indians, Jefferson introduced a plan that could lead to nothing but conflict. Indians' "disposition to exchange lands" would be encouraged by getting "the good and influential among them run in debt" at government trading houses. These debtors would "become willing to lop them [debts] off by a cession" of tribal lands.

Alarming as this was, Jefferson's second point, Indian removal, was more so. If indebtedness failed to work, he explained, recalcitrant Indians would be given little alternative: "They will in time either incorporate with us as citizens of the United States, or remove beyond the Mississippi." Jefferson concluded that "should any tribe be fool-hardy enough to take up the hatchet at any time, the seizing of the whole country of that tribe, and driving them across the Mississippi, as the only condition of peace would be an example to others, and a furtherance of our final consolidation."

A problem for Jefferson, who considered himself a student of Indian languages and life, was his closed-mindedness and lack of sensitivity when dealing with real Indians. He never seemed to ask why Native Americans should choose to leave the land where they were born, had buried their dead, and with which they had strong spiritual connections. Why would they agree to give up their hunting territory and move to small, constricted farmsteads where even whites often lived at subsistence level? Indians already produced a fairly lucrative "cash crop" by trapping and hunting animals. They ate the meat, drying much for later consumption, and traded the hides and furs for manufactured necessities.

Jefferson also missed some gender-related considerations, which, in all fairness, escaped most white observers of the era. Among many Native American groups, women grew corn and other staple crops so they did not need white-style farming. Nor did numerous women want to move from the fields into their homes. Jefferson made the usual, but mistaken, assumption that women would "gain by quitting the labors of the field for those exercised indoors." In reality, Indian women would lose prestige, for as farmers they showed themselves as blessed by the Great Spirit with being the reproductive ones. Also they would lose power in decision making. Women who farmed had a great deal of control over a group's food supplies and stores, often dictating whether men needed to hunt and raid, or not. And women were traders, exchanging farm produce and their closely woven baskets and other craftwork for items that could not be purchased with hides and fur. A parallel misconception was that Indian men who hunted, raided, and fought in wars enjoyed leisure in between, which ignored or trivialized such men's duties as participating in councils and various rituals—including sweat lodges and war games—and manufacturing bows, arrows and arrowheads, spears and spearheads, and related war goods. Because in many groups, women designed, erected, and owned and cared for such dwelling places as tepees and wickiups, while men owned their weapons and tools, the attaining of white-style wealth may have seemed undesirable. Perhaps understandably, many Native American women and men were not anxious to redo the gendered order of things.

Jefferson was not easily deterred, however. Through both of his presidential terms, he continuously sought ownership transfers of land from Native Americans to the U.S. government. On November 3, 1805, he reported to Congress that the United States now controlled "the whole of both banks" of the Ohio River, making the area "safe to our citizens settled and settling on its extended waters." Jefferson next turned his attention, often acting personally, to lands south of the Ohio, especially those held by Cherokees. By the end of his second term, he had acquired a total of almost two hundred thousand acres, in some cases at one to two cents per acre. These cessions lay largely in the present-day states of Alabama, Arkansas, Indiana, Illinois, Georgia, Michigan, Mississippi, Missouri, and Tennessee, and affected tribes from the Cherokee in the south to the Chippewa in the north. A map shows that these land deals opened and protected the Ohio and Mississippi Rivers for white trappers, traders, land speculators, and settlers.

As a self-proclaimed colonialist, Jefferson was in sync with his time. His policies matched British, French, and Spanish colonial policy. Although the overwhelming success of these powerful empires does not justify Jefferson's schemes, they did provide a comfort zone for the colonialist philosophy he espoused during his lifetime and bequeathed to those who would enlarge his ideas into the national mania termed "Manifest Destiny." At the same time, his beliefs inundated Native American policy and documents, as well as the minds of a trained network of government officials, politicians, military leaders, diplomats, frontier governors and agents, and others who were ready to think and act as he did. Jefferson also provided convenient rationalizations for thousands of other whites, in his own era and later in the nineteenth and twentieth centuries, who wanted to expand, move to, or speculate in western real estate once owned by Native Americans.

JEFFERSON AND THE TRANS-MISSISSIPPI WEST

As Jefferson acquired land east of the Mississippi, his eyes were increasingly drawn to the trans-Mississippi region, or Louisiana Territory. As a result, he began to think about organizing and sending a "scientific" expedition to parts of the West that the United States did not own. As early as June 1801, Jefferson added a potential star to his constellation when he invited a young military man named Meriwether Lewis to serve as his personal secretary. Although it is debatable whether Jefferson intended Lewis eventually to lead a western expedition, it is true that Lewis lacked the skills, training, and political experience for the position as Jefferson's secretary. But the Virginian Lewis soon proved invaluable to President Jefferson. Lewis was efficient, curiously able to charm people into cooperation with his employer's requests, and willing to take on unexpected tasks, such as reading Jefferson's State of the Union address to Congress because Jefferson abhorred public speaking. Lewis also had numerous outdoor skills; he was an exceptional hunter, an avid student of nature, familiar with military matters, and knowledgeable about the then-frontier, the Ohio country. While Lewis lived in the White House with Jefferson during his two years of service, Jefferson and his friends in the American Philosophical Society tutored Lewis in keen observation, detailed reporting, and political finesse. It seems clear that Jefferson hoped that Lewis would take charge of planning, supplying, and staffing what would become Jefferson's dream, the Lewis and Clark expedition—or the

Corps of Discovery, as Jefferson named the party he created to explore what lay beyond the Mississippi River.

Unfortunately, there was a major obstacle to launching such a project: Spain owned most of the area that Jefferson hoped to explore. The situation changed dramatically when Jefferson learned, late in 1802, that Spain had secretly transferred the Louisiana Territory to France. In his message to Congress on December 15, 1802, Jefferson announced the shift. On January 18, 1803, he sent to Congress a covert message seeking twenty-five hundred dollars "for the purpose of extending the external commerce of the United States." This appropriation was in fact to finance Lewis's trek. At the caution of his advisors, the president downplayed his hope of expanding into Indian-held lands, emphasizing instead science and commerce. Jefferson also demonstrated his interest in trade by initiating the Cumberland Road bill, the first federally financed internal improvements project, which he later signed in 1806.

Meanwhile, Jefferson realized the journey would go more smoothly if France, apparently the current owner of the Louisiana area, would sell the United States a part of its new holdings. He targeted New Orleans because, as a U.S. possession, New Orleans could be useful in protecting American shipping and keeping the Mississippi River open. As such, its purchase would be relatively easy to justify to Congress and the public. Accordingly, on April 13, 1803, Jefferson wrote to the U.S. minister plenipotentiary to France, Robert R. Livingston, asking him to explore the possibility of America's buying from France the port of New Orleans, which, he wrote, shipped approximately three-eighths of the backcountry's production to market and would soon move as much as one-half. The president dispatched James Monroe to assist Livingston; but when Monroe reached Paris, he learned that Livingston had already negotiated a prime deal. Because Napoleon Bonaparte's government sorely needed funds, Napoleon had offered to sell the entire Louisiana Territory to the United States for $15 million.

When Jefferson learned of Napoleon's offer, he hesitated, not because of the $15 million, for he had already asked Congress for around $10 million to buy New Orleans alone, but because he did not have the constitutional power to add foreign territory to the United States. As a strict constructionist of the Constitution, Jefferson believed that elected leaders should not surpass the authority granted them by that document. Yet, as the nation's leader at an opportune time, he thought he would be foolish not to act. Although he first considered pursuing a constitutional amendment, he soon realized that that process would cause such a delay that he might lose the opportunity to buy Louisiana at all. Thus, Jefferson turned to Congress for support. After extended debate, on October 10, the U.S. Senate formally approved the Louisiana Purchase by a vote of fourteen to seven. Jefferson had to be elated. Not only would his as-yet-undisclosed Corps of Discovery traverse (mostly) American land, but agrarian interests would be thrilled and would, he hoped, vote for his reelection in 1804.

At the same time, Jefferson readied Lewis for a huge undertaking. Assuring Lewis that all was well with Spain, who in truth adamantly declared invalid France's sale to the United States, Jefferson asked Lewis to avoid revealing their plans and to help develop a special code to be used between them. The president gave Lewis many of the maps he had collected, and procured for him British and French passports. When the Spanish minister to the United States refused to grant Lewis a passport, he told Jefferson that he was aware of the "secret" expedition and that his government would surely "take umbrage." In response, Jefferson trotted out his maxims regarding science and trade. At the same time, he continued to reassure both Congress and Lewis that Spanish officials were unconcerned. Obviously, Jefferson intended to explore Louisiana Territory, even if Spain did not countenance the sale.

In June 1803, Lewis headed for St. Louis. He planned to gather information regarding trade and Native Americans in the area; hold training exercises; and purchase, sort, and pack supplies and trade goods. On June 19, Lewis wrote to frontier scout William Clark, inviting him to join the undercover journey. To Clark, he described a trip of "about 18 months" that would winter about two hundred or three hundred miles up the Missouri River. Lewis added that purposes of the trek included making acquaintance with western "tribes" and impressing them "with a just idea of the rising importance of the United States" as well as providing "a tribute to general science." On Jefferson's behalf, Lewis offered Clark "a Captain's commission and a portion of land."

It was December before Lewis, Clark, and their party established a winter camp, called Fort Dubois, east of St. Louis. The following June, they and their men set out for the unknown American West. And the rest, as they say, is history, the details of which are reported in Lewis's notes and his letters to Jefferson, as well as in the published journals of the Lewis and Clark expedition that began to appear in 1814.

Unnoted by the journal keepers, however, was the continuing wrath of Spain. Between 1804 and 1806, the Spanish government initiated four attempts to seize Lewis and scuttle the expedition by military force. Apparently, Lewis was unaware of his Spanish trackers as he moved across what Spain considered contested territory. The presence of the Spanish was revealed much later by researcher and writer

Warren L. Cook in his *Flood Tide of Empire* (1973). Based on archival research in Seville and Madrid in Spain; in Mexico City in Mexico; and in Santa Fe, New Mexico, Cook stated that Spain's expeditions involved considerable numbers, which in several instances came close to nailing Lewis and Clark, but ultimately failed.

Back in Washington, President Jefferson also appeared uninformed regarding the Spanish campaigns, but took Spain's opposition to the sale seriously, repeatedly warning Spain that the Americans would protect the Louisiana Territory and would perhaps attack the Spanish-held Floridas as well. Late in 1805, Jefferson even complained to the Senate regarding Spain's transgressions. Although not usually a warmonger, Jefferson agreed with war advocates in considering an armed conflict with Spain that might end Spanish aggression and procure at least west Florida for the United States.

During these Louisiana-dominated years, it appears that Jefferson was not always as open and honest as his admirers would like to believe. As a former secretary of state and as president, Jefferson knew the effectiveness of, and was willing to employ, secrecy and outright falsehood in arranging the purchase and exploration of the Louisiana Purchase. He also played on animosities between nations. One result of his intrigue was a less than fully organized expedition born of conflict, secrecy, perfidy, and antagonism to all things Spanish and Mexican, including the Spanish borderlands. Looking ahead to such presidents as Andrew Jackson and James K. Polk, it can be seen that Jefferson's tactics, ranging from plots to falsehoods, established precedents for American leaders during the first half of the nineteenth century.

In addition, Jefferson's creation of an unsettled situation led to charges and countercharges, criticism and retorts, and speculation regarding the future of the West—all of which contributed in part to unsuccessful plots to separate portions of the West from the United States, or even Mexico from Spain, by such national leaders as Alexander Hamilton, James Wilkinson, and Aaron Burr. Jefferson compounded the confusion by stating, early in 1804, that, "whether we remain one confederacy, or form into Atlantic and Mississippi confederacies, I believe not very important to the happiness of either part." Is this the same Jefferson who spoke so stirringly for the union and stability of the new United States? His statement revealed an attitude that failed to give the situation the stability it so patently needed.

In the end, Jefferson himself was not totally pleased with the findings of the Corps of Discovery. In his 1806 message to Congress, he commented that the journey of Lewis and Clark "had all the success which could have been expected." He went on to list the exploration of the Missouri and the Columbia Rivers, collection of data regarding lands and peoples, and an expanded understanding of commerce as their gains. In private, however, such western phenomena as towering mountains, vast deserts, and the lack of a Northwest Passage to the Pacific coast disappointed Jefferson, while public attacks, often by Federalists, ridiculing him and questioning his relationship with his black slave, Sally Hemings, further disillusioned him. Lewis's failure to produce a publishable manuscript concerning the trek also frustrated Jefferson. Overall, Lewis and Clark's trip was not the public relations triumph for which Jefferson had hoped. For 150 years, interest in Lewis and Clark's achievement would ebb and wane until more enlightened writers began to celebrate the trek.

With historical perspective, we can render our own judgment of Lewis and Clark. The expedition legitimized the Louisiana Purchase, consisting of 828,000 square miles, or 529,920,000 acres, at a cost of less than four cents an acre then and less than forty-two cents an acre in today's terms; removed foreign nations from the Mississippi River and environs; and made possible further westward expansion. The Corps of Discovery also fulfilled its charge, reporting on land and peoples in detail, supplying sketches by Lewis and maps by Clark, and providing specimens of plants and animals. Jefferson was delighted with the latter; in 1806, he added an Indian Hall to Monticello to display Indian artifacts and specimens that proved the existence of an "empire of science" in the West. On a much broader plane, the ephemeral West became a real place, authentic yet mysterious, and intriguing to people all over the world. The revelation of the West as a land of wonder elicited interest and enthusiasm from explorers, scientists, artists, and writers, notably in Europe where people seemed enamored with the West and its magic. Soon, such artists as George Catlin and Karl Bodmer would travel parts of the still-"wild" West, painting Jefferson's "noble savage" and the West's primal scenery.

Another significant accomplishment of the Corps of Discovery, one with far less happy consequences, resulted from white "parleys" with Native American tribes and their leaders. Gifts and trade goods ranging from blue glass beads and brass buttons to knives, kettles, textiles, needles, and widely used awls were presented, showing that some white men, thanks to trader-advisor Pierre Chouteau back in St. Louis, understood the importance of including women's goods among presents. Lewis and Clark also hung medals stamped with a likeness of Jefferson around the necks of male leaders who were, in general, not taken with the men of Lewis and Clark's party.

Yet Lewis and Clark did their best to impress. As historian James P. Ronda points out in *Lewis and Clark among the Indians*, they left Native American leaders little room to demur or even dissemble. Shortly after encountering a group of Indians, Lewis and Clark, dressed in formal attire, would parade troops who presented a stunning show while carrying the latest weapons. Lewis would then take to the stump where, speaking for Jefferson, he informed the assembled Indians that white Americans were now "fathers" of the West's Native peoples, a term smacking of paternalism and racism. Most Native American leaders, who thirsted for a regular supply of manufactured goods, tried to believe Lewis's assertions that the Father in Washington wanted commerce rather than land, but they clearly heard the implied violence in Jefferson's declarations that Americans were "as numerous as the leaves of the trees" and "are strong . . . are all gun-men."

To achieve his goals, Jefferson depended on explorers other than Lewis and Clark. Because he recognized that the Corps of Discovery findings would not be enough to definitively establish boundaries of Louisiana, in 1804 he appointed scientists William Dunbar and George Hunter, both of Scottish birth, to travel the southern reaches of the Louisiana Purchase. Even though Spanish officials again denied passports to American explorers, the two men and their party spent the fall of 1804 and the winter of 1805 along the Ouachita River, producing journals laden with information that Jefferson desired. A possible 1805 follow-up trip did not materialize for a number of reasons, one being that both men were in their fifties and hesitant to make another dangerous and demanding journey.

Jefferson then got busy looking for someone to replace Dunbar and Hunter in probing the southern Louisiana Territory. He finally settled on Irish-born civil engineer Thomas Freeman to head what he called his "Great Excursion" into the Southwest. He also invited Peter Custis to serve as the first trained naturalist and ethnographer on an American exploration of the West. Freeman, Custis, and others set out on May 2, 1806, hoping to find a waterway to Santa Fe. Although the group spent four months on the Red River, it failed to locate a water passage to Santa Fe. The existence of the party did, however, further annoy Spain, which mounted armed resistance to American entry of any kind into the Spanish borderlands.

During these years, President Jefferson also worked on exploration with the head of the U.S. Army, General James Wilkinson, who initiated a number of forays himself. The most notable of the groups Wilkinson sent out was led by Zebulon Montgomery Pike Jr. Although Wilkinson was a spy for Spain, no evidence exists that Pike was also an agent or that he knew of Wilkinson's espionage. Pike seems to have been guilty only of trusting his friend and superior, Wilkinson, and accepting questionable assignments from him. In 1805, Wilkinson sent Lieutenant Pike with a party of twenty men up the Mississippi River one month behind Lewis and Clark. Pike's group spent the winter in Minnesota, then returned to Wilkinson, who, after alerting the War Department and his alternate employer, Spain, dispatched Pike down the Red River directly into Spanish-held territory. Apparently unclear about the objectives of this July 1806 to June 1807 trip, Pike visited a Pawnee village, pursued a detachment of Spanish soldiers, built a fort, and got lost at least once or perhaps several times, which eventually earned him the nickname "The Lost Pathfinder."

Even though early writers underestimated Pike's achievements, or dismissed him entirely as one of Wilkinson's spies, more recent scholars have established Pike as a positive influence on Jefferson's expansion into the Southwest. Notably, Pike's second journey resulted in exactly the kind of information that Jefferson wanted, including highly useful maps, geographical and other data, trade statistics, assessments of Native peoples and cultures, and a description of an imposing mountain, which Pike's party did not scale but was later named Pike's Peak. When Pike's journals were published in 1810, they opened American eyes to the possibilities of the Red River country, thus making American expansionism into the region not only desirable but attainable. In his *Life of Zebulon Pike*, historian Jared Orsi takes this idea one step further, arguing, that although virtually all early explorers were inspired by Jefferson's "empire of liberty," it was Pike who helped turn the area into an "empire for commerce." According to Orsi, Pike alerted American minds to the potential rewards of trade, thus providing a material basis for Jefferson's more philosophical ideas regarding the West.

JEFFERSON IN RETIREMENT

In spring 1809, Jefferson retired and retreated to Monticello. He seemed exceptionally pleased to put the public realm behind him, explaining that "I am tired of a life of contention and of being the personal object for the hatred of every man who hates the present state of things." Throughout his career he was the anti-hero to many Federalists, including Alexander Hamilton; was verbally flayed by early reformers for his western land and Indian policies; and, in an age that largely condoned slavery and its ills, was criticized for his liaison with his slave, Sally Hemings. It is little wonder that he was anxious to escape to the relative peace and security of Monticello. "Being chained to a writing table" was another torture he hoped to leave behind. Rather, he planned to indulge himself with "the blessings of domestic society" and "pursuits" of his own choice. He even hoped that the "serious debts" he carried home from his years in office might be ameliorated at Monticello.

Jefferson's respite did not turn out as he hoped, for hordes of people, ranging from well-wishers, admirers, and former associates to folks he had never met or invited, descended on Monticello, staying days or even months, literally eating out his substance, eroding his time, and increasing his debts. As a result, Jefferson, never known as an astute financial manager, was, at the time of his death, not solvent enough to free his slaves as he had hoped.

During the fall of 1809, as Jefferson settled into retirement, the public perception of his western explorations received a blow when Meriwether Lewis died tragically and under suspicious circumstances. After giving William Clark and Meriwether Lewis their promised ranks and land grants, Jefferson had appointed them to posts in St. Louis. Clark married, took up his job as superintendent of Indian affairs for Louisiana, and appeared content. Lewis took over for General Wilkinson as territorial governor of Louisiana, with a determination to enforce trade and other agreements and to act in an equitable manner in all Indian-related matters. In St. Louis, where opportunities in the fur trade flourished, thousands of landless men vied for land, and corruption was rife, Lewis's attitude soon earned him respect in certain quarters and vitriolic enemies in others.

After Lewis's violent death on October 11, which was ruled a suicide, he was buried in an unmarked grave with one person present and no Christian ceremony. In 1848, the State of Tennessee reburied Lewis and placed a monument over his grave with a brief epitaph: "Of courage undaunted, possessing a firmness and perseverance of purpose which nothing but impossibilities could divert from its direction." It was a sad ending for so adventurous and important a man, as well as for Jefferson's grand scheme to know the West.

In the meantime, firmly ensconced in retirement at Monticello, Jefferson was at once an American hero of great repute as well as an able politician of a slippery nature. He had been known to pursue projects in secret, to change his mind and his policies, and even to lie outright. His duplicity was a result of his dual nature—homebody and philosopher on one hand and public activist on the other. Now at Monticello, he reveled in the enjoyment of home and family, a pleasure he had first extolled while married to Martha Wayles Skelton, who bore him six children, two girls surviving to adulthood. Between their marriage in 1772 and her death in 1782, the couple shared such a close bond that when she asked him not to remarry because she trusted no one with her children, he had promised not to take another wife. Jefferson's love of domesticity, coupled with his deathbed promise to Martha, may explain in part his long-term relationship with Sally Hemings, who was a half-sister of Jefferson's wife and, according to one account, arrived at Monticello shortly after Martha's death.

Besides domesticity, in retirement Jefferson sought the life of the mind. Aside from performing agricultural-related tasks that had immediate, visible outcomes, he walked miles across his land and the surrounding countryside, ruminating as he went. Once again, he was the Sage of Monticello. In this milieu, Jefferson had long demonstrated his abilities as an exceptional thinker. His ideas were visionary, humane, and inspiring. As such, he had given the American people such enduring concepts as "life, liberty, and the pursuit of happiness." Later, he had spoken out against racism and mistreatment of such groups as blacks and Native Americans.

At the same time, in retirement Jefferson did not appear content with memories of that other part of his life: public activism. Because he was so disenchanted on many scores with politics, he decided to commit his remaining energies to creating the University of Virginia. He had once believed that he could make a difference by putting his philosophies into action in the political arena. Unfortunately, he had soon discovered that the rationality of the Enlightenment thinkers he so admired disappeared in the midst of conflict, contention, and calumny. Either in writing or in raised voices, demands were made, charges leveled, lies told. In these situations, Jefferson's idealism receded a bit, and reality took center stage. The resulting duality explains how he could be a strict constructionist of the Constitution yet seize the power to buy the Louisiana Purchase; how he could condemn slavery as an immoral system yet own slaves; and how he could pursue an almost reverential study of Indians and their culture yet advocate destroying their way of life by "civilizing" them or "removing" them beyond the Mississippi River. This assessment of Jefferson's inner conflict does not excuse him; it only makes him a more sympathetic figure.

During his retirement, between 1809 and his death on July 4, 1826, Jefferson did set pen to paper but seemed to avoid the tough issues. He seldom referred to the burgeoning West he had literally created, even though back in Washington, many of those who came after him—including William Henry Harrison, governor of the Indiana Territory; Lewis Cass, governor of the Michigan Territory; and William Clark, governor of Louisiana Territory—perpetuated Jeffersonian innovations, including government sales of public lands, surveying new lands by townships, and, especially, Jefferson's use of purchase or seizure to obtain western lands from Native Americans. But Jefferson remained largely in the background, as he thought appropriate for a retired president.

The credos regarding the trans-Appalachian and trans-Mississippi areas and its inhabitants that Jefferson had brought to the presidency no longer dominated his writings as they had in the 1790s and early 1800s. He did obliquely refer to his purchase of Louisiana Territory, justifying his decision to buy Louisiana without explicit constitutional permission by stating his belief that "saving our country when in danger" was far more important than "strictly following written laws." In 1816, obviously forgetting the secrecy and falsehoods surrounding the purchase, he wrote, "Never suffer a thought to be harbored in your mind which you would not avow openly. When tempted to do anything in secret ask yourself if you would do it in public." If not, do not, he concluded.

Jefferson retained considerable interest in Native Americans, finally resolving his ambivalence. He remembered Indians fondly, as people for whom he had early acquired "attachment and commiseration . . . which have never been obliterated." His attention to Native peoples was now primarily scholarly, as he pursued Indian history, languages, and lexicology, and in 1817 he gave what papers remained after an earlier theft to the American Philosophical Society. Some years later, Jefferson wrote to William Clark, asking that he donate Native American artifacts to the new University of Virginia museum. Clark replied that he would search for some, then shifted to a plea stemming from his work as superintendent of Indian affairs. Clark explained that "it would afford me pleasure to be enabled to meliorate the condition of those unfortunate people placed under my charge." He implored Jefferson to send "his views on the subject, which would enable me to use the Small Means in my power" to improve the situation of Native Americans. The great man did not reply.

Jefferson's quest to apply the scientific method to everything, especially in exploring the American West, softened a bit as well. As he became aware of the physical limitations imposed on him by age, he cut back on travel and, after seventeen years of service, in 1814, he resigned as president of the American

Philosophical Society in faraway Philadelphia. In 1816, he mentioned that he was "rather feeble to walk much, but ride with ease, passing two or three hours a day on horseback." Still, he found the energy to consult on the mapping of the state of Virginia. He wrote the governor a twelve-page letter that revealed his technical expertise in cartographic matters. He also maintained the Indian Hall at Monticello, adding to it bits of Americana and leaving it all to the University of Virginia at his death.

Increasingly, Jefferson's real world existed only at Monticello, where surely none of his horde of visitors brought up controversial issues in his presence. Reminiscences written by his grandson Thomas Jefferson Randolph, his granddaughters Virginia Trist and Ellen W. Coolidge, and Monticello slave Isaac Jefferson are overwhelmingly positive. In this comfortable setting, Jefferson apparently forgot his use of such methods as secrecy, falsehood, and personal influence to get his way. Rather, he wrote that "I never did, or countenanced, in public life, a single act inconsistent with the strictest good faith; having never believed there was one code of morality, for a public, and another for a private man."

Gradually, the former patriot and president reconstructed his personal history, remembering what seemed true and significant to him. When he wrote the epitaph for his gravestone, he chose to emphasize only three accomplishments: the Declaration of Independence, the Statute of Virginia for Religious Freedom, and the University of Virginia. He ignored everything from the political realm, including the stellar achievement of serving as the third president of the United States.

JEFFERSON'S WESTERN LEGACY

It is probable that Thomas Jefferson, like most people of his era, did not realize the scope, resources, and commercial opportunities that came to the United States through the Louisiana Purchase. Although he created a West that doubled the size of the nation, served as space for American democracy to flourish and avoid factionalism, protected the young country from foreign control, and opened the way to further expansion to the Pacific Ocean, he mentioned none of this in later writings. His "empire of liberty" image had not only come to be, but had expanded to an "empire of science" and an "empire of commerce," yet he noted none of this. Nor did he seem to remember his earlier, prepresidential contributions to western policies. The sale of government lands, the township survey system, the equality of new western states, and, most importantly, the resistance to slavery in much of the West stemmed directly from him.

Despite this lack of attention from him in retirement, Jefferson's American West lived on, in so many ways an unparalleled contribution to the nation he loved. Even though he failed to recognize his less attractive attributes and actions, they contributed to the West as well, affecting generations of common people and uncommon leaders and bequeathing such significant problems as the reservation system and all its ills to the contemporary American West. For better and sometimes for worse, there is no doubt that Thomas Jefferson not only created, but significantly influenced the great American West.

FOR FURTHER READING

Ambrose, Stephen E. *Undaunted Courage: Meriwether Lewis, Thomas Jefferson, and the Opening of the American West.* New York: Simon & Schuster, 1996.

Carlson, Laurie Winn. *Seduced by the West: Jefferson's America and the Lure of the Land beyond the Mississippi.* Chicago: Ivan R. Dee, 2003.

Cook, Warren L. *Flood Tide of Empire: Spain and the Pacific Northwest, 1543–1819.* New Haven: Yale University Press, 1973.

Ellis, Joseph J. *American Sphinx: The Character of Thomas Jefferson.* New York: Vintage Books, 1998.

Harris, Matthew L., and Jay H. Buckley, eds. *Zebulon Pike, Thomas Jefferson, and the Opening of the American West.* Norman: University of Oklahoma Press, 2012.

Holmes, Jerry, ed. *Thomas Jefferson: A Chronology of His Thoughts.* Lanham, MD: Rowman & Littlefield, 2002.

Jackson, Donald. *Thomas Jefferson and the Stony Mountains: Exploring the West from Monticello.* Urbana: University of Illinois Press, 1981.

Jefferson, Thomas. *Notes on the State of Virginia.* 1785 edition.

Kennedy, Roger G. *Burr, Hamilton, and Jefferson.* New York: Oxford University Press, 1999.

——. *Mr. Jefferson's Lost Cause: Land, Farmers, Slavery, and the Louisiana Purchase.* New York: Oxford University Press, 2003.

Kukla, Jon. *A Wilderness So Immense: The Louisiana Purchase and the Destiny of America.* New York: Alfred A. Knopf, 2003.

Meacham, Jon. *Thomas Jefferson: The Art of Power.* New York: Random House, 2012.

Orsi, Jared. *Citizen Explorer, The Life of Zebulon Pike.* New York: Oxford University Press, 2017.

Owsley, Frank Lawrence, Jr., and Gene A. Smith. *Filibusters and Expansionists: Jeffersonian Manifest Destiny, 1800–1821.* Tuscaloosa: University of Alabama Press, 1997.

Peterson, Merrill D. *The Jeffersonian Image in the American Mind.* Charlottesville, VA: Thomas Jefferson Memorial Foundation, 1998.

Ronda, James P. *Jefferson's West: A Journey with Lewis and Clark.* Monticello, VA: Thomas Jefferson Foundation, 2000.

———. *Lewis and Clark among the Indians.* Lincoln: University of Nebraska Press, 1984.

Wallace, Anthony F. C. *Jefferson and the Indians: The Tragic Fate of the First Americans.* Cambridge, MA: Belknap Press of Harvard University Press, 1999.

ANDREW JACKSON, 1829–1837

LC-USZ62-59182

Chapter 2

ANDREW JACKSON
ENCUMBERING THE AMERICAN WEST

On January 15, 1815, Andrew Jackson led his motley army of approximately five thousand men, including regular soldiers, frontiersmen, free black volunteers, Kentucky muskets, Tennessee long rifles, and Jean Lafitte's pirates, to handily defeat some seven thousand classically trained British regulars, leaving a huge number of them wounded or dead. In an era before radio, television, or the Internet, news about the Battle of New Orleans flew from person to person, house to house, tent to tent, and barracks to barracks. One oft-repeated story told of a Jackson man who, stunned by an explosion, regained consciousness to see bands of scarlet and ash-gray wavering around him. "I thought I had died and gone to hell," he later explained. When the young soldier recovered his wits, he realized that the ground was covered with injured or dead Redcoats, sometimes two and three deep, while gun smoke tinged the air. Although this is probably an apocryphal tale, the final count showed that this engagement cost the British two thousand casualties, while the Americans suffered eight dead and thirteen wounded.

Jubilant Americans reveled in the victory. To them, Jackson's stand at New Orleans was a prime example of Americans' exceptional courage. General Jackson and his men had challenged all would-be invaders to stay at home; indeed, no country ever again invaded the United States. In the following weeks, enthusiastic songs, shouts, and jokes celebrating Jackson and his triumph were everywhere, from taverns to riverboats to humble cabins and fine mansions.

Jackson, now known as the Hero of the Battle of New Orleans, rose to great heights of glory—and of political influence. Americans believed him to be a true hero from the reaches of the then-frontier, western Tennessee. He was tall and striking in figure, fiery and charismatic in personality, and always ready to scrap in temperament. If anyone could have foretold the future, they would have known that this episode marked the beginning of the astounding climb of an uncommon common man to become the nation's seventh president.

Unfortunately for the American West, which was rapidly spreading westward across the Mississippi River, Jackson's tumultuous presidency included some actions that encumbered the region far more than they helped. His most destructive policy was moving Native Americans to what would become Oklahoma Territory, which included the infamous Trail of Tears tragedy, forcing thousands of Indians from their homes in the East and dumping them in the West.

AN UNCOMMON COMMON MAN

Jackson's life was always full of chaos and drama, even as a child. He was born on March 15, 1767, in the Waxhaw district along the present-day border of North Carolina and South Carolina, three weeks after an accident had killed his father, Andrew. Growing up, he erratically attended an old field school; at home, he soaked up his mother Elizabeth's tales of her Indian captivity, which she repeated again and again. In addition, he witnessed or heard horrifying details about frequent Indian wars, often said to be British-incited. Little wonder that he grew up despising Native Americans and the British. At thirteen, he demonstrated his hostility toward the British by serving in the American Revolution, probably as a courier.

Soon after his return from the battlefield, his mother died of cholera and Andrew was on his own. As an orphan at fourteen, Andrew needed to plan his future, but he lacked kinfolk willing to give him support and direction. He kicked around a while, living at one or another of his uncles' homes. He briefly tried his hand at teaching school, quickly deciding he preferred to study law. He knew the frontier needed lawyers and judges to establish law and a legal system, but law had other attractions for him as well: he would travel, making friends and contacts as he went; would be in line for promotions to such posts as prosecutor and judge; and might even enjoy the conflict and contention involved. Yet he was an indifferent student, devoting a good deal of time to his social life. Fortunately, he learned enough law to pass the bar in 1787 and establish a backwoods practice that provided adequate income.

The year 1788 brought a significant change in Jackson's life. When a friend offered him a public prosecutor's position in Tennessee, he snapped up the opportunity. In addition to the prosecutor's job, Jackson practiced law in Tennessee and tried his hand at a wide variety of other enterprises. In 1794, he joined his friend John Overton in a land-speculation company, which occasionally bought land owned by Chickasaw and Cherokee Indians. He also tried shopkeeping, opening the first general store in Gallatin, Tennessee, in 1803. The following year he purchased 640 acres of land twelve miles from Nashville, where he established the plantation he called the Hermitage. A fine, southern-style mansion became the Jacksons' home and around it he developed a cotton plantation that eventually grew to 1,050 acres and required the energy of 150 slaves.

The Hermitage was perhaps Jackson's favorite project, for he wished to provide his beloved wife, Rachel Donelson Jackson, with peace and seclusion. He had met Rachel shortly after his arrival in Tennessee in 1788, while he lodged at Donelson's boardinghouse. Because he and Rachel believed her to be divorced, the couple married in 1791. Upon learning that her divorce had not been final, they remarried in 1794. Local gossips labeled Rachel a bigamist and worse. Some women even pulled the bottoms of their skirts aside when she came in view so that their skirts would not be sullied by touching hers. Jackson hoped to leave such scandal and rumormongering behind in Nashville when he and Rachel moved to the Hermitage.

During the Hermitage years, Rachel helped her husband in his many political undertakings and offices. Jackson worked energetically on behalf of statehood for Tennessee, which he now considered his home state. The offices he held ranged from attorney general of the Nashville district and member of the Tennessee supreme court to the state's first representative to the U.S. House of Representatives and to the U.S. Senate. During Jackson's successful campaign for the presidency in 1828, Rachel suffered greatly from personal diatribes against her from Jackson's opponents. Sadly, Rachel did not live to see Jackson as president; she died of a heart attack shortly after his victory.

JACKSON AS PRESIDENT

Although Jackson lost in an 1824 run for the presidency, four years later, he gained a majority of votes and became president on a wave of public acclaim. A rollicking campaign had downplayed such divisive issues as slavery and states' right, presenting Jackson as an archetypal westerner and a highly successful common man. His western image, which derived largely from his Tennessee background and his prowess as an Indian fighter, led to such designations as "the frontier president" and "the first president from the American West." There was also a claim that he was the first president born in a log cabin, which is probably untrue. His actual birth place somewhere along the Carolina line went unrecorded. But nicknames continued to suggest a tie with things western: Hero of the Battle of New Orleans, Old Hickory, and Sharp Knife. The last name was given to him by Creeks and Choctaws, who enhanced Jackson's western reputation among white voters by describing him as a frontier demon who easily spilled Indian blood and walked away without looking back.

The second representation—common man—came from Jackson himself. He often supported mid- and low-born American males in his speeches. By this term, Jackson meant white male artisans, workers, farmers, and planters who deserved increased rights and better opportunities to get ahead. He clearly modeled his idea of a common man on his own background. The ultimate goal of Jackson's drive for reform was to make it possible for men like him, from poor families and with little formal education, to climb the fabled American ladder of success. To accomplish this, Jackson planned to attack upper-class elites who, according to him, wielded wealth and power for their own advancement. He also disliked what he referred to as the wealthy class's "grasping institutions," meaning banks. According to Jackson, elites and their minions caused corruption and financial distress throughout American cities and countryside alike. Taking such people down would lead to pulling up millions of others.

Although these portrayals appealed to voters, they were highly inaccurate. By 1828, when Jackson was elected to the presidency, he was, in reality, a southern planter, slave owner, and member of a moneyed class. He proudly possessed a cotton plantation near Nashville, a rapidly growing town trying to shed its frontier past, while the surrounding area of western Tennessee was no longer part of the backcountry. In addition, rather than being a common man, he was a skilled politician who could sway a crowd with his oratory or adapt his policies to suit an immediate need. He did not travel beyond the Mississippi River, nor did he very often read or talk about the trans-Mississippi frontier. One might say that the well-being of the American West was not one of Jackson's major concerns.

Nor did Jackson look or act the part of a frontiersman or a common man. People who expected to see a rough-looking individual encountered instead a graceful six-foot-one figure who weighed between 130 and 140 pounds and had an impressive shock of white hair and exceptional blue eyes. He typically clad his sparse frame in black suits with extravagantly ruffled white shirts. Besides his imposing appearance, Jackson soon proved to be as much a personality as he was a president, meaning that he often used personal force to get his way. For instance, Jackson's manners were courtly and he employed them to good effect. Acting as a genteel southern gentleman, he was fond of sweeping over the hands of ladies who stood barely five feet or less and delivering a kiss on their tiny hands, followed by eloquent compliments. Yet Jackson's vitriolic temper was also legendary. Those who observed him closely remarked on his ability to control himself when it was to his advantage, or to allow his anger to erupt in order to stun an opponent, muddle proceedings, or stop activity altogether. Perhaps most confounding was his penchant to say little or nothing about a particularly troubling issue, sidestepping or ignoring even a crucial and volatile topic, hoping it would somehow resolve itself.

As a result of Jackson's histrionics and obfuscation, it is difficult to separate out his western policies. Documentary evidence lacks any proof that Jackson thought much about the way his actions might shape the future of the American West. Thus, it can be fairly be said that Jackson took the older trans-Appalachian, and especially the newer, trans-Mississippi, West into account only incidentally as:

gaming chips in the struggle regarding the expansion of slavery into western territories,

a convenient place to deposit inconvenient Native American peoples, and

a source of specie when his economic manipulations led to trouble for America's economic situation.

JACKSON, SLAVERY, AND THE WEST

When Jackson became president in 1829, he had little to say about slavery and less about the West, both of which became crucial, intricately intertwined issues during his two terms as president. In his inaugural address, Jackson stated that he would countenance absolutely "no discord" or "wrangling" over "delicate topics," by which he meant slavery. Jackson believed that arguments between the North and South could destroy the very fabric of Union. Although he did not mention the West, he was quietly effective at turning western territories into chips in a game of political poker. As soon as the question of the extension of slavery into western territories became a major point of intersection between the president and the West, Jackson made it clear that he was unwilling to bend in his long-held view of slavery. To him, slavery's extension into western territories might provide the balance to keep the nation part slave and part free.

After all, like Thomas Jefferson, Jackson came to adulthood in a plantation culture where owning slaves could improve a man's life socially and economically. Jackson had accepted the system's opportunities and limitations, and had built his personal fortune and way of life on the exploitation of an enslaved workforce. Although Jackson's contemporaries judged him a "humane" owner who housed his slaves in larger-than-normal family units and provided ample food and medicine, this may have been a smoke screen on Jackson's part. During the late 1820s, many of the slave-owning class increasingly attempted to ameliorate public criticism by presenting themselves as beneficent "employers" of an unfortunate group of people—black slaves—who could not fend for themselves. This sentimentalized trope emphasized that slave owners took care of aged family slaves no longer fit to work so they would not fall victim to less-high-minded masters. They also claimed to purchase slaves in family groups that included siblings or maintained a slave marriage, and to avoid buying young children. These same slave owners claimed, like Jackson, that they provided ample medical care, clothing, housing, and food. Reportedly, Jackson even provided knives, guns, and fishing gear so that his slaves could supplement their diets. Yet a close look at the Hermitage records indicates that a fair number of its slaves voted against its system by running away. Jackson's retainers issued posters offering rewards for the return of wayward slaves and punished, with vigorous and sometimes life-threatening whippings, those who had the bad fortune to be sent back.

In fact, Jackson quietly supported slavery and tried to refurbish its public image. To him, slaves were a special class of public property who could be bought and sold, needed care and confinement for their own good, and, as a condition of their race, had no entitlement to "rights." Jackson was far from alone in this attitude. His own vice president, John C. Calhoun of South Carolina and a slave owner like Jackson, not only advocated slavery as a positive, paternalistic institution, but gradually developed a political theory justifying its existence. Like Jackson, he wanted to preserve the Union, but increasingly saw limited government, free trade, and states' rights, including the right to nullify any action of the majority that hurt the minority (meaning slaveholders), as the way to do so. Calhoun further alienated Jackson by objecting to a high protective tariff; arguing for a state's right to neutralize a federal law; insisting that a state could, as a last resort, secede from the Union; and vocally and aggressively supporting slavery.

As president, Jackson was hardly in a position to openly advocate slavery. Instead, during the 1820s and 1830s, his reaction to the increasingly heated slavery debate was pure Jackson. A poker player might say that Jackson knew when to hold his cards and knew when to fold them. He was definitely holding, surely fully aware that presidential silence gave tacit approval to the spread of slavery in the South and to the extension of slavery into western territories. Jackson's policy, or lack thereof, became a nagging worry to people living in trans-Appalachian and trans-Mississippi regions who opposed slavery and its extension into their home areas. Unfortunately for them, Jackson's continued adherence to pro-slavery principles meant that the president of the United States as much as approved of slavery in western territories.

Jackson further complicated his stance by refusing to acknowledge slavery as a human rights' issue. Rather than admitting that the challenge to the morality of slavery might be at the root of secessionist threats and of eventual civil war, he insisted that secession and war were political matters, caused by the current states' rights versus nationalism split. He classified the burning question of his era not as a moral issue, but as power-related: who would be the ultimate ruler in the United States—individual states or the federal government? Although he had come to the presidency with states' rights leanings, he soon recognized that being at the helm of the nation meant, first and foremost, holding it together. Over everything, he wanted to balance states' rights and nationalism and to avoid secession and civil war, but addressing slavery might lead to the opposite result. For the West, Jackson's goals meant expanded rights for states, yet they also created the potential for extending slavery.

Jackson's hopes of stimulating America's economic growth involved him in another conundrum. To hold the Union together, he realized that the country had to sustain economic growth. Because agricultural products, which included a low percentage of cotton, accounted for about 66 percent of U.S. exports at the time, he planned to increase American output by opening as much new farmland as possible in the North and, especially, in the South and Southwest. Yet it was clear that economic development demanded affordable, dependable workers of all kinds. In addition, such workers, mostly white, needed adequate wages to survive and usually disdained plantation labor as overtaxing and as "slaves' work." But, because Jackson hoped to accelerate the production of cotton to feed the machinery of the Industrial Revolution in the North and in England, he felt that the nation needed more slaves. Worse yet, because of the 1808–9 prohibition against importing slaves, planters had to rely on increasingly expensive American-born slaves, smuggled slaves, or kidnapped free blacks. The latter was quite possible, given that in 1830 the federal census counted over six thousand free blacks living in Washington, D.C., alone, and quite available for abduction.

Jackson must have asked himself a number of crucial questions. How could he, a southern planter, in good conscience oppose slavery? If he did oppose slavery, how could he plunge himself, as well as his neighbors, colleagues, and constituents, into economic destitution and social upheaval? Would the abolition of slavery not also cause the nation's economy to career toward destruction? The Union would surely crumple, and he would be responsible for the division of the nation. He apparently concluded that if the American economy had to grow on the backs of black people, so be it.

Many people, including numerous westerners, expressed outrage that the president avoided taking a decisive stand on slavery and its extension, but if they had looked back, they would not have been caught off guard. In 1816, for example, Jackson had clearly revealed his regard for slavery. As a major general in the American army, he was called upon to handle the crisis at Fort Negro, a Florida fortification and its compound abandoned by the British at the end of the French and Indian War in 1763 and now occupied by runaway slaves who had fired on a U.S. naval force, killing four American sailors. Jackson sent troops to Fort Negro to destroy what he called a threat to southern safety and property composed of land and, especially, slaves. On July 27, 1816, troops literally blew the fort to oblivion, sending three hundred black men, women, and children to their deaths. Later, Jackson ordered the fort rebuilt on a nearby site to keep "safe" the border between southern states and Spanish-controlled East and West Florida. The new Fort Gadsden was to ensure that no American slaves ran away to the Floridas or to Creek Indians willing to shelter them. Jackson's actions indicated that he deeply believed in protecting slavery in the South.

In 1819, Jackson showed himself once again by supporting the Missouri Compromise, which drew a line at 36 degrees, 30 minutes north latitude across the trans-Mississippi West, providing that territories above the line would remain free but those below could decide for themselves. In other words, he favored slavery extension into the western territories. Even ten years after the Missouri Compromise, the president continued to desperately hope that somehow the balance could be maintained, that the Union could survive half-slave and half-free, which Republican President Abraham Lincoln, who was not a cotton planter, would later declare an impossible state of affairs.

In the meantime, the growing demand for cotton and the tendency of cotton to rob the soil of its nutrients fueled the quest for more arable land and more slaves to work that land. In 1830, census takers counted over two million black slaves, a sharp increase over the nine hundred thousand counted only twenty years earlier. Because cotton was a crop demanding intensive cultivation, the majority of slaves worked cotton; that is, planting cottonseeds, then weeding, hoeing, and keeping the plants insect- and disease-free until picking time. Jackson's response as a southern planter was to add slaves to his personal workforce; legend says that at one point he owned as many as three hundred slaves, including some from severed families.

In spite of the fraught situation, Jackson appeared oblivious of the import of current happenings. The emergence of growing and vitriolic opposition to slavery should have put him on notice. In 1831 alone, two events occurred that surely caused thoughtful men and women to take pause. One was the establishment of an abolitionist newspaper, *The Liberator,* by a fiery and committed white editor, William Lloyd Garrison. The second occurred on August 22 of that year. A slave rebellion in Virginia led by black slave Nat Turner resulted in the death of fifty-seven white people. The punishment for Nat Turner's rebellion was swift and harsh; he was hanged on October 30, 1831.

Shortly afterward, Jackson confronted what he thought of as the final defection of his vice president, John C. Calhoun. In 1831, a long exchange of hateful letters between Jackson and Calhoun ground to a halt, while a cabinet scandal involving Secretary of War John Eaton and his wife, Peggy, led to Calhoun's becoming the first vice president in history to resign his office. Calhoun continued to be involved in conflicts regarding the tariff and nullification, while he fleshed out his view of slavery as a positive good. According to Calhoun, black people were destined to be permanent laborers, but white paternalism protected them from exploitation and harm.

These and other happenings caused the abolitionist crusade to escalate to a national level, eventually dragging President Jackson into the controversy. In 1835, the actions of Northern abolitionism disrupted the U.S. post office and the U.S. House of Representatives. Early that year, Northern abolitionists began sending anti-slavery tracts by U.S. mail to Southerners. Most recipients judged the materials to be "incendiary literature" and asked that post offices suppress such mailings, which they lacked power to do. On July 29, a mob of three hundred Southerners forced their way into the Charleston post office, seized abolitionist tracts, and destroyed them. In crafting his response, Jackson was caught between pro-slavery Southerners and anti-slavery Northern Democrats. To extricate himself gracefully and placate both sides, he ordered the U.S. postmaster to give southern post offices the discretionary power to deliver the offending material, or not. Most post offices chose not to deliver the tracts, averting a crisis in the South. At the same time, Jackson criticized Northern abolitionists for their inflammatory tactics.

Jackson may have breathed a sigh of relief, but that was not the end of the matter. In December 1835, abolitionists submitted petitions to the U.S. House of Representatives, asking it to pass legislation stopping the slave trade and slavery in Washington, D.C. When Southern pro-slavery members denounced the people behind the petitions as "ignorant fanatics," Northerners responded that submitting petitions was a constitutional right. The volatile situation was diffused by using the House's recently adopted resolution, or gag rule, saying that petitions regarding slavery would not be read, but would be tabled instead. Jackson was pleased because he did not want the slavery debate to upset the presidential campaign of his personal choice as his successor, Martin Van Buren.

Besides, Jackson had an ace in the hole that might resolve the slavery argument to his satisfaction. For some years, the Mexican government had tried to develop its northern state of Tejas by offering land to settlers, especially Americans. The majority of takers, who numbered some thirty-five thousand whites with three thousand slaves between 1821 and 1835, wanted to escape worn-out lands and contention over slavery in the American South. When they brought slaves with them or purchased them after they had settled, their actions discomfited the Mexican government, which by Spain's order had abolished slavery in 1811. Jackson tried to resolve the conflict by sending, as ambassador, Anthony Butler to buy Tejas from Mexico for $5 million. Unfortunately for Jackson, Butler was a corrupt bumbler who offered bribes, threatened, and attempted to "deal." After Butler had totally annoyed and alienated Mexican officials, Jackson recalled him.

The friction between Mexican leaders and American settlers continued. In 1830, Mexico banned additional immigration. Shortly, General Antonio López de Santa Anna came to power and instituted a new anti-slavery constitution, which upset American settlers who relied on slave labor for their incomes. In 1835, settlers who wanted independence from Mexico initiated a revolution. Although they suffered a tremendous defeat at the Alamo, the insurgents went on to wrest their freedom from Mexico. In 1836, the leaders declared Texas, as they now called it, an independent pro-slavery republic, and applied for admission to the United States as a slave state.

Jackson had watched this grueling and destructive process in relative silence. In 1835, his inaction was taken as implicit approval of the Texas revolution. After all, the American pro-slavery states had much to gain. Whether intact or divided into smaller states, Texas would give the South increased leverage in the Senate, as well as overall. But when the Texas document reached Jackson, he refused to raise the slavery issue because, for him, the timing was wrong. Again, he wanted to minimize opposition from such people as Senator Henry Clay from Kentucky until Martin Van Buren was successfully elected to the presidency. After Van Buren's election, Jackson left the question of Texas statehood to the new president. But, on March 3, 1837, Jackson's last day in office, he showed his support of Texas by formally recognizing it as an independent republic.

After Van Buren became president, however, he would reject his mentor's guidance. Instead, he would oppose the extension of slavery into the West, including Texas. At that point, former President Jackson would break with his favorite. What Jackson left behind for Van Buren was obviously controversial, but what he left for the West was a chaotic situation in which some people opposed slavery while others argued for its extension westward, thus pushing the West down the path to involvement in a civil war not of its own making.

JACKSON, INDIAN REMOVAL, AND THE WEST

In the meantime, Jackson was creating an irredeemable blot of historic proportions on America's honor. In the Age of Romanticism that stressed individual thought and action, Jackson had adopted as his operating motto, "I know what is right and I will fight for it." In relation to Native Americans, many of whom still lived on their original lands, he seized the position of a moral arbiter who believed that removal from their homes would prevent the extinction of Indian peoples and their cultures. In his contacts with Native Americans, Jackson styled himself a paternalistic figure called the Great Father, who knew what was best for his children. In spite of Jackson's seeming sincerity, his removal programs resulted in a massive loss of life, widespread ruin of personal property, and the end of life as Indians and their ancestors had always known it. Even if Jackson's motives were authentic, he was guilty of careless planning, an impossibly low budget, and virtually no presidential oversight.

In truth, another unstated and far less altruistic motive also inspired Jackson. For him, Indian removal was integrally tied to slavery. The westward removal of Indians would free land for white farmers and planters in the Southeast. Because white Southerners were growing in number and wearing out much of the available fields, Jackson saw removal of Native Americans from their relatively fresh land as a perfect solution. Although Jackson did not hope to add additional areas to the United States as had Thomas Jefferson, he felt it was imperative to retrieve by purchase vast tracts of Indian-owned land, especially in the Southeast. Thus did Jackson become an expansionist of sorts, creating what might be called "internal expansion."

Jackson failed to give much consideration to what removal might do to Native Americans or to areas to which they were deported. Any thinking person would have recognized that evicting thousands of Native Americans from their homes would create a huge dispossessed population that, short of outright extermination, had to be transported and settled somewhere. Jackson, who had spent many years negotiating Indian treaties, had to have known the dangers of removal. He was especially culpable of haste in achieving his goals. He did not examine the logistics of removal nor did he follow up the process as it developed. The president put removal into motion and let it roll its catastrophic way westward.

Jackson's haste and carelessness appear odd, given the fact that removal was one his long-term goals, and one that he believed had the potential to resolve the South's problems. Indeed, when he first had become president, he had immediately advocated what he saw as the "necessity" of removal. As early as his inaugural address in March 1829, the new president informed a crowd of twenty thousand spectators that he would be careful and kind: "It will be my sincere and constant desire to observe toward the Indian tribes within our limits a just and liberal policy, and to give that humane and considerate attention to their rights and their wants which is consistent with the habit of our Government and the feelings of our people."

Jackson also promised that Native Americans would be relocated where they would always be "*free* from the influence of White men and undisturbed by the local authority of the states." If true, this statement meant that future white settlers would have to accept Indian possession of land. Yet recent events had shown that white settlers were perfectly capable of encroaching on Indian lands through dishonesty or force. Nor, Jackson pledged, could local governments intervene in Indian affairs. Control would belong to federal authorities, who would supposedly have agents on the ground to help and protect the relocated Native Americans.

The new president hoped that Native Americans would view removal favorably and would voluntarily relocate in the West. In an early message directed to the Cherokees, he assured them that he felt compelled to "save" their people by relocating them to "fine and fertile country," where the federal government "could and would protect them fully in the possession of the soil, and their right of self-government." If they agreed to move, Jackson continued, they would someday be the "equals" of whites "in privileges, civil and religious," but those Cherokees who stayed on their tribal lands in the Southeast would bring "destruction upon their race," a result that he could not alter unless they relocated.

What Jackson meant by "destruction" was the continual interference of self-serving whites. Southeastern tribes were suffering evils similar to those they had confronted in Thomas Jefferson's time. Greedy whites cheated Indians out of their land or moved into Indian areas and refused to leave. White traders illegally sold whiskey to Indians and even opened "drinking houses." And on Cherokee land, where gold was discovered in 1828, thousands of white men literally dug up the ground looking for the precious metal. Apparently on orders, American troops refused to interfere, even though treaties had guaranteed the military protection of Indians.

By mid-1829, Jackson decided that federal action had to be taken to help what he called this "much injured race." Of course, he meant removal. To make the plan succeed, he explained, Congress must become involved immediately. Prior to that time, Native Americans had been relocated by presidential action. The Senate had been asked only to approve treaties and the House to pass an occasional appropriations bill, as were the duties of each house according to the Constitution. Now, after much consultation, Jackson sent a strongly worded message to Congress requesting removal legislation. He asked that Congress set aside a land area in the western, unsettled portion of the Louisiana Territory for a new Native American homeland. To get this legislation passed, Jackson relied on such Democratic stalwarts in Congress as Hugh Lawson White of Tennessee, who chaired the Senate's Committee on Indian Affairs, and John Bell of Tennessee, who headed the House of Representatives' Committee on Indian Affairs. Both committees were packed with pro-removal Southerners. Also important to Jackson's cause was Speaker of the House Andrew Stevenson, who three times broke a tie vote, thus saving the removal bill. Although the debates in Congress were political, sectional, and acrimonious, spurred on by pressure from Jackson, the Removal Act was approved. On May 28, 1830, the president signed it into law.

The Removal Act had several key provisions. It allowed Jackson to trade as yet unsettled land in the West for Indian-held land in the Southeast, reimburse Indians for improvements they had made on their original lands, pay the expenses of removal, give Indians perpetual title to their new holdings, and assure them they would have whatever "aid and assistance as may be necessary for their support and subsistence" during their first year in the West. The act also provided the woeful amount of $500,000 to fund this ambitious program. In *The Legacy of Andrew Jackson* (1988), the eminent Jackson scholar Robert V. Remini states that the actual cost of removal soared into "tens of millions of dollars, and took 100 million acres of Indian land east of the Mississippi River at a cost of sixty-eight thousand dollars, as well as 32 million acres west of the Mississippi that had been reserved for Indians by treaty." Remini adds that, "in terms of human life and suffering," the cost was incalculable.

At first, because Jackson hoped that Indian leaders would agree to the move, he personally met with chiefs and elders. When he encountered Indian resistance, he reacted with surprise, acting as if Native Americans should be happy to leave the harmful impositions of the white world. When Jackson learned this to be untrue, he said that Indians could remain on their lands if they were willing to abide by the rules of their states. "Brothers, listen," Jackson responded to Chickasaws who refused to leave: "To these laws, where you are, you must submit." When leaders asked Jackson why this was so and what had become of their existing treaties with the U.S. government, he implacably replied that individual states "claim a right to govern and control your people as they do their own citizens. . . . where you are, it is not possible you can live contented and happy." The president predicted that, in such circumstances the extinction of Native Americans was inevitable. Jackson offered them no viable choice, and they knew it.

Gradually, some leaders and their groups acquiesced, yet others remained hesitant. In disgust, Jackson turned matters over to his friend and supporter, John H. Eaton, whom he had purposely appointed as secretary of war to help him with removal. Eaton would eventually mediate a fair number of the approximately seventy treaties signed during Jackson's two terms. Although the negotiations often entailed bribes, intimidation, and outright force, Eaton always reported to Jackson that the transactions had been on the up-and-up. Whether Jackson believed this, he accepted Eaton's reassurances and gave the necessary orders to get a particular relocation in motion. Jackson, intent on haste and impatient with recalcitrant Indians, moved ahead as rapidly as possible, which left little room for second thoughts or recasting incomplete plans.

Corruption on all levels compounded existing weak spots. Fraud and theft seriously marred preparations. For instance, money set aside for blankets was so depleted by illegal withdrawals by various officials that there was only enough money left to purchase "shoddy blankets" made of cuttings and threads from a textile factory floor that were soaked and dried to form a substance commonly used for the linings of coats. On the westward trail, rain and snow caused these blankets to return to their original components. In addition, food and medical supplies were totally inadequate.

Tragically, the winter of 1831–32 was a fury of cold, snow, and ice. Accounts of this first westward trek of the Indians made its way back east through word-of-mouth, letters, newspapers, and magazines. Pleas and petitions soon poured into the president's office from the travelers; they detailed abuses, including perplexing and dangerous conditions both during the trek and after arrival. Lands had not been surveyed, supplies had not arrived, and federal payments were in arrears. Added to this was the antagonism of tribes already living in the area, some of whom were indigenous and resented the newcomers. Newcomers reported that antagonistic tribes stole their stock, depleted their hunting reserves, and mounted punitive raids against them. The military protection that Jackson had promised was not in evidence, and, in some cases, the situation had degenerated into mayhem. Seemingly shocked at reports of the carnage, Jackson switched the operation from civilian to military hands, but with little system-wide reform.

Back in the Southeast, leaders of the "civilized" and white-educated Cherokee Nation were appalled at what faced them. After all, they had taken on white ways, including language, law, clothing, and housing, yet their success at assuming Anglo civilization earned them no consideration. To keep their lands, they appealed to the American public and fought two cases to the Supreme Court—with no result but to raise Jackson's ire. After extended wrangling, some Cherokees left Georgia, while others remained until their two-year deadline expired. During that time, they were harassed by white intruders, were restricted from digging gold on their own land, saw their chiefs and councils deprived of power, and were denied military protection.

Finally, it would be left to Jackson's successor, Martin Van Buren, to send seven thousand troops to dislodge the Cherokees and escort them westward. Local militiamen armed with rifles and bayonets, forced Native American men, women, and children from their homes and herded them into a stockade, where they were to wait for their removal. They had nothing but what they carried. Looters stole things left behind, including stock, then destroyed what they could not carry off by torching the Indians' homes and buildings. At the same time, Cherokees were divided into groups of one thousand. They would be forced to walk the last eight hundred miles and were ordered to leave their dead and dying along the side of the road that they named "The Trail of Tears." Of the some eighteen thousand Cherokees who set out upon the hellish and deadly path to the West, it is estimated that between four thousand and eight thousand died before reaching their destination.

Removal left a disastrous legacy for Native Americans but also for the American West. Rather than the peaceful life that President Jackson predicted for those who relocated, the aftermath for the Indians included broken treaties; widespread poverty and liquor addiction; incursions by white settlers, especially growing numbers of immigrants; increasing anti-Indian prejudice on the part of whites; lack of military protection; and shrinking boundaries of the Indian reserve. In Indian Territory, soon to be Oklahoma Territory, removal meant an influx of thousands of poverty-stricken residents, who were often ill, starving, or liquor-addicted. When federal assistance was late or failed to materialize at all, someone had to fill the breach, from sympathetic individuals and missionaries to religious, reform, and benevolent groups.

Other desperate situations quickly developed. White incursions and prejudicial attitudes led to legal entanglements, notably regarding land rights and boundaries. As white settlers immediately started to whittle away at the boundary lines of Indian Territory, demanding more cessions to provide for white settlement, Indian holdings were continually redefined and reduced. Those who were too poor to move, or who wanted to stay where they were, found themselves left behind in areas that were turning white, where they were unwelcome. Other Indians were moved again, but as Indian Territory shrank, Indians having different languages, cultures, and expectations were pushed together and often lived in discord.

The federal government, especially through the Bureau of Indian Affairs

(BIA), tried to help all relocated tribes, but Jackson's removal program led to numerous and complex problems. In 1840, Indian Territory was not organized as a formal territory with its own constitution and government. Thus, the BIA back in Washington, D.C., had to try from afar to understand Indian needs and controversies. At the same time, white BIA agents on the ground too often reacted to immediate conditions in impatient and even corrupt ways, further complicating matters and causing bitterness on the part of local whites. All of this resulted in a volatility that impacted virtually every aspect of western society, from health care and education to violence and crime. Thanks to Jackson, such difficulties set the stage for the reservations that eventually grew out of removal settlements. Over the years, most of these early ills turned into modern-era social and economic concerns for both Native American and western leaders.

JACKSON, THE AMERICAN ECONOMY, AND THE WEST

As he had with the controversial topics of black slavery and Indian removal, Jackson used his inaugural address of 1829 to raise questions related to the American economy. According to him, "the paper money system and its natural associations—monopoly and exclusive privilege" were so deeply rooted in the American economy that only "vigilance and control would eradicate the evil." Because Jackson saw common people as the "bone and sinew of the country," he hoped to protect them from what he called the greed and selfishness of such elitist classes as industrialists and bankers.

Unfortunately, the president was uneducated in the finer points of economics and acted on his prejudices. Even when more knowledgeable advisors offered their input, he refused to listen and went his own way. Jackson brought to office a deep-seated belief that banks and the men who ran them were at the core of America's economic ills. Accordingly, in late 1832 Jackson wrote, with the help of his disciple, Representative James K. Polk (who in 1845 would become president in his own right), a veto message to kill the bill that would have chartered the Second Bank of the United States for another twenty-year term. Jackson accused the Bank of such practices as accepting devalued paper money for public lands and of serving only the wealthy. Although the Bank had four years in which to disband, in 1833 Jackson ordered that government funds and other Bank revenues be deposited instead in state banks of his choosing, called "pet banks." Because these state banks had no regulatory system, they used the increased funds to issue easy loans and print virtually worthless paper money. This triggered a dramatic inflationary whirlwind that encouraged individuals and speculators to buy even more public land, especially in the West, with highly inflated paper money.

On the Bank controversy, Jackson faced formidable opposition, especially from Senator Henry Clay of Kentucky. Also a supporter of a strong American economy, Clay raised Jackson's hackles with his "American System," which was based on a higher tariff to stimulate American industry; a comprehensive federally funded program supporting such internal improvements as roads and canals; and a strong national bank. After Jackson destroyed the Second Bank of the United States, Clay successfully urged Congress to sanction the president. Although Jackson later had this action reversed, the incident did nothing to reconcile the two men. In fact, as Henry Clay became more attuned to western concerns and needs, he picked up nicknames of his own: Henry of the West and the Western Star.

Still, the president remained impervious to suggestions from Clay and others. Jackson, who had once said that his greatest fear was that he might fail to ensure the "future prosperity of our beloved country," responded to the mega-inflation he had helped create with yet another horrible policy. In July 1836, the Specie Circular ordered that public lands must be paid for in specie (silver or gold coins) rather than with paper money. This led to a disastrous credit crunch. Investors and speculators used the specie they had to pay what loans they could and defaulted on the rest. Many existing companies, such as those that had funded internal improvements during the 1820s and 1830s, crashed. Twenty-six state governments, which had also invested heavily in such projects as roads and canals, declared bankruptcy or almost did so. Exports fell and unemployment was rife.

The following year, the Panic of 1837 erupted, with calamitous impact. At the same time, the British economy experienced a similar decline, which caused its demand for imports—most notably cotton—from the United States to drop. It is ironic that the South, which Jackson so favored, took the first hit. Planters in the Cotton Belt who had purchased land and slaves on credit went under, and even the formerly prosperous economy of New Orleans declined. The North suffered extensive damage as well, with bank losses in New York alone topping $100 million. The West held out slightly longer, largely because of demand for its agricultural goods and because westerners could eat their own products. But the Specie Circular caused hard money to flow from west to east, leaving abject poverty in its wake in the West.

In response, Jackson asked that the Specie Circular be given a bit longer to take effect, while he continued to claim that the "perfidy and treachery" of bankers had caused the economic reverse. Much of the American public blamed Jackson, however, for his manipulation of national currency and banking. To his dismay, the bitterness followed him into retirement, with disillusioned citizens holding him personally responsible for the Panic of 1837.

JACKSON AND RETIREMENT

In March 1837, Jackson retired to a flood of gifts and enthusiastic acclaim from thousands of people who applauded his programs, especially Indian removal. He moved to the Hermitage near Nashville, Tennessee, and, shortly thereafter, joined the First Presbyterian Church of Nashville. But if Jackson wished to live in peace, it was a short-lived hope. Without his wife, Rachel, he felt lonely and forlorn. Poor health frequently kept him down. And his friends and neighbors stayed away because they judged him guilty for the Panic of 1837 and its aftermath, which had so curtailed their lives.

At the same time, other national controversies worrisome to Jackson continued to escalate and intensify. For instance, in 1838, a mob burned Anti-Slavery Hall in Philadelphia, bringing closer to reality Jackson's remark that the slavery question would someday be settled by the "thunder of the sword." And, as threats of secession and civil war grew more strident, an unbending Jackson continued to advocate a strong federal union of the states, saying, "I will die with the Union." Only his policy of removal gained acceptance from many white Americans who held anti-Indian prejudices and saw great value in obtaining Indian lands.

Gradually, his long interest in political gambles and deals faded. On June 8, 1845, Andrew Jackson gave up the game. The most immediate cause of his death was heart failure, with chronic tuberculosis and dropsy as contributing factors. In his will, Jackson left the Hermitage to his adopted son, Andrew Jackson Jr.

JACKSON'S WESTERN LEGACY

What this giant of a personality bequeathed to the trans-Mississippi West was legion. Although, when alive, Jackson showed little interest in the West, his programs had tremendous impact on the region. For the white male population of the West, Jackson's reputation as a western hero and advocate of expanded democracy established a model of white male westerners who were strong, courageous, and democratic. As he argued for the democratization of the nation, its peoples, and its government, so did Jackson democratize the white male West. It was in the West that his version of democracy especially took hold among people who, for a variety of reasons, had faith in his ideas of majority rule and of elected officials as the agents of common folk. And Jackson deserves credit for pushing western states to grant universal white manhood suffrage, opposing property requirements for voting, and supporting labor reform for white men. At the same time, Jackson's use of the veto and a strong personal presence increased presidential influence immensely, bringing the West more closely under presidential supervision and policy. Although many westerners resented power being located in the distant East, the majority of white men in the West were often strong supporters of Jackson's newly formed Democratic Party.

Of course, given the era, Jacksonian democracy excluded peoples of color. Because of Jackson's vigorous removal policy, Native Americans spring to mind first. White westerners especially posed difficulties for Indians who had been removed to the region. Looking for a rationale in responding to Native Americans, whites often turned to Jackson. They held him up as the Indian fighter, as an American hero whose reputation had accompanied him to the presidency. Copying Jackson's "heroic" actions, numerous white westerners treated Indians despicably. The results were disastrous for Native Americans, who suffered loss of their homelands, splintered families, fear and even hatred of white people, poverty—and the addiction, poor health, and crime that so often accompany poverty.

Among Cherokees, for example, injustice appeared to be integral to white policy. Indians were not allowed to sell their land to a white man, a crime that carried the death sentence. A white man, however, could purchase allotment land if he was married to a Cherokee woman, a rule which led to a number of fraudulent marriages and easily obtained divorces. Predictably, whites clamored for Congress to open Indian areas for settlement. Some whites even settled among Cherokees, which could have led to federal fines of a thousand dollars, had there been enough federal marshals to enforce the law. Besides, only white officers could arrest whites or Native Americans if the crime was against a white person. Cherokee police could not restrain whites in any circumstances, but could take into custody other Cherokees. Gradually, Cherokees established mounted police units called the Lighthorse Police, who could judge and convict prisoners or take them to district courts.

Native Americans' troubles were so pervasive and entrenched that, despite the efforts of reformers, religious groups, and others, many of these difficulties still exist today. In addition, many descendants are tied to reservations by their dependency on the monolithic federal government back East and by anti-Indian prejudice on the part of many white westerners who hem them in on all sides. Although numerous whites deplore the situation, it is a problem with intricate historical dimensions, dropped on their predecessors in the 1820s and 1830s by President Jackson. Its roots are deep and its branches are many, confounding reasonable solutions.

Another ill-used group was black westerners, some slave and some free, who often lived in poverty and experienced discriminatory treatment in housing, education, and employment. By supporting the extension of slavery into the western territories, as well as permitting prosperous Cherokee leaders to take slaves with them into Indian Territory during the western removal, Jackson had split asunder westerners who soon replicated the rest of the nation by dividing into pro-slave and anti-slave factions. Unfortunately for blacks, whites often looked upon them as physical symbols of the controversy over the extension of slavery, and, thus, they became the targets of white ire. What Jackson left behind for the white West was an uncertain and unrestrained situation; his policies not only created a vitriolic debate over slavery in the West but caused the region to become crucial to the coming of the American Civil War.

In the economic realm, the results of Jackson's experiments hurt the West. During the Jackson years, the West had an unstable economy, further weakened when land speculation reached a frenzied peak in the mid-1830s. The Panic of 1837 then hit the West hard; farms and businesses failed, the value of paper money fell to little or nothing, and European markets dried up. When Jackson's Specie Circular caused gold and silver to flow eastward, foreclosures occurred like dominos falling. And when the Bank of England raised interest rates, denied new loans to Americans, and called in existing loans, the West approached collapse. When westerners defaulted, they angered British bankers, who were no longer willing to finance American settlers or those thronging to the American West from European countries.

The West was left largely to its own financial and economic devices to absorb thousands of newcomers. Jackson, a strong opponent of Henry Clay's American System and other internal-improvement proposals, had vetoed the Maysville Road bill in 1830 and afterwards refused federal funding for any new projects. Consequently, the West lacked a transportation network to help move thousands of settlers and the goods they needed. As these migrants pushed westward, they forged their own paths and supplied their own needs. While this did not seem to slow the tide of settlers, it led to numerous hardships and even disasters.

In sum, most of Jackson's western policies encumbered the West in its development, much like an unexpected blow to the solar plexus. Yet one positive and usually overlooked fact exists. Outgoing president Jackson signed the first act of Congress protecting a natural resource in the American West. As early as 1673, the explorers Marquette and Joliet had visited the area and claimed it for France. After it passed to the United States in the Louisiana Purchase, President Jefferson had sent scientists Dr. George Hunter and William Dunbar to explore the territory in 1804; they reported no permanent settlement as yet. In 1818, the Quapaw Indians ceded the area to the United States. In 1832, President Jackson signed legislation creating the first federal reserve, made up of four parcels of land with hot mineral springs, called Hot Springs, Arkansas Territory. This suggests that Jackson may have been somewhat more aware of the future of the American West than was shown by his other actions as president.

FOR FURTHER READING

Buchanan, John. *Jackson's Way: Andrew Jackson and the People of the Western Waters*. New York: John Wiley & Sons, 2001.

Brands, H. W. *Andrew Jackson: His Life and Times*. New York: Anchor Books, 2008.

Cole, Donald. *Vindicating Andrew Jackson: The 1828 Election and the Rise of the Two-Party System*. Lawrence: University Press of Kansas, 2009.

Green, Michael D. *The Politics of Indian Removal: Creek Government and Society in Crisis*. Lincoln: University of Nebraska Press, 1982.

Langguth, A. J. *Andrew Jackson and the Trail of Tears to the Civil War*. New York: Simon & Shuster, 2011.

Leckie, Robert. *From Sea to Shining Sea: From the War of 1812 to the Mexican War; The Saga of American Expansion*. New York: Harper, 1993.

Magliocca, Gerard N. *Andrew Jackson and the Constitution: The Rise and Fall of Generational Regimes*. Lawrence: University of Kansas Press, 2007.

Meacham, Jon. *American Lion: Andrew Jackson in the White House*. New York: Random House, 2008.

Remini, Robert V. *Andrew Jackson*. New York: HarperCollins, 1999.

———. *Andrew Jackson and His Indian Wars*. New York: Penguin Books, 2001.

———. *The Battle of New Orleans: Andrew Jackson and America's First Military Victory*. New York: Penguin Books, 2001.

———. *The Legacy of Andrew Jackson: Essays on Democracy, Indian Removal and Slavery*. Baton Rouge: Louisiana State University Press, 1988.

Wallace, Anthony F. C. *The Long Bitter Trail: Andrew Jackson and the Indians*. New York: Hill & Wang, 1993.

Wilentz, Sean. *Andrew Jackson*. New York: Times Books, 2005.

JAMES K. POLK, 1845–1849

LC-USZ62-23836

Chapter 3

JAMES K. POLK
EXPANDING THE AMERICAN WEST

To say that Tennessee Democrat James K. Polk was a compromise candidate for the presidency in 1844 would be understating the matter. As the election campaign neared, the Democrats favored Martin Van Buren for their presidential candidate and hoped to win by advocating the immediate annexation of Texas, a slaveholding republic at the time, to the United States. But Van Buren caused political havoc by releasing a letter to Washington newspapers declaring his emphatic opposition to the annexation of Texas. Just a few days earlier, Polk had come out strongly on the side of annexation.

Despite the suspicious timing, James K. Polk actually did support Texas. Like his mentor, Andrew Jackson, he argued that, if the United States did not act, Britain was hovering on the cusp, waiting to take Texas and place itself directly on U.S. borders. Even given this scare tactic, Polk's nomination came only on the ninth ballot cast by wary delegates to the Democratic convention. Yet Polk won the presidency with 170 electoral votes to 105 for Whig Henry Clay, who had opposed the admission of slave Texas.

Polk's presidential priority was set; that is, until outgoing president John Tyler pulled the political rug out from under him. Seeing that a majority of Americans appeared to favor the annexation of Texas, President Tyler grabbed the glory for himself. He finagled a way to push through a Texas annexation bill by supporting a joint resolution that was highly dubious constitutionally. Nevertheless, Tyler signed the legislation three days before Polk's inauguration. Polk hardly blinked. On March 4, 1845, he delivered a forceful inaugural address that devoted over one-third of its message to continental expansion all the way to the West Coast. The Jacksonian Democrat had triumphed and obviously intended to pursue the Manifest Destiny leanings of American voters.

What remained to Polk was dissuading Mexico from trying to hold on to Texas. Mexican officials had stated that an American move toward Texas would constitute a cause for war. In his inaugural address, Polk warned Mexican officials to leave the matter alone, stating that the Texas Republic and the United States were "independent powers and foreign nations have no right to interfere with them or to take exception to their reunion." Two days later, Mexico's liaison in Washington collected his credentials from the State Department and effectively severed U.S.-Mexico relations by boarding a ship and sailing home.

In response to Tyler's action, Polk's course took a different direction than he had anticipated. Instead of Texas, he turned his attention to the Oregon country, which the United States held jointly with Britain. The annexation of Oregon would be the first issue of his term.

THE YOUNG POLK

None of this combativeness was presaged by Polk's early life. Born in 1795, he spent his early years in Mecklenburg County, North Carolina, where land hunger raged. His father, Samuel, was a planter, surveyor, and land speculator, yet was driven to achieve more. When Cherokees relinquished their holdings in middle Tennessee, the Polk family relocated to Maury County, where Samuel would amass some fifty slaves and eight thousand acres of land. But young James was never suited to country life or outdoor activities. Chronic illness kept him by the side of his mother, Jane, who home-schooled him and passed on her stern Presbyterian beliefs and the ability to endure, no matter how difficult the situation.

In 1812, Polk's life changed when, at seventeen, he traveled on horseback with his father to Danville, Kentucky, to consult with a physician of growing repute by the name of Dr. Ehpraim McDowell. The doctor's work in abdominal disorders was pathbreaking but pain-inducing. With only brandy as anesthesia for his patient, McDowell surgically removed from James a urinary bladder stone. Remarkably, the young man made a complete recovery. Although he would never be a frontiersman, much less an Indian fighter, he thereafter enjoyed moderate good health and left domestic seclusion behind.

Because Samuel realized that his son would probably not be a planter either, he fostered James's educational aspirations. From a year at the Zion Church Academy, Polk went on to two years at the University of North Carolina at Chapel Hill, learning oratory and scoring honors along the way. In 1818, James returned to Tennessee to study law with the well-known attorney Felix Grundy. Two years later, he passed the bar exam and established a law practice in the county seat of

Columbia. In 1823, at age twenty-seven, Polk won a seat in the Tennessee House of Representatives, where he aligned himself with the unsuccessful reform causes of a democratic state constitution and an equitable tax system. He also courted and, in 1824, married Sarah Childress, a staunch Presbyterian much like his mother. Because the couple never had children, perhaps because of James's surgery, Sarah assisted him in his career. They were an attractive political couple, for what James lacked in charisma and humor, Sarah made up for with her genteel background and innate grace.

Soon Polk caught the eye of Andrew Jackson. With Jackson's help in the political arena, the youthful politician moved in 1825 from the Tennessee House of Representatives to the U.S. House of Representatives, where he became one of Jackson's close friends and advisors. By 1828, when Jackson swept the South and the West, winning the presidency by a two-to-one margin in the electoral college, Polk considered himself a "Jackson man." In following years, he supported Jackson, following him in turning away from the influential Democratic senator John C. Calhoun of South Carolina over nullification. Also, as chair of the House Ways and Means Committee, Polk gave crucial support to Jackson's destruction of the Second Bank of the United States. He later served as Speaker of the House from 1835 to 1839 and as governor of Tennessee from 1839 to 1841.

During these years, Polk added another dimension to his career, that of absentee planter. Because he had recognized that public officeholding was neither steady nor lucrative, he experimented with the land and the slave laborers that his father had left him. In 1834, he sold his fledgling Tennessee cotton plantation and established another in Mississippi. In a revealing study, *Slavemaster President* (2003), historian William Dusinberre employs overlooked evidence to show that Polk was a slave owner for profit rather than for such lofty goals as taking in family retainers, keeping slave families together, or enjoying a planter's lifestyle. Dusinberre adds that Polk recognized the political pitfalls in owning slaves. As a result, he was secretive about his plantation, his buying and selling of slaves, and the relatively high number of deaths and runaways on his place. When he ran for president in 1844, his friend and large landholder Gideon Pillow wrote publicly that Polk had taken in family slaves from his parents' and brother's families and had bought only "one slave," a woman he wished to reunite with her husband. In truth, Polk had already purchased twenty-nine slaves that year, including a number of teenage boys as field laborers, all bought separately from their families. As president, Polk continued the deception, swearing his agents to secrecy about his slave purchases, saying that "the public have [sic] no interest in knowing it, and in my situation it is better they should not." On occasion, Polk even had agents take title to slaves and later transfer bills of sale to him.

Polk's subterfuge reflects the volatile nature of the issues of slavery and its extension into western territories during the 1840s. The influential Democrat, John C. Calhoun, increasingly took an opposite view from Polk, in that Calhoun repeated the argument that slavery was a beneficent system. Calhoun downright disagreed with Whig Henry Clay, who held that Americans were in "opinion and feeling" against slavery as an evil and immoral system. Rather, Calhoun touted slavery as a "positive good" that preserved order and protected black people. Understandably, Calhoun's ideas appealed to many southerners, but caused controversy elsewhere.

In part, Polk avoided speaking favorably of slavery because he knew that he needed more than southern support. To gain a national office, he would have to appeal to the West as well. Although Polk knew much about the South and its needs, he had little experience with the West. When he lived in Tennessee, it was no longer frontier or backcountry. The "West" had largely moved across the Mississippi River, with some American settlers living as far away as Oregon and California, neither one yet a part of the United States. Nor did Polk grow up with frontier experiences. He did not live through Indian wars, as did Thomas Jefferson and Andrew Jackson, nor was he physically able to work on his father's farm. As a lawyer and politician, his milieu was Tennessee, then Washington, D.C. One of his biographers, Sam W. Haynes, put it this way: "Polk knew little of the world beyond rural Tennessee and showed no particular inclination to learn."

Nor was Polk, like Thomas Jefferson, a political theorist or, like Andrew Jackson, a military hero and a brawler. Rather, he was a serious man of Jacksonian principles who was devoted to seeing "right" done. To this end, he spent hours with friends and advisors, listening to each man's views before revealing his own. Polk went against advice only if he believed his position was correct. In personality, he was taciturn, humorless, and increasingly dependent on his wife Sarah's charm to get him through social engagements and ceremonial occasions.

Polk also lacked personal style. His dress and demeanor spoke of a slightly fusty gentleman or perhaps a businessman from middle America. He was slim and of moderate height, had brown hair that he wore in no particular fashion, favored plain black suits that were usually outdated, and used his capacious pockets in lieu of a briefcase. But he was meticulous in other ways. He spent hours at his desk routing mail, completing mundane documents, and doing other tasks so they would be done right.

Obviously, Polk was not an engaging or imposing man. On seeing him, people did not immediately judge him of great character or of some importance. Polk himself was aware of his shortcomings and made attempts to fix them. For instance, to lighten his speeches he added humorous quotes and anecdotes. Yet he knew that he was not the ilk of a Jefferson or a Jackson, especially when he failed in 1841 to win a second term as governor of Tennessee. Thus, he did not aspire to the presidency of the United States. In that momentous event, both fate and Polk's mentor, Andrew Jackson, would play major roles.

THE FIRST "DARK HORSE" PRESIDENT

In 1844, however, Polk did hope to advance his career, perhaps by attaining the office of vice president of the United States. Because Martin Van Buren appeared likely to be the Democratic candidate for a second term as president, Polk showed outward loyalty to him. When Van Buren's fortunes flagged because of his refusal to immediately annex Texas, Polk realized that the Democratic Party was deeply divided along sectional lines. Then, a still-influential Andrew Jackson suggested Polk as a presidential candidate, reasoning that Polk was the "most available man." In addition, Polk favored the Democratic cause of annexing Texas.

At the end of May, factionalized Democrats met in Baltimore to choose a candidate for the presidential election of 1844. When the posturing and arguing ended, James K. Polk received the nomination on the ninth ballot. He had come out of the backfield like a dark horse to grab the prize. Part of his success stemmed from his agreement to several conditions: he would continue to support the annexation of Texas, and he would take Oregon Territory away from Great Britain, which held it jointly with America. Just as he had anticipated, his campaign would be in the South first and the West second. On a more personal level, Polk made a highly unusual commitment: he would not run for a second term, thus giving the Democrats four years to resolve their problems and mass behind a single candidate.

Because individual states scheduled voting on different days, the ballots came in erratically. When the count was final, Polk squeaked by the Whig candidate, Henry Clay, who had discredited himself in the North by trying to backpedal on his declaration against the annexation of Texas. As president-elect, the first thing that concerned Polk was making cabinet appointments that would appeal to intraparty contingents. He traveled to Nashville to pay Jackson homage and consult with him on choices. Polk's final list reflected both the South and the North. The critical position of secretary of state was problematic, in that it was held by the esteemed and not easily displaced Calhoun, even though Calhoun was growing more extreme in his pro-slavery views by the day. Fortunately for Polk, Calhoun stepped down, allowing Polk to appoint the more amenable Pennsylvanian, James Buchanan, as his secretary of state. In the Senate, it appeared that Polk had another break, for his recent opponent, Henry Clay, stepped aside, at least temporarily. In 1848, he retired to Ashland, his home in Kentucky, but the following year, he was again elected to the U.S. Senate, where he would oppose the Mexican-American War and seek compromise in the fracas over slavery.

POLK AND THE OREGON TREATY

In the meantime, the newly inaugurated president searched for grounding. Because the twenty-ninth Congress would not meet until December 1845, he had time to plan his program carefully. On the domestic side, Polk chose to attack the high tariff, which, looking ahead, would result in the passage of the more moderate Walker Tariff that encouraged the trans-Mississippi West's sale of agricultural products abroad. Polk also decided to continue Jackson's opposition to internal improvements—roads, railroads, and waterways—and to define them as the states' responsibilities. This policy would rile western states, ranging from the "old" frontier that included Tennessee and Kentucky to the newer trans-Mississippi states, including Missouri, which needed transportation networks but lacked money and know-how to build them. As a third domestic goal, Polk set the creation of an independent treasury to replace the Second Bank of the United States that Jackson had destroyed. This idea would cause less debate and pass with relative ease.

In foreign affairs, Polk was on less solid ground. Two huge issues demanded attention: pursuing the annexation of Oregon and completing the annexation of Texas that Tyler had begun. Both of these goals were of tremendous import to the trans-Mississippi West. The Oregon question regarded a possible U.S. takeover of the Oregon territory held jointly by the United States and Great Britain. Because negotiations were ongoing and escalating, Polk was expected to step in as soon as possible to manage heated discussions between the two expansionist nations.

Polk was aware of Americans' fears of Great Britain on U.S. borders, in this case, the border being Oregon. America's mistrust of Great Britain dated back to the American Revolution, and was gaining steam by the 1840s. Andrew Jackson, a longtime enemy of the British, wrote to Polk, admonishing him that "War is a blessing compared to national degradation." Jackson predicted that a British hold on any part of North America "would cost oceans of blood and millions of money [*sic*] to burst asunder." Even after Polk's inauguration, when the new president had announced that America's claims to the entire Northwest area were "clear and unquestionable," Jackson urged Polk not to falter, but to stand strong against Great Britain.

Yet, for weeks after the inauguration, Polk avoided discussing his annexation plans. Silence was perhaps a ploy he had learned from Jackson. A cabinet member, Secretary of the Navy George Bancroft, said that Polk kept "his mouth as effectively shut as any man I know." Because Polk was not a person of introspection or self-examination, he was perhaps startled by his new role as advocate for the American West, specifically in the matter of the Pacific Northwest. But the gauntlet had been flung down by an "All Oregon" plank in the Democrats' 1844 platform, so Polk was committed to bringing an end to the quarrel.

Still, he seemed to be waiting for Manifest Destiny to work its magic on his behalf. This philosophy went back to President George Washington, who, in 1783, described the infant nation as a "rising empire." Similarly, President Thomas Jefferson referred to the growing country as "an empire for liberty." In its simplest form, Manifest Destiny meant that Americans believed they had the God-given mandate to spread into other people's countries, bringing with them white "civilization," prosperity, and Christianity. When Manifest Destiny became outright imperialism, it lost supporters, notably John Quincy Adams, Abraham Lincoln, and Ulysses S. Grant. Other Americans thought Manifest Destiny irreligious, inevitably leading to war and subjugation of indigenous peoples. Because Manifest Destiny was thus contested, it never became a specific policy or a formal philosophy.

The term "Manifest Destiny" came from a young journalist, John L. O'Sullivan, writing in the the *New York Morning News* in 1841. He not only gave the fuzzy yet propelling concept a name, he also argued that America must "overspread the continent allotted by Providence for the free development of our yearly multiplying millions." He added that the goal was "the development of the great experiment of liberty and federated self-government." In 1846, Senator Thomas Hart Benton expanded on O'Sullivan's ideas by phrasing them even more boldly: "It would seem that the White race alone received the divine command, to subdue and replenish the earth, for it is the only race that has obeyed it.." Today the hubris of these statements seems overwhelming, perhaps even humiliating, but in their day, men like O'Sullivan and Benton supplied a rationale for many policies and plans.

Even though Polk firmly believed in Manifest Destiny, it was July 1845 before he broke his silence regarding Oregon. He asked Great Britain to reopen talks and suggested a limited proposal, which so offended the British that they refused to resume negotiations. Polk, believing in the fairness of his offer, stated that the United States must, "firmly maintain our rights, and leave the rest to God and country." Thus, when the British offered to reinstate negotiations, Polk refused.

In his annual State of the Union address later that year, the president clarified his expectations. He urged Congress to end joint occupation of the Oregon Territory, giving Great Britain one year's notice of the American takeover. He added that forts should be built along the Oregon Trail to protect incoming settlers, especially from Native Americans, and that a generous land program be enacted to encourage American settlement when joint control ended. It looked as if America, whose claims to Oregon were not as clear-cut as Polk stated, was on the brink of war with Great Britain. In fact, Polk's demand that the boundary be at 54 degrees, 40 minutes north latitude became a rallying cry: "Fifty-four forty or fight."

The escalating contretemps over Mexican-owned Texas saved the United States from war with Great Britain. Affairs with Mexico had gotten into such a muddle that "war fever" against Mexico erupted all over the country. Unexpectedly, the two aging senators, John C. Calhoun of South Carolina and Thomas Hart Benton of Missouri, joined in opposing war, predicting that it would bring the turmoil of slavery to a head. In the meantime, the British drafted a compromise proposal regarding Oregon. They would accept the forty-ninth parallel as a line of division if Vancouver Island remained British. Although the offer failed to give the United States all of Oregon, it was favorable enough to consider. As the possibility of war with Mexico loomed large, Polk and his advisors decided to accept Britain's offer. In early June 1846, the Senate formally ratified a peaceful Oregon Treaty with Great Britain.

The reaction in the Far West was mixed. The "All Oregon" supporters charged Polk with promising one thing but accepting another. Others accused the Polk administration of caving in to Great Britain. One western legislator proclaimed: "Whilst we bluster and bloat over imbecile Mexico, we present the ridiculous attitude of yielding to England what we have asserted to be our just right." In spite of such criticism, without going to war, Polk had achieved sizable gains for the western United States: ports along the West Coast, land for settlers, and free use of the Oregon Trail without fear of British incitement of Indians.

This decision was far from the end of the matter, for the argument over extending slavery into western territories once again raised its ugly head. In 1847, Polk encouraged Congress to establish a territorial government for Oregon. The House of Representatives, with more free-state representation than the Senate, formulated a nonslavery bill based on the Northwest Ordinance of 1787, which prohibited slavery in new territories. To Polk's disgust, Calhoun confused the issue by claiming that Congress lacked the constitutional right to restrict slavery anywhere in the territories. Accordingly, neither could slave-owning citizens be barred from entering the territories with their slaves. And there was the opposite suggestion put forth by the Democratic senator from Michigan, Lewis Cass, that people in new western territories should go to the polls and vote whether to be slave or free. In other words, let popular sovereignty solve the problem in Oregon, and later, territory by territory.

Polk was further disconcerted when the Whigs entered the arena. Formed in the early 1830s by a group of disillusioned northern Democrats, the Whigs now joined the Free Soil Party—composed of erstwhile members of the Liberty Party—to support former Jacksonian Democrat Martin Van Buren for president. When Polk heard the news, he was shocked and prophesied that regional parties were "dangerous to the harmony if not the existence of the Union itself." As for Van Buren's actions, Polk damned them as "selfish, unpatriotic, and wholly unexcusable [*sic*]."

In spite of Polk's belittling the Free Soil candidate, the party's manifesto appealed to many, especially moderate anti-slavery proponents. The Free Soil approach ignored abolitionism, morality, and equality. Instead of getting into philosophical tangles regarding what the Founding Fathers intended or the ethical consequences of slavery for the United States, Free Soilers maintained that the crux of the matter was the economic threat that slavery posed to white settlers and entrepreneurs in the western territories. Was the West not the place where ambitious people could pursue the American dream of bettering themselves? And was the West not the region that, once developed, would carry the nation to prosperity? If yes, then free labor needed protection from forced slave labor. The party banner carried the slogan "Free Soil, Free Speech, Free Labor, Free Men." In 1848, the Free Soil ticket, which also promoted limited internal improvements, a homestead law, paying off the public debt, and a moderate tariff, would pick up 10 percent of the vote in the presidential election.

Meanwhile, Polk's Senate remained stymied—until news arrived of a tragic situation in Oregon. White settlers pouring into Oregon, literally by hundreds and soon by thousands, seized lands belonging to Native Americans. As usual, violence resulted when Indians resisted. The latest outburst had occurred at the Whitman

Mission, founded in 1836 near Walla Walla. After several disappointing years trying to convert Cayuse Indians to white ways, Marcus and Narcissa Whitman revised their goal drastically; they would help white settlers traveling the Oregon Trail into the Willamette Valley. In 1843, Marcus Whitman led a wagon train of some eight hundred people over the Oregon Trail, explaining, "I have no doubt our greatest work is to be to aid the white settlement of the country." Outraged Cayuse Indians tried to save their valley by first pleading with, and then threatening, Whitman, but Marcus had become an ardent proponent of Oregon expansionism. Early in November 1847, a small group of Cayuse attacked the mission, ruthlessly killing the Whitmans and twelve other people, as well as taking some fifty more captive. White retaliation followed, with as much violence and cruelty as the whites claimed the Cayuse had displayed.

In May 1848, the bearer of these bad tidings reached Washington, D.C., galvanizing senators into recognizing that the Oregon Territory must have a government and soon. Near the end of the summer session, the Senate voted in favor of the original House resolution, which stated that, based on the Northwest Ordinance, slavery would not exist in Oregon. Although President Polk saw this as a one-time solution, he signed the legislation. He appointed Joseph Lane of Indiana as governor and Joe Meek of Oregon as U.S. marshal for Oregon. He also urged the extension of federal control over the rest of the Oregon Treaty lands: present-day Idaho, Washington, and portions of Montana and Wyoming.

MR. POLK'S WAR

Meanwhile, in Mexico City, the status of Texas was hotly debated. Mexican officials, who had repudiated Texas independence, agreed to recognize the Republic of Texas, if Texans promised to remain independent, meaning they would reject American offers. In Texas, President Anson Jones suggested that the proposal be submitted to voters. Polk moved quickly. To warn the British and the Mexicans alike, he ordered sixty-two-year-old General Zachary Taylor to relocate his army from Louisiana to the south bank of the Nueces River in Texas.

Polk's action defined the legal basis of the war that would soon erupt, for both Mexico and Texas claimed the land between the Nueces River in the north and the Rio Grande in the south. Polk also seized the opportunity to show concern and sympathy for Texans. Even though American claims to the trans-Nueces were weak—one might even say phony—Polk asserted that the United States intended to protect Texas—in other words, he would hold the disputed section for Texas.

Avoiding the word "war," Polk proclaimed, "I am resolved to defend and protect Texas as far as I possess the constitutional power to do so." President Jones later remarked that "Texas never actually needed the protection of the United States," and that there had been little real reason that Texans would reject America's advances. Still, Polk was heartened when, in early summer 1845, the Texas Senate unanimously repudiated Mexico's deal by voting for annexation and statehood, scheduled for December of that year.

About the same time, a newly elected representative from Pennsylvania, David Wilmot, raised the extension-of-slavery question once again. Wilmot introduced into the U.S. House of Representatives a blanket proposition drafted by an Ohio abolitionist that no slavery would exist in areas taken from Mexico, in this case, Texas. Although the Wilmot Proviso garnered support in the West and the North, it failed to pass in the House. Still, it reopened a badly infected wound in Congress. Acrimonious debates concerning the westward extension of slavery punctuated congressional sessions for the next four years, until the issue would be put temporarily to rest by the multipart Compromise of 1850.

During the summer and fall of 1845, rumors were rife: Great Britain was planning to make Texas a protectorate; Mexicans were preparing to invade Texas; and, farther afield, Mexican-owned California was experiencing a separatist movement. It appeared that Polk had his eye on other western lands, especially California and its San Francisco and Monterey Bays. Although he denied that he intended war with Mexico, it seemed to his detractors that he was already considering Mexico's losses. In the meantime, General Taylor and his men waited south of the Nueces River in contested territory.

In November 1845, without going through proper diplomatic channels or observing ceremonial niceties, Polk sent Minister John Slidell on a secret mission to Mexico to negotiate the disputed boundary and to offer to buy parts of California and New Mexico for $25 million. Mexican officials were startled and indecisive. Aware of the heft of the United States and the strong opposition of northern Mexicans who could sweep them from office, they knew they had to either accept these demands or expect war. To stave off disaster, they refused on a technicality to accept Slidell's credentials. Shortly before Slidell returned to Washington, D.C., in March 1846, he wrote to Polk saying, "[W]e can never get along well with them, until we have given them a good drubbing."

As winter 1845–46 dragged on, people tried to decide where they—and where President Polk—stood. There were many reasons for going to war with Mexico, depending on political party affiliation, section of the country, economic status, race, ethnicity, and religious beliefs. But, inarguably, slavery was one of the most important reasons. Slaveholders in Texas wanted their rights to slave labor protected, not prohibited, as the Mexican government had done in 1829. Because of its nearness to the South and its ability to produce cotton, Texas was regarded by American slaveholders as a fair field for the expansion of slavery. Those who suffered from worn-out land especially looked to Texas for relief. Another factor was that Texas would provide a market for the South's surplus slaves.

Many of Polk's critics assumed that the president's motivations were tied to slavery. Despite Polk's attempts at secrecy, numerous people knew that he owned a Mississippi cotton plantation. Whig leaders accused him of wanting additional Texas land for settlement by southern planters/slaveholders who would spread slavery and expand southern society. Polk, of course, had never advocated slavery, its extension, or the superiority of southern culture. In addition, the plantation records that Polk left behind reflect a man who viewed his plantation not as a defining feature of his character or as a way of life, but as a source of necessary income for someone without family money or regular employment. In 1844, for example, Polk mentioned that plantation income would cover his campaign expenses. He also hoped the plantation would support his wife if she became a widow. Although he drew on plantation profits to finance aspects of his political career, he never used his presidential salary to purchase additional slaves. Also, he showed no intention of perpetuating plantation culture or southern values. Still, his opponents associated him with the "Slave Power" in the matter of wresting Texas from Mexico.

Others charged President Polk and his supporters with experiencing the adrenaline rush of Manifest Destiny. This belief was intensified for Polk, his political colleagues, and all manner of other Americans, by what scholars have come to call the "Black Legend," a prejudicial view of Spanish-heritage peoples dating back to non-Spanish, non-Catholic Europe. Because of the Spanish Inquisition, Europeans often saw Spain as overbearing, fanatical, superstitious, dark-natured, and unenlightened. When Spain and the Catholic Church successfully established a thriving empire, Europeans added the labels "greedy," "violent," "cruel," and "imperialistic" to the Black Legend.

European immigrants carried these disparaging opinions to the Americas, including the American West, where what they saw of Spanish peoples seemed to reinforce their biases. For instance, white people were often astounded when they encountered mestizos, mixed-heritage men and women, usually of Spanish and Indian background. Whites frequently responded in outrage, stating that such "mixed-breeds" were "degenerate" and deficient in morals. In 1846, the editor of the *New York Herald,* James Gordon Bennett Sr., put the matter harshly when he blamed the "degradation of the Mexican people" on the "amalgamation of the races." He added that "the idea of amalgamation has always been abhorrent to the Anglo-Saxon race on this continent."

During the mid-1840s, such vilification of Mexicans and those of Mexican heritage proved convenient, for these beliefs further rationalized Polk's possible seizure of Mexican lands. Yet opposition to Polk's growing war stance existed as well. Many Whigs, especially in the North, disapproved of war because they wanted vertical growth through industry and banking rather than horizontal growth by adding more farmland, especially if it might support cotton plantations and slavery. "Conscience" Whigs and abolitionists were especially outspoken. Boston poet and abolitionist James Russell Lowell branded the war "a national crime committed in behoof [*sic*] of slavery, our common sin." And Senator Thomas Corwin, a leading Whig from Ohio, prophetically warned that one war would lead to another; that the North and South would be "brought into collision on a point where neither will yield."

Despite the voices lifted against war, by early 1846 Polk and his supporters agreed that the United States had much to gain and little to lose by fighting a war against a nation widely believed to be deficient in principles and morals. Accordingly, Polk sent a war message to Congress, where Democratic stalwarts pushed it through. Americans who disregarded Mexico were elated, but others maintained that it was unfair to wage war on a new republic that had just achieved independence from Spain in 1821, whereas the United States had been a republic since 1776. Moreover, Mexico had experienced a series of lesser revolts since independence, with the presidency changing hands six times between June 1844 and September 1847, while the United States had a stable presidency. Mexico's economy was shaky as well, partly because it had a population of only seven million people, comprising four million Indians and three million mestizos and Europeans, to develop that economy. The United States, on the other hand, had an expanding economy based on a population of twenty million, including three million slaves.

Yet when President Polk declared war against Mexico, Mexican leaders judged their country to have the upper hand. They expected Mexico to have an easier time than America in moving men and supplies to the front, in what is today the American Southwest. They also had great hopes for Mexico's army of thirty-two thousand men, many of them experienced in warfare. Mexican leaders failed to consider that their men carried antiquated weapons and that the government had no funds to purchase later models. As it turned out, the crucial task of feeding and providing medical care often fell to mothers, sisters, daughters, and wives who straggled after their men to do what they could. As a result, Mexican troops deserted at a significantly higher rate than did American troops. Because these deserters were often poor men far away from their homes, they were ignorant of the reasons for war and had little interest in fighting it. They also lacked loyalty to the unstable Mexican government and had no fealty for their presidents, especially Veracruz native Antonio López de Santa Anna, who circulated through the presidency a number of times during the war.

Mexican leaders also underestimated the United States. Men from all over America responded to Polk's call, from the trans-Mississippi West first, the South second, and the North last. Many of the commanding officers were West Point graduates, who knew how to run a professional army. Also, the majority of the soldiers had shooting, riding, and hand-to-hand fighting in their backgrounds. The West alone supplied some forty thousand men out of a total of almost seventy thousand volunteers who came from such hard-fighting groups as the Texas Rangers, the Mormon Battalion, and the Army of the West from Missouri. Westerners had access to the field of battle and, because they envisioned the land the West would gain from Polk's war against Mexico, they fought vigorously.

In Washington, Congress usually approved measures that would help the United States win the war. As a result, although American troops experienced an unusually high casualty rate from accident and disease (eleven thousand men lost), they were generally better dressed, supplied, nursed, and fed than their Mexican counterparts, who sometimes were not only hungry, but even lacked shoes. Also, American rifles were of the spiral smooth-bore type, more accurate than the old smooth bores that Mexicans used. Later in the war, cavalry and officers carried improved Colt Walker revolvers. Also, the "flying artillery," or horse artillery, proved decisive in a number of battles. Consisting of a cannon pulled by horses ridden by armed soldiers, the equipage burst on the scene of the battle, killing as it went. The Mexicans had nothing like it, and no effective way to stop it. Many Mexicans ended the war feeling that President Polk had unleashed a mighty power that had rolled over their undeveloped and unprepared country.

In an important sense, it was Polk's war. After ordering General Taylor to cross the Rio Grande and then move southward to wrench Monterrey from the Mexican hold, Polk had worked as diligently at overseeing the war as he had at everything else in his life. As president, he had been industrious, even spending twelve-hour days at his desk. He once said that "No president who performs his duties faithfully and conscientiously can have any leisure." Polk took on the war with the same determination. Although he had little military training and experience, he did everything—making and executing battle plans, hiring and firing generals, and keeping a finger on the pulse of the fighting. His efforts redefined the vague concept of commander-in-chief, making presidential supervision and guidance high priorities in wartime. Polk also contributed a wide vision, leading to the 1846 invasion of the far north of Mexico by American troops. Under the leadership of Captains John C. Frémont and Stephen Watts Kearny, the United States brought New Mexico, a gateway to trade in the Southwest, and California, with its invaluable ports and goldfields, to America's side.

Americans at home avidly followed these developments, for the invention of the telegraph made it possible for journalists' reports to quickly reach President Polk, his Congress, and the public. Polk was more aware of faraway events than any president to his time. Reporters even formed the Associated Press to make transmission more reliable. At the same time, the print revolution made cheap newspapers, known as the "penny press," widely available. Newspaper accounts of American victories caused great excitement and were celebrated with fireworks, impromptu parades, and the ever-popular activity of drinking alcoholic beverages. Also, Generals Taylor and Scott were so lionized by the press that they would both later run for the presidency of the United States.

In 1847, President James K. Polk judged the war's end to be imminent. Accordingly, he dispatched the chief clerk of the State Department, Nicholas Trist, to negotiate a treaty with Mexico that would bring an end to the war and assess appropriate reparations. Polk could not have picked a better man. The Virginia lawyer had a long career in politics that tied the three expansionist presidents of the early nineteenth century together and provided him with tremendous expertise in diplomatic affairs. First, he had served as the aged Thomas Jefferson's secretary, married Jefferson's granddaughter, and was executor of Jefferson's estate. Next, he acted as personal secretary to President Andrew Jackson, then headed the State Department office for President Polk. Additionally, Trist was fluent in Spanish. No less a person than Secretary of State James Buchanan urged Polk to send Trist to Mexico as his executive agent. Yet, partway through his assignment, just as he was making progress, Trist received a recall notice from Polk, no reason given. After great deliberation, Trist refused to obey, supplying his reasons in a letter. Above all, Trist feared that the resulting chaos in the Mexican capital would make a treaty impossible and that all his gains would be lost. He therefore chose to remain in Mexico, continuing to act in an official capacity.

About the same time, the war moved toward Mexico City, which Polk intended to conquer. Under General Winfield Scott, American soldiers invaded Veracruz, opening access to Mexico City. On September 19, 1847, Scott's troops marched triumphantly into the capital, proclaiming the defeat of the Mexican republic. Scott's army thus began a hostile occupation, which would extend from September 1847 to June 1848. This discordant interlude did nothing to resolve relations between the two countries. Rather, it would leave much anti-American sentiment behind among Mexicans, as well as supply the American military with a surplus of anti-Mexican attitudes to take home.

As treaty negotiations approached, the question on American minds was how much Mexican territory should be taken by the United States as reparations for war costs and losses. While some Americans believed the country should claim no land, a position that Polk rejected, others called for the annexation of "All Mexico," of which Polk was unsure. The latter cry had grown through the war, particularly as Mexico's silver lodes, other mineral deposits, and agricultural production were recognized as potential boons, especially to the trans-Mississippi West. The idea also had its dissenters who pointed out that total annexation would mean that millions of Spanish-speaking, Catholic Mexicans would have to assimilate into an English-speaking, predominantly Protestant United States. It was suggested that this would have to be accomplished through military occupation or colonization, neither of which appealed to the majority of Americans.

In 1848, Polk's representative to Mexico, Nicholas Trist, initiated the final treaty, virtually dictating provisions to the devastated Mexican government represented by only three ministers. The terms located the U.S.-Mexican border at the Rio Grande rather than the Nueces River and awarded the United States the present-day states of California, Nevada, and Utah, as well as portions of New Mexico, Arizona, Colorado, and Wyoming, all in the trans-Mississippi West. In return for what was about 55 percent of Mexico, the United States would pay $15 million and assume $3.25 million in debts that Mexico owed to American citizens. As the Mexican envoys signed the initial agreement, one remarked to Trist that he must feel very proud of himself and his nation. Trist let the remark go, but later said that if the man could have seen his heart he would have known how ashamed Trist felt at the rapacity of the United States. Trist was the only American to negotiate and sign the treaty. Had he left Mexico as Polk had ordered, there might never have been such a treaty.

When Polk received the treaty, he felt forced by circumstances to accept the terms that Trist had negotiated, so he sent it to the Senate for ratification. At a pen's stroke, thousands of Mexicans suddenly found themselves living in what is now the American Southwest rather Mexico. Because the Treaty of Guadalupe Hidalgo's Article X, which protected Mexicans' property rights, was stricken by the U.S. Senate before they would ratify the treaty, Mexican landowners lost everything, from small homes to large ranches. In California alone, many of the 500-plus land grants originally given by the Mexican government were ruled invalid in U.S. courts. Those Mexicans who had once owned the land often spent years in American courts trying to prove their claims, but they lacked the written deeds and other paperwork that American officials demanded. Those who finally attained clear title were deeply in debt for court costs and related expenses.

After the war, Mexicans faced other difficulties. In programs and policies, Polk and his colleagues did little to diffuse the tremendous anti-Mexican attitudes of many Americans or to help Mexicans adapt to their new country. In the American West, many Mexicans lived in segregated areas and, even if allowed to vote, were discouraged from voting or told how to cast their ballots. The rights of Mexican women were also curtailed. For example, those who had owned and operated businesses fell victim to U.S. laws that prohibited married women from undertaking such enterprises. Meanwhile, Mexicans who stayed in Mexico crossed the border to supply much-needed labor in the American Southwest. They worked in low-level jobs, receiving what was called a "Mexican wage," which was less than the going rate, but higher than they would have received in Mexico. Neither group felt that America and its president had treated them as neighbors.

POLK'S UNTIMELY DEATH

The presidency took a heavy toll on Polk. By the time he left the presidency, he had lost weight and his face was lined and pallid. Although he was only fifty-three, he looked much older. On a goodwill visit to the South, he contracted cholera in New Orleans, from which he never fully recovered. At the suggestion of supporters, Polk went on a monthlong tour through the South, where huge, cheering crowds met his stops. When he returned to Nashville on April 2, he was again met by spirited fans. His health improved a bit until late May, when the cholera epidemic hit Nashville. Polk grew ill again, and on June 15, 1849, he died at Polk Place, only three months after his retirement. His wife, Sarah, continued to live at their home for more than forty years, supported by its cotton production. In his will, Polk stipulated that his slaves were to be freed after he and his wife had both died, but the Emancipation Proclamation of 1863 would free them first.

POLK'S WESTERN LEGACY

Although Polk was not a western-oriented president or especially sensitive to the region beyond the Mississippi River, he left it an immense legacy, most of which still influences the West today. Most notably, he added 1.2 million miles of land beyond the Mississippi River. Yet Polk put in motion far more than geographic growth. By catapulting the United States onto the international stage, he brought the West along as well. Also, because of the West Coast ports acquired with the annexation of Oregon and California, the West increased its international trade and had the opportunity to make contacts abroad. And, just days before California's transfer to the United States, gold was discovered there, which led to the largest gold rush ever known in this country. No longer was the trans-Mississippi West a younger sister to the rest of the United States; it was approaching adulthood in its own right.

As another outcome of Polk's aggressiveness, the West now encompassed a huge number of new territories that brought to a head several existing issues. The question of whether slavery would be extended into western territories taken from Mexico created a national crisis. No longer a sectional dispute that could be resolved, at least temporarily, by compromises, the sheer mass of the new western territories demanded an answer from the federal government regarding the westward extension of slavery. Although Mexican negotiators at Guadalupe Hidalgo had implored Nicholas Trist to add to the treaty the prohibition of slavery in the lands Mexico was losing, Trist made it clear that President Polk and his supporters would not even consider the provision, let alone include it. After the treaty, Texas leaders immediately reestablished slavery in Texas. Reportedly, even slaves freed by the 1829 Mexican edict reverted back to slave status. At the same time, talk of the failed, but not forgotten Wilmot Proviso, was everywhere. To say the least, the slavery issue demanded a resolution.

At the same time, the West was experiencing a migration of gigantic proportions. When Polk opened Oregon and Texas for settlement, thousands of settlers flocked over the Oregon Trail, the Santa Fe Trail, the Mormon Trail, and less well-known routes. The West's population was turbulent in many ways. Polk's addition of unimaginable amounts of land at one time led to such rapid settlement that it was seldom orderly. Unlike Thomas Jefferson, Polk had not thought ahead to land surveys, ordinances, and other provisions. As a result, boundaries of the American West allowed open range without fences; open towns without law and order; and an open society of enormous flexibility and change. Although some people took advantage of the near-chaos to profit, many others craved sheriffs, deputies, and officers of courts. Most were happy to see federally built forts rise across the West to protect settlers, who crowded around such installations as Fort Worth and Fort Bliss, thus establishing the towns of Fort Worth and El Paso. Although forts and towns were a stabilizing influence, they also had about them a climate of violence and bloodshed. Certainly, they, along with the local saloons, encouraged excessive drinking, especially on paydays.

In addition, settlement included immigrants, especially from Europe, who gave the West some of their best qualities, ranging from a strict work ethic to different kinds of art and music. The West became not the agrarian "empire of liberty" that Jefferson had advocated, but a Polk-inspired jumble of peoples, cultures, products, and political and economic goals. The West was now home to people with specific needs and goals. One faction was composed of veterans of Polk's war, who approached their lives in the West with new confidence and skills. After the war, they went aggressively, and often successfully, into such fields as farming and ranching, banking, business, law enforcement, and politics. And they supplied leaders for America's next conflict, the Civil War. Another segment of settlers was people of color—Mexicans, Mexican Americans, black Americans, Native Americans, and Asians—who fared less well. Because Polk was not one to assess and try to improve racial and other differences, his neglect of reform issues helped create a climate of mistrust. For those who lived on reservations or in barrios or ghettoes, the American Dream failed to materialize.

Mexicans and Mexican Americans particularly served as targets of negative white attitudes. Because Polk had allowed the war to be fought with personal and racial animosity and because it ended with a hasty and punitive treaty, tremendous tension, even hatred, existed between whites and people with Mexican backgrounds. Encouraging this situation was the growth of the Black Legend, which worsened after the war's end by the addition of exaggerated wartime stories about Mexican soldiers. In the postwar West, whites often made it clear that they looked down upon Mexican Americans who, as a result, frequently suffered ill treatment. Mexican men now supplied necessary labor in western farming, ranching, and cotton cultivation; Mexican women entered into domestic service. But these men and women were usually paid little and treated badly. And after the 1848 discovery of gold in California, Mexican miners were not tolerated by white miners. By 1850, 163 Mexican miners had reportedly been lynched by their white counterparts.

Mexicans and Mexican Americans would long feel betrayed by President Polk and the Treaty of Guadalupe Hidalgo. Although contemporary Americans hardly recognize the event known as the "Mexican War," there are those Mexicans and Mexican Americans who remember the conflict as what some of them call "an exercise in American imperialism," "a capitalist invasion," or "the war where the gringos stole our land."

During the 1840s, Native Americans also faced such disasters as forced relocation on inadequate reservations or in prisons, outright neglect, and even extermination. Neither Polk nor his Congress had much concern for Indian welfare. In addition, Polk had inherited a corrupt bureaucracy riddled with federal, regional, and local authorities who embezzled, stole foodstuffs and other provisions intended for Indians, and diverted Indian annuities to their own pockets. Rather than initiating reform, Polk went along with the existing system and perhaps even made it worse through his inappropriate appointments. Although he resented the demands of patronage-seekers, Polk conscientiously spent many hours making appointments. But, because he had not accepted the need for reform, many of his people were lackluster at best. For instance, Polk's commissioner of Indian affairs, Ohio Democrat William Medill, was inexperienced, poorly informed, and prejudiced. In addition, Polk's precipitous takeover of the Southwest disrupted or removed local administrations. Native Americans in the La Puebla area near Santa Fe, New Mexico, had adopted Catholicism, blending it with their own religious beliefs, but after the Mexican War they had to face Protestant missionaries who tried to change them again.

And what of that important, yet often overlooked, footnote to Polkian history, Nicholas Trist? How fared the man who ended the war on such favorable terms to his country? Unfortunately, Trist caught the president's wrath, which reveals something more about Polk, who seldom brooked opposition to his will. When Trist returned to Washington, the president summarily fired him for insubordination and refused to pay any wages incurred after October 1847. As a career civil servant, Trist was mortified, to say nothing of broke. For the next twenty-two years, he worked at low-level office jobs in Philadelphia, Wilmington, and Baltimore. In 1870, Trist received an appointment as the postmaster of Alexandria, Virginia, and payment of the back wages that Polk had denied him. He died in 1874, having never received acclaim for a treaty that enlarged the United States by about two-thirds and brought an end to the highly controversial war between Mexico and the United States. Today, few Americans would recognize his name.

Polk's image has fared slightly better. He is remembered as an educated, meticulous man who set agendas and pursued them. Although he had worked closely with Andrew Jackson for many years, he evidently never picked up Jackson's penchant for quick decisions or combative outbursts. Rather, Polk was said to be cautious, reasoned, and very much a detail person. Today, many scholars rank Polk as the last strong president before Abraham Lincoln. Certainly, for the American West, Polk's presidency was critical, on both the positive and negative sides. In support of Polk is the fact that he fulfilled his expansionist promises, increasing the trans-Mississippi West with the addition of the present states of California, Nevada, Utah, the bulk of Arizona, approximately half of New Mexico, about one-fourth of Colorado, and a small part of Wyoming. Against Polk are such charges as creating a divide between Mexico and the United States that left behind a long-term bitterness between Americans and Mexican Americans. How these results balance each other depends on who does the judging.

FOR FURTHER READING

Comer, Douglas C. *Ritual Ground: Bent's Old Fort, World Formation, and the Annexation of the Southwest*. Berkeley: University of California Press, 1996.

Dusinberre, William. *Slavemaster President: The Double Career of James Polk*. New York: Oxford University Press, 2003.

Engstrand, Iris H. W., Richard Griswold del Castillo, and Elena Poniatowska. *Culture y Cultura: Consequences of the U.S.-Mexican War, 1846–1848*. Los Angeles: Autry Museum of Western Heritage, 1998.

Haynes, Sam W. *James K. Polk and the Expansionist Impulse*. New York: Pearson, 2006.

Merry, Robert W. *A Country of Vast Designs: James K. Polk, the Mexican War, and the Conquest of the American Continent*. New York: Simon & Schuster, 2009.

Morrison, Michael A. *Slavery and the American West: The Eclipse of Manifest Destiny and the Coming of the Civil War*. Chapel Hill: University of North Carolina Press, 1997.

Robinson, Charles M., III. *Texas and the Mexican War*. Austin: Texas State Historical Association, 2004.

Winders, Richard Bruce. *Crisis in the Southwest: The United States, Mexico, and the Struggle over Texas*. Latham, MD: Rowman & Littlefield, 2002.

ABRAHAM LINCOLN, 1861–1865

LC-USZ62-12950

Chapter 4

ABRAHAM LINCOLN
DEVELOPING THE AMERICAN WEST

On the last conscious day of his life, April 14, 1865, Abraham Lincoln finished his work in the late afternoon and joined his wife, Mary, for a carriage ride. He was in an unusually buoyant mood and told her that "we must be more cheerful in the future." Lincoln had already issued the Emancipation Proclamation, ending black slavery, and pushed through the Homestead Act, making possible mass settlement of the American West, yet he had plans for the rest of his second term. His conversation with Mary now turned toward California, in which he had more than a casual interest. He assured Mary that they would be visiting the state soon.

Apparently, as the Civil War ground to an end, Lincoln's thoughts had turned to other matters—in this case, the West. Because he hailed from the "old" frontier states of Kentucky, Indiana, and Illinois, it was not surprising that he would think often of the West. After all, he described himself as having been a frontier lad and later a prairie lawyer. Although as a young man he preferred to spend his time educating himself through reading and studying, he also did the work of a frontiersman, developing a proficiency in splitting rails.

When Lincoln finally decided on politics as his career, admirers associated his good qualities, such as honesty and lack of pretension, with his frontier upbringing. In fact, when he ran for president in 1860, the Republican Party presented him as "The Rail Candidate" for his strength and respect for hard work. Certainly, the West thought of him as one of their own. In that year, the votes of western states combined with those of northern states to give Lincoln 40 percent of the popular vote and a decisive victory in the electoral college. Lincoln had still another tie to the West. Despite the claims of earlier presidents, he was the first to be born in a log cabin.

At the time Lincoln was inaugurated on March 4, 1861, he had two priorities. The first was bringing the recent secession of Confederate states to a satisfactory resolution: "I shall do all that may be in my power to promote a peaceful settlement of all our difficulties. . . . The man does not live who is more devoted to peace than I am." His second objective was implementing a growth curve in the American West that would leave the Panic of 1857 and its aftermath as little more than a bad memory.

Lincoln's visions were not easily achieved. When the Civil War erupted at Fort Sumter, South Carolina, on April 12, 1861, its horrendous events pitted American against American and compelled Lincoln to take on the overwhelming task of commander-in-chief. He chose to train himself in military matters and become the war's primary strategist, which temporarily pushed to the back of his mind his dream for the West. Fortunately for the region, before Lincoln's assassination in 1865, he put a number of his goals into effect, thus changing the essential course of the American West, as well as altering its fundamental nature.

FRONTIER LAD

Abraham Lincoln was a child of the then-frontier, born on February 12, 1809, in Hodgenville, Kentucky, in a one-room log cabin. Like Andrew Jackson, Lincoln grew up hearing stories describing a Native American's brutality to a family member, which had occurred in 1786, over twenty years before his birth. In 1854, Lincoln wrote to a cousin that his grandfather's tragic death in Kentucky, followed by the killing of the Indian attacker by Lincoln's fourteen-year-old Uncle Mordecai, was the "legend more strongly . . . than all other imprinted upon my mind and memory."

Bitter land controversies were also part of Lincoln's childhood. In 1816, such a dispute drove the family to relocate to Indiana. Abraham later described the new place in verse: "When first my father settled here, / 'Twas then the frontier line; / The panther's scream filled nights with fear, / And bears preyed on the swine." In 1859, he recalled that he had grown up in "a wild region, with many bears and other wild animals still in the woods."

As a lad, Lincoln experienced major changes. In 1818, his mother died, and his father married a widow, who took to nine-year-old Abraham and helped with his self-education. Ten years later, his beloved sister, Sarah, died in childbirth. In the meantime, he grew to dislike his father, who was distant and harsh. Still, Abraham turned his wages over to his father until he was twenty-one. In 1830, the family moved again, to Macon County, Illinois. When the Lincolns removed yet again to Coles County, Abraham parted from them and settled in New Salem, Illinois. One of his first jobs was taking goods to New Orleans, where he saw slavery firsthand and decided he disliked black bondage.

Young Abraham also felt strongly about marrying and having children. He forged a relationship with Ann Rutledge, who died in 1835 at age twenty-two, probably of typhoid fever. In 1836, he met Mary Owen, whom he briefly courted, and in 1836 encountered Mary Todd, who came from a wealthy, slaveholding Kentucky family. After an erratic courtship, they married on November 4, 1842. Two years later, the couple bought a house in Springfield, where they had four sons, only two of whom survived.

PRAIRIE LAWYER

Lincoln tried several occupations, ranging from storekeeper to county surveyor and postmaster. He served for three months with the Illinois militia in the Black Hawk War before entering politics. In 1832, running as a Whig, he lost his bid for a seat in the Illinois House of Representatives. He then decided to become a lawyer and prepare, on his own, for a legal career. In 1834, he won a seat in the Illinois House of Representatives, which he held until 1842. In 1836, he passed the Illinois bar exam and moved to Springfield, where he gained a reputation as a talented attorney.

In 1846, Lincoln entered politics on the national level by gaining a place in the U.S. House of Representatives for a two-year term, beginning in 1847. Calling himself a "Western free soil man," he supported the Wilmot Proviso, which would prohibit slavery in areas taken from Mexico in 1846. He also gained notice for his opposition to the Mexican-American War because, in his view, Mexico had not menaced or molested the United States in any way. In January 1848, Lincoln delivered a wordy, legalistic speech to the House, asking that President James K. Polk designate the exact spot where the war began, so "he can show that the soil was ours where the first blood of the war was shed." Many jeered at Lincoln, who thus lost face and support because of his so-called Spot Resolutions.

Without regret, Lincoln returned to Springfield and his law practice, but during the 1850s, the rising outcry over slavery piqued his interest. He rejected abolitionism, which he thought did more harm than good, and favored the containment of slavery to one area, believing that if the institution was constricted it would eventually weaken and die. He was especially adamant that slavery be prevented from spreading into free western territories. He was incensed when, in 1854, Illinois senator Stephen Douglas proposed the Kansas-Nebraska Bill, which would nullify the Missouri Compromise of 1820, stipulating that in new western territories voters could approve or reject slavery. In response, Lincoln delivered many speeches, but one in Peoria, Illinois, stands out. Although he remained respectful of the U.S. Constitution's protection of existing slavery, he emphasized instead the Declaration of Independence's equality of rights.

The following year, Lincoln, who described himself as an Old Whig and an admirer of "The Great Compromiser," Henry Clay, helped establish the Republican Party, which started in a frontier schoolhouse in Ripon, Wisconsin, in 1854, and was formalized later that year at a well-attended convention in Jackson, Michigan. The name "Republican" derived from Thomas Jefferson's Democratic-Republican Party, dedicated to freedom and equal opportunity for all. As Lincoln put it, all men were clearly not "equal in color, size, intellect, moral development, or social capacity," but they should be so in such human rights as "life, liberty, and the pursuit of happiness."

Lincoln reentered politics full bore in 1857, after the Supreme Court handed down the *Dred Scott v. Sandford* decision, which held that slaves were not citizens, had no right to sue in federal courts, could not be freed by transport into a nonslave state or territory, and could not be excluded from western territories by Congress. In 1858, the Republican Party nominated Lincoln as a challenger to Senator Stephen Douglas, who was running for reelection as a Democrat from Illinois. The two men engaged in what are said to be the most famous political debates in American history. While Douglas argued popular sovereignty, that is, letting the voters in each of the western territories decide to adopt slavery or not, Lincoln maintained that slavery was inherently evil. In a Springfield appearance, Lincoln admitted that he was doubtful about total white/black equality and that he opposed the "amalgamation of the races." All people were not equal socially and politically, he explained, but all people were free, independent, and exempt from rule by others.

Although Lincoln lost that race to Douglas, his growing hostility to slavery entangled him in secession issues and the status of slavery in the West, while his defense of the Republican Party made him a viable candidate for the upcoming presidential campaign. In an early 1860 speech at New York City's Cooper Union, Lincoln revealed his passion against slavery and for the growth of the West. He asserted that extension of slavery into the territories was the crux of the argument: "The new territories are the newly made bed to which our children are to go, and it lies with the nation to say whether they shall have snakes mixed up with them or not."

After a grueling campaign that focused on popular sovereignty, a homestead act for western settlers, and a transcontinental railway connecting east and west, Lincoln gained election as the sixteenth president of the United States. The contested Northwest (today the Midwest) supported Lincoln, as did Oregon and California. But seven states in the lower South, where numerous large cotton plantations were located, seceded from the Union before Lincoln's inauguration.

As early as 1858, his "House Divided" speech had stated that the Union could not endure half-slave and half-free; it had to be one or the other. Yet he tried to save the Union and avoid war by assuring the South that he would not interfere with existing slavery.

LINCOLN AND HIS WARS

In 1861, the issue of secession led to an incredibly brutal civil war that destroyed lives, families, and loyalties. In part, this occurred because the South was beyond negotiation or compromise. The "Slave Power" had much to lose if black laborers were liberated. In 1860, cotton constituted nearly 60 percent of American exports and was valued at $200 million annually. This wealth benefited an influential upper class, mostly planters, for slaveholding was more concentrated than it had been earlier; only 25 percent of households now owned slaves as compared with 36 percent in 1830.

At the same time, President Lincoln opposed secession, which thereby split the Union into two hostile parts—on the one hand, the South and the lower West, on the other the North and the upper West. In his inaugural address on March 4, 1861, Lincoln had explained that one section of the country believed slavery was right, while the other thought it wrong and certainly not to be extended into western territories, which were largely democratic and anti-slavery in sentiment. "This is the only substantial dispute," he concluded. Frequently, Lincoln repeated that his goal was to keep the Union together and that the war was not about slavery. But, for decades the preservation of the Union had been tangled with states' rights, secession, slavery, and western expansionism, with no apparent way to separate them.

Lincoln turned to his cabinet for advice and ideas, but probably not support. As historian Doris Kearns Goodwin reveals, Lincoln appointed his rivals, including several who had vied with him for the Republican presidential nomination, and through his political genius gradually shaped them into something of a team. In 1861, however, the cabinet was riddled with suspicion and intrigue. The top slots had not only gone to men who had earlier opposed Lincoln, but some still had presidential aspirations, which encouraged them to criticize Lincoln. Nor were any from the trans-Mississippi West, some of whom may have supported Lincoln's western plans.

Given these advisors, it is little wonder that Lincoln's annual reports indicate that he seldom took cabinet recommendations, depending on himself to know what was "right." At first, Lincoln considered one of his earlier ideas—compensated emancipation with colonization of freed slaves in Liberia in Africa—but this proved unpopular and unworkable. Within a year of the war's beginning, Lincoln acknowledged that the Union could not be saved unless slaves were freed. The president planned to end slavery by freeing slaves in parts of the South, hoping that other states would have the will to follow, thus reducing the threat of slavery in the West as well.

Lincoln crept up on the issue. In June 1862, he endorsed a congressional ban on slavery in all federal territories, located mostly in the West. In July, he approved Congress's passage of the Second Confiscation and Militia Act, establishing procedures to free slaves owned by anyone assisting the rebellion. That same month, Lincoln consulted with his cabinet regarding a draft of the Emancipation Proclamation, which he released on September 19, 1862. The proclamation was to take effect on January 1, 1863, liberating slaves in areas under Confederate control.

The Emancipation Proclamation was a war measure that Lincoln issued under his powers as commander-in-chief. It was intended to create runaway slaves who would cause havoc in rebellious states and along Confederate military lines, and to encourage border and western states to release their slaves. The proclamation was also meant to discourage Great Britain, who had freed their slaves in 1833, from helping the South. Intensifying the impact of emancipation were past hurts and humiliations experienced by North and South; sectional pride and honor, especially in the South; the militant reformism that emerged from Jacksonian democracy and became abolitionism, especially in the North; and the question of whether North or South would rule the West and establish either free labor or slavery there.

With the Emancipation Proclamation, Lincoln gave the war a moral dimension and turned Union troops into liberators by declaring emancipation "an act of justice." By freeing the slave, he said, freedom was also given to the free. In November 19, 1863, in the Gettysburg Address, Lincoln proclaimed that the Civil War had a new objective, a rebirth of freedom in the still-divided nation.

Lincoln's next step was to propose a constitutional amendment prohibiting slavery, including in the long-disputed western territories. Given evidence of public support, the Senate in April 1864, and the House in January 1865, passed the amendment and sent it to the states for ratification. On December 6, 1865, the Thirteenth Amendment became part of the U.S. Constitution, thus protecting western territories from further threats of slavery. As a result, the West was no longer a pawn in the great contest between pro-slave and anti-slave factions. Just as black slaves were free at last, so was the American West.

Even though Lincoln did not believe in racial equality, his always-evolving thoughts recognized the need to extend a modicum of civil rights to black citizens.

The Civil War was his crucible, bringing forth instances of needed change for black people. It is fair to say that Lincoln engaged in an additional "war" concerning free black Americans in the North, South, and West. He initially focused on black men who wanted to fight for the Union. Because they were prohibited from military service by 1792 federal legislation, Lincoln included in the 1862 version of the Emancipation Proclamation a provision allowing black men to serve in the Union military, both army and navy, that operated in all theaters of war, including the West. Accordingly, the War Department established the Bureau of Colored Troops, which supplied much-needed manpower for Union forces. Also, black enlistment would reduce the number of freed blacks, who were called "contraband" and who swarmed around Union camps looking for assistance, living in tent camps or worse, and receiving food handouts from government and private sources.

Enrolling contraband men would also allow these men to send a little money to their families and to gain respect for themselves. At first, black recruits worked as manual laborers to free white soldiers for training and combat, but as they proved themselves, they were asked to serve in battle. The First Kansas Colored Volunteers was the initial black regiment to engage in combat, and in a western battle that set a precedent for the use of black combat troops in the region. In October 1862, at Island Mound, Missouri, the First Kansas repulsed Confederate troops. Another triumph for the First Kansas occurred at Honey Springs, in Indian Territory, present-day Oklahoma. In July 1863, after leading black soldiers in a two-hour battle against Confederates, General James Blunt declared, "I never saw such fighting as was done by the Negro regiment." As Lincoln hoped, black troops distinguished themselves in all theaters of the Civil War, including the trans-Mississippi West.

As a result, black men became an important segment of the U.S. military, especially in the Indian wars following the Civil War. This was the beginning of the renowned Buffalo Soldiers who served in the West. Because of Lincoln's foresight, black men protected Native Americans living on reservations. They also captured rebellious Indians, defended white settlers, safeguarded whites on the trail to the goldfields in Montana and Colorado Territories, constructed roads and forts, defended railroad workers, and enforced law and order. They faced racial prejudice within and outside the military, and the westerners they protected were not always grateful. Yet blacks reenlisted at a higher rate than whites, suggesting that blacks found more benefits within the western military than without.

Lincoln was interested in mobilizing black troops in the West; but he also wondered whether this war would draw the West toward the Union. Overall, he was a hands-on planner who kept his finger on the pulse of Civil War in the

West. When the name Abraham Lincoln is invoked, many people recall such places as Gettysburg, Pennsylvania, and Antietam, Maryland, where decisive struggles occurred. They have forgotten, or perhaps never knew, that the Civil War was also fought in the trans-Mississippi West, an arena of combat that was Lincoln's to command.

Early in the war, Lincoln recognized the necessity of building roads, supply depots, and forts for the use and protection of Union troops stationed in the West. At his behest, the Union Army Corps of Engineers constructed many military installations in the region. In 1863, for example, the Union built Fort Stevens with its extensive earthen ramparts to provide coastal defense in the Pacific Northwest, along the Columbia River, and in Puget Sound.

Lincoln was also clever about using his presidential power of patronage in the West. In the trans-Mississippi region, he appointed numerous Republicans to territorial and local offices, men who then acted as his information pipeline, sent him status reports, advocated his programs, and, above all, supported the Union. The Oregon country provides an excellent example. Although Oregon had become a state in 1859, Lincoln kept in touch with friends and former appointees there, men whom historian Richard W. Etulain describes, in *Lincoln and Oregon Country Politics in the Civil War Era*, as numerous and usually loyal. Lincoln often warned his Oregon contacts to suppress all Confederate sympathizers. In addition, Etulain adds, Lincoln used patronage to spread the Republican Party in the rest of the West.

The president also listened to his people in the West; he learned about tension points and Confederate plans to capture the region so the Confederate empire could spread to California and the Pacific coast, while gaining the West's resources and ocean ports. Although most battles in the trans-Mississippi West theater, as it was designated, occurred in Missouri, Arkansas, Louisiana, and west Texas, fighting also took place in present-day day Arizona, where the Battle of Picacho Pass was fought on April 15, 1862, north of Tucson in what was then western New Mexico Territory. Lincoln concentrated on New Mexico Territory, composed of present-day Arizona and portions of Nevada. Because this location was crucial to trade between the North and the West via the Santa Fe Trail and as a gateway to the South, Lincoln viewed it as tremendous asset.

Accordingly, the most important clash in the trans-Mississippi West erupted at Glorieta Pass in the Sangre de Cristo Mountains in eastern New Mexico Territory. As part of the Confederate's New Mexico campaign, on March 26, 1862, eleven hundred Confederate soldiers attacked thirteen hundred Union men, hoping to seize the Santa Fe Trail and break the Union's hold on the West. The fray lasted three days, ending with a Union victory, which saved the West for the Union and soon gained the title, "The Gettysburg of the West." Later, a panel of government-appointed experts ranked Glorieta Pass as third only to Gettysburg and Antietam in overall significance.

In these western encounters, as he did back east, Lincoln faced a problem finding volunteers. In 1863, he signed into law a conscription act, or military draft, which was opposed by the "Peace Democrats," and led to draft riots, notably in New York City. Lincoln also tried other sources. He found westerners quick to volunteer. New Mexico Territory alone contributed eight thousand volunteers. Later in the war, Lincoln's administration turned to Native Americans. In an undated recruiting poster headed "Message to Indian Territories" located in present-day Oklahoma, Lincoln appealed to Native Americans to enlist. This plea was followed by other equally ineffective broadsides.

Unfortunately, Lincoln's relations with Native Americans in the West were difficult for a number of reasons. Obviously, he was busy managing the Civil War and his campaign for black rights. He had also inherited an Indian system long riddled with corruption and disorganization on every level. In *Lincoln and the Indians* (1978), historian David A. Nichols describes exploitation of the Indian system and of individual Indians by self-interested agents and other officials. According to Nichols, the political "machine" bestowed upon Lincoln fought reform because its leaders wanted to keep their own, often immoral or illegal, benefits in place. For example, such local interests as the Tucson Ring riled up Indians, so that there would be no loss of local forts and the commerce they generated.

Lincoln soon recognized the need for change, yet he continued the policies of removal and concentration of Native Americans that had brought so many Indians poverty, ill health, disease, and early death. Like previous presidents, he often made ineffective appointments. For the crucial office of commissioner of Indian affairs, Lincoln chose a man who had little knowledge of Indians, lacked experience, and held white prejudices. Lincoln's commissioner William P. Dole supported the old ideas of placing Indians on reservations and "civilizing" them. On one occasion, Dole did request troops and supplies to assist Indians and was disheartened when "unprecedented demands" on the War Department prevented it from complying, but he was generally unsympathetic to his Indian constituents.

Another difficulty that Lincoln faced—one that usually goes unnoted—was financial. During the early years of his presidency, the government literally had no money. Lincoln could not have paid annuities to the Indians had he wanted to. The legacy of the Panic of 1857 and a federal debt of $40 million meant Lincoln had no way to pay for the Civil War. In July 1862, he pled with Congress for war funding. Secretary of the Treasury Salmon P. Chase had estimated that the Civil War would cost $320 million. Chase thought he could raise $300 million in loans and asked Congress for $20 million. The strapped Congress responded with the Revenue Act of 1861, which combined a raise in some import duties, a new property tax, and the nation's first income tax measure. Although Lincoln quickly signed the bill, enforcement was so poor that these measures failed to produce the anticipated revenue. The system was reformed in the Revenue Act of 1862, which also set up the Internal Revenue Service (IRS) and a sliding tax scale. Even after the war, when the national budget decreased noticeably, 44 percent went to servicing the war debt and 9.5 percent to veterans' pensions.

Making matters worse, during the war a national debt of 2 percent rapidly spiked to 13 percent. When Lincoln and Chase appealed to New York bankers, they discovered that interest rates would be in the usurious range of 24 to 36 percent. Near despair, Lincoln moaned, "[T]he bottom is out of the tub." He responded by signing into law the First Legal Tender Act of 1862, which created "greenback" paper bills as legal tender. He also signed the National Banking Act of 1863, which levied taxes on paper currency distributed by private banks, thus driving such bills out of circulation. Furthermore, Lincoln increased the use of tariffs and bonds. These actions helped stabilize the economy and put some money in the U.S. Treasury. In 1864, still looking for funds, Lincoln turned to the West. In that year, he reportedly pushed Nevada into statehood and removed its Indians to reap the new state's electoral votes and the silver its taxes would feed to government coffers.

Meanwhile, Native Americans waited, not realizing that the president was essentially broke. Clearly, it would have been unwise for Lincoln to broadcast this or to cry poverty to Indians, who were so penurious that they died daily from malnutrition, starvation, and disease. At that point, the one thing Native Americans understood was that, despite treaty promises, government annuities were late in coming or never arrived, which spelled grinding destitution for them.

In 1862, Sioux Indians in Minnesota vented their rage at the government through a series of horribly destructive attacks on white settlers and their property. Reports described thousands of attacking Indians; hundreds of dead whites; and wholesale destruction of homes, land, animals, and crops, all of which resulted in widespread panic and white flight from the state. Governor Alexander Ramsay telegraphed Lincoln, asking for federal assistance: "This is not our war. This is a National War." In 1862, Lincoln created the Department of the Northwest and again made a poor appointment by shifting General John Pope, whom he found unsatisfactory on the battlefield, from the war front to Minnesota as the head of the new department. Even though Pope had no experience or knowledge of Native Americans, including their military tactics, Lincoln told Pope to take care of the rebellion in Minnesota.

Pope joined forces with his former partner, Henry J. Sibley, whom he appointed head of the Minnesota militia. In a six-week-long crusade, Sibley defeated the insurgents, taking more than a thousand prisoners. Pope and Sibley took it upon themselves to conduct mass war trials, condemning 303 Indian men to hanging. Pope telegraphed a list of the names of the condemned to Lincoln, anticipating the president's quick approval. Instead, the shocked president replied: "Please forward, as soon as possible, the full and complete record of these convictions." Lincoln's investigation into the records revealed that the "trials" had been fifteen to twenty minutes long and the accused were allowed no defense. To his credit, Commissioner Dole disparaged a mass execution as "contrary to the spirit of the age and our character as a great magnanimous and Christian people."

Lincoln was caught between political pressures and voices of reason. After deliberation, he crafted a compromise: thirty-nine of the rebels, who had committed rape and murder, would die and the rest would go to prison. After one received a reprieve, the remaining thirty-eight men were hanged on the day after Christmas. Today, many Native Americans curse Lincoln's action as "genocide" and a "mass execution," while others defend his ruling as the greatest act of clemency in the nation's history. Of course, the result for the trans-Mississippi West was the same: an increase in bitterness, blame, and animosity between Native Americans and white Americans, then and now.

A listing of Indian treaties and tragedies during the Lincoln years contains many lamentable events that occurred with startling regularity. For instance, in 1863 and 1864, Union General James Carleton, with some help from Colonel Kit Carson, invaded Navajo lands in western New Mexico Territory, killing Indians and burning their houses, barns, and crops. They set the remaining Navajos, along with some Apaches, on what the Indians called "The Long Walk," to the Bosque Redondo Reservation at Fort Sumner, also in New Mexico, where the Indians discovered polluted water, rampant disease, arid land, and their long-term enemies, Mescalero Apaches, as their immediate neighbors. In November 1864, yet another devastating calamity occurred at Sand Creek in eastern Colorado when U.S. Colonel John M. Chivington led the Third Colorado Regiment volunteers in an attack that left some four hundred Cheyennes and Arapahos dead.

Where was Lincoln? Indeed, he experienced bouts of sympathy for Native Americans. For example, when Bishop Henry Whipple, bishop of the Episcopal

Church in Minnesota, begged him to help Dakota Sioux Indians, Lincoln felt "the rascality of this Indian business . . . down to my boots." Yet he did not act. In some ways, he was a prisoner of his era, which he unwittingly revealed upon occasion. In an 1852 speech in Peoria, Illinois, he defended Andrew Jackson's earlier removal of Cherokees from Georgia via the Trail of Tears to Indian Territory. He noted that Jackson had gained "the applause of the great and good of the land" and was hardly a "fool." Later, in an 1863 meeting with Sioux leaders at the White House, Lincoln acted like a stereotypical white, referring to white Americans as "pale-faced people," calling the White House a "wigwam," and warning his visitors that acculturation into the white world was their only path to survival. The following December, Lincoln used his third annual address to Congress to assure legislators that the "measures" they had provided for Indian "removal" and access to "large and valuable tracts of land" for whites had been "carried into effect," adding the ingenuous statement that he "hoped that the effect of these treaties will result in the establishment of permanent friendly relations" with the tribes involved.

Lincoln tried mightily to reconcile the needs of Native Americans with his own dreams of western settlement and economic development, but he failed to find a way to preserve Indian peoples and boost the white West. His decision was clear, in actions if not in words: the Indians lost; the West won. Result: the cruel and unconscionable Indian wars of the post-Civil War years in the American West.

LINCOLN AND WESTERN LANDS

In the meantime, President Lincoln showered concern on white settlers in the West. He expended time and energy advocating and calling upon his supporters in Congress to create a program of free or cheap western lands to be given to settlers. With Southerners who had opposed a free-labor West now out of Congress, Lincoln encouraged the body to pass the Homestead Bill, which he promptly signed into law on May 2, 1862. This legislation made available plots of 160 acres to claimants who were U.S. citizens, or had declared intentions to become citizens, and were at least twenty-one years old, or head of his or her household. Homesteaders agreed to live on and improve their lands for five years, then go to a land office to "prove up," or finalize, the title to the claim and pay a modest filing fee, typically under twenty dollars. With the war on his doorstep, Lincoln could have let the homestead plan die, but he wanted to reward veterans and to attract to the West European immigrants as well as white Americans and those of color—and to appeal to single women, giving them an alternative to working in home and factory and, perhaps, an edge in the marriage market.

Once Lincoln's Homestead Act was in place, government agents and surveyors set up land offices and laid out townships. The Land Ordinance of 1785 had provided the scheme of townships of six miles square, subdivided into 160-acre lots. One lot was set aside for a school. Although this system sounds orderly and fair, many exploited it. For example, as many as 40 percent of homesteaders, who did not have the cash for the final filing fee or hesitated for some other reason, let the filing date drift beyond the five-year mark. Such delays often resulted in unscrupulous men claiming the land out from under the original claimants, getting improved farms in the process. Another common hoax was perpetrated by one person using multiple names to claim several adjoining plots of land. These deceptions were possible because western land offices relied on the written testimony of absentee witnesses as to the land tenure of a claimant. Unsurprisingly, some of these claims turned out to be false. Timber and mining companies also were quick to "homestead" an area rich in trees, oil, or water.

As a result, the effects of Lincoln's homestead plan were mixed. As the president had hoped, numerous families who could not afford a farm or business in their former homes thrived on their little piece of the West, but others went broke and returned home or moved farther west. Women faced gender-related trials on these isolated homesteads; one woman lost three children to diphtheria in two days; another faced an unwanted pregnancy after having seven children, only two of whom had survived. Some women reportedly "lost their wits" and went back home, or to a western asylum. Nor was life always peaceful. Conflicts with Indians as well as "range wars," contests over location of a county seat or of a railroad, and family and clan wars kept things stirred up. And the climate on the plains did little to help, bringing fierce blizzards, riveting rainstorms, hordes of locusts, and a scarcity of water.

In spite of the drawbacks, Lincoln's homestead plan proved instrumental in settling the plains states of Kansas, Nebraska, Indian Territory (later Oklahoma), and Dakota Territory (later North and South Dakota), where settlers established farms; lobbied for law and order; and built schools, churches, and towns. Also, migration created rich cultures with, for example, Finns settling in Minnesota, Swedes and Norwegians in Minnesota and the Dakotas, Volga Germans in Kansas and what became North Dakota, and German Jews in Oregon. Religions also varied, ranging from Protestant sects to Catholicism and Judaism. Adding to the mix were single women called "girl homesteaders," who went west on their own, and free blacks, many of them freed slaves, who took up land and founded all-black towns such as Nicodemus, Kansas, and Bliss, Nebraska.

Also in 1862, legislators passed the Morrill Land-Grant Colleges Act, which would give tracts of government land to states to sell and establish endowment funds for the support of agricultural colleges. In 1857, James Smith Morrill had unsuccessfully introduced such legislation to Congress. In 1861, he submitted an enlarged bill, providing that land grant institutions would teach not only agriculture, but also engineering and military tactics. Given Lincoln's interest in education, especially in the West, and the absence of Southern recalcitrance, the bill passed Congress. Lincoln signed it into law on July 2, 1862.

The western state of Iowa almost immediately accepted the terms of the Morrill Act. In 1864, Iowa opened the State Agricultural College and Model Farm, now Iowa State University. When the war robbed the new college of male students, the grant's coeducation clause went into effect. White women eagerly enrolled, often finding themselves taking unusual courses. In military science, they wore uniforms with skirts and toted rifles while drilling on the commons, even though Lincoln would not allow women to join the Union Army. In 1869, domestic science replaced military science for female students, many of whom remained after veterans returned from the war.

The Morrill Act offered numerous benefits. Land grant schools nudged western agriculture toward the emerging revolution in scientific farming and established coeducation and public education, although black Americans were still excluded. And agricultural colleges moved education in general from a sole emphasis on classical studies, for practical education was now valued. After the Civil War, the program encompassed the former Confederate states.

Also in 1862, Lincoln cooperated with Congress in establishing the Department of Agriculture to put into effect federal policies concerning land, farming, stock raising, and forestry. This bureau collected new types of seeds and plants and compiled agricultural statistics. Under its first commissioner, agriculturalist Isaac Newton, its programs encouraged farmers to move from traditional methods to more scientific ones, sometimes called chemistry in farming, and to use improved farming methods and machinery throughout the West.

Another piece of legislation that Lincoln favored concerned the building of railroads. On July 1, 1862, he signed into law the first Union Pacific–Central Pacific land grant. The act's full name showed that Lincoln had in mind more than just transport of goods: "An Act to aid in the construction of a railroad and telegraph line from the Missouri river to the Pacific ocean [*sic*], and to secure to the government the use of the same for postal, military, and other purposes." To guarantee that private companies would extend rail transport and wire communication into the West, the act provided for thirty-year government bonds at 6 percent interest and enormous grants of federal land. Best known of these were alternate land grants that set up separate sections on each side of a company's tracks and could be sold by the company. In subsequent years, four more railway acts established standard-gauge tracks and refined the provisions of the original legislation. Between 1850 and 1871, the railroads obtained 175 million acres, or about one-tenth of the United States. Of all the presidents involved, Lincoln granted more land to railroads in the West than did any others.

Although Lincoln did not live to see it, western railways proved largely successful. In 1869, the Union Pacific Railroad, built westward from Council Bluffs, Iowa, especially by Irish workers, and the Central Pacific, built eastward from Sacramento, California, by mostly Chinese laborers, met at Promontory, Utah. A golden spike was driven into the ground to commemorate the occasion of the first transcontinental railway in the nation. During this decade, additional rail lines appeared with amazing speed so that the United States, which had had thirty thousand rail miles in 1860, had well over fifty thousand in 1870. Beyond that, nearly all railroad companies paid their government loans on time and with interest.

Lincoln's foresightedness, combined with the expansion of the railroads, stimulated westward migration and tourism. Companies advertised widely; offered free inspection trips to potential settlers; sold land to settlers; and provided immigrant boxcars so that a family could transport themselves, their animals, and goods in one compact car, which the railway would pull off the track at their chosen place so they would have a "home" while getting settled. As for leisure pursuits, tourists began to travel via railroad cars, called observation cars, appointed for their comfort while viewing the West. Thus, railroads played a significant role in stimulating the tourist industry in the West.

Railroads also encouraged the production of many consumer goods, especially cattle. Western ranchers who had driven their cattle over land routes to markets now drove them to railheads, where they used stock cars to transport them to eastern consumers, who paid prices ten times higher than they had earlier. By 1866, these loading places included St. Louis, Kansas City, and Sedalia, Missouri; and soon after, Abilene, Kansas; Cheyenne, Wyoming; and Dodge City, Kansas. In the process, the American cowboy emerged as the icon of the West.

Other pieces of Lincoln's dreams for the West also came to fruition. Railroads proved a prime factor in moving the West toward capitalist agriculture, big business, banks, and federal assistance. Although railroad officials sometimes acted badly, the situation often turned out well. For example, because rail companies received government subsidies for each mile of track laid, they got more money for winding, indirect routes that reached small towns, which would have been ignored, and who happily paid railroad companies additional bonuses. But in other cases, heinous corruption raised public ire. Railway magnates and investors looking for huge profits caused such scandals as the Credit Mobilier, in which the Union Pacific company gave stock to members of Congress in exchange for favorable votes. On the local level, farmers and ranchers lodged complaints against companies that charged more for a short haul than a long haul.

"THE PRESIDENT IS DEAD"

During his presidency, Lincoln often doubted his popularity. In 1862, when he told Harriet Beecher Stowe, author of *Uncle Tom's Cabin,* that "Whichever way it [the Civil War] ends, I have the impression that I shan't last long after it's over." Two years later, he penned a frequently expressed sentiment: "I long ago made up my mind that if anybody wants to kill me, he will do it." His 1864 run for reelection posed additional questions for him. In July, he said, "It is very strange that I, a boy brought up in the woods, and seeing, as it were, but little of the world, would be drifted into the very apex of this great event."

As in 1860, Lincoln's quest for the presidential nomination in 1864 was problematic. In a sense, he proved a dark horse in both elections, with a split party behind him. In 1859, he had described himself as "in height, six feet, four inches nearly; lean in flesh, weighing on average, one hundred and eighty pounds, dark complexion, with coarse black hair, and gray eyes—no other marks or brands recollected." Now, four years later, he understandably looked thinner and more harassed. Yet many people thought him wonderfully eccentric. His long legs often sparked comment, especially when he slid so far down in his chair that his legs were parallel with the floor, or when he rested them on the mantle of his office fireplace. And his advice and humorous stories, most with salient points, are repeated over and over to this very day.

But in 1864, Lincoln worried that his policies and the war would do him in. He wrote that "It seemed exceedingly probable that this Administration will not be re-elected." The Democrats were still split into factions; one faction, calling themselves Peace Democrats, supported one of Lincoln's generals, George McClellan, while the faction supporting Lincoln—for this one election called the National Union Party—endorsed his successes and the impending end of the war. To Lincoln's surprise, he won by a landslide, carrying all but three states and receiving 55 percent of the popular vote compared to McClellan's 45 percent. The election looked like a referendum for Lincoln and the Civil War. The soldier vote, which was only 4 percent of the total cast, went to Lincoln by 78 percent, which was a mandate in that it bypassed the general whose party repudiated the war, and fell to the commander-in-chief who defended the war.

After the election, Lincoln was his usual gracious self, avoiding rubbing salt into Democratic wounds. Instead, he remarked, "[N]ow that the election is over, may not all, having a common interest, reunite in a common effort to save our common country?" In his second inaugural address, Lincoln made his well-known plea for "malice toward none; charity for all" in order to achieve "a just and lasting peace." He could not have known that there was a viper named John Wilkes Booth in the crowd. Then, in April, in the last speech he gave, Lincoln supported the idea of suffrage for black men who had served in the military. Perhaps he foresaw a virtual war between races and wanted to use his time to gain as much protection for black Americans as possible.

At Ford's Theatre on the evening of April 14, 1865, the bullet fired by Southerner and Lincoln-hater John Wilkes Booth robbed the nation of Abraham Lincoln's commitment to humanitarian reconstruction of the nation and to racial progress. After lying unconscious all night, Lincoln was declared dead on April 15. Six days later, his funeral train pulled out of Washington, D.C., heading for Springfield, Illinois. At twelve stops, perhaps a million people viewed the president as he lay in state. In between stops, another seven million Northerners silently regarded the train as it passed by.

LINCOLN'S WESTERN LEGACY

Westerners were deprived of this physical act of mourning for the president who had changed their lives and futures in so many ways, giving them incredible largesse, despite his energies being consumed by war. The results were legion. Western migration and settlement of the West increased exponentially, drawing veterans, women, free blacks, and Europeans. The established, orderly way of surveying federal lands in the West into townships and sections was retained. Settlement brought investment in transportation, which improved means of travel, transport of goods, and communication between the West and the larger world, as well as promoting the new business of western tourism. Lincoln's policies encouraged territories to become states, which could escape presidential patronage, elect officials, make laws, and appropriate resources. Lincoln's support of education encouraged western colleges and universities to teach and research agricultural methods and issues; these schools also offered women higher education. Lincoln encouraged federal subsidies to the West; these subsidies set a precedent for federal aid to education, to overland mail delivery, to maintenance of forts and roads, and to land surveys and land offices.

Of course, there was a negative side. Although Lincoln's homesteading acts opened the West to black military units and free blacks as settlers, they also increased the bitterness, poverty, illness, and early death experienced by Native Americans. Also, Lincoln's monetary programs, designed to help stabilize economic conditions, proved unpopular in the West, which typically supported hard money, used the gold dollar as a standard of value, and accepted Lincoln's greenbacks only at discounted rates. Further, Lincoln's policies involved an increase in taxes and in government "red tape," both having lists of rules and regulations. Westerners came to resent and even block federal intervention in banking, transport, and environmental controls. And no one can claim that the bulk of westerners showed enthusiasm for Lincoln's concepts of the income tax and the draft—then or now.

It is also sad that the programs of a president known as "Honest Abe" aided the emergence of corruption throughout the West. A combination of rapid growth, federal monies, explosion of big business and big government, and rudimentary regulation encouraged numerous westerners, including some officials and government employees, to foment schemes to line their own pockets. Local cabals were always ready to pick up forfeited claims, especially in timber, mining, and ranching areas. Across the West, groups composed of attorneys, judges, legislators, and speculators gained from the misfortunes of others by investing in former Indian lands, failed settler claims, and the results of other misfortunes. In New Mexico Territory, a Santa Fe group of bankers, judges, lawyers, and land investors sought any investment that might turn a profit. After the war and into the 1870s, they were called the Santa Fe Ring, and as such received mention in New York newspapers as an example of scandalous corruption in western territories. Members of the Santa Fe Ring later participated in the Lincoln (named for President Lincoln) County War, which flared among unscrupulous investors competing for the business of supplying New Mexico's Fort Stanton and the nearby Mescalero Apache Reservation, and made Billy the Kid the West's favorite bad boy.

Dwarfing this good-versus-bad list is the significant way that Lincoln physically reshaped the West in a manner that reoriented the entire polarity of the United States. When Lincoln came to the presidency in 1861, the country operated on a north-south axis, with controversies, issues, compromises, and solutions originating with the North or the South. Although growing rapidly in population, economic systems, and influence, the West was not a direct player in national affairs. Even though one of the key points in the argument over secession and slavery concerned the extension of slavery into western territories, few seemed to ask what westerners wanted. After Lincoln's sudden demise, the country found itself operating on an east-west axis, with migration, railroads, and commerce flowing from east to west. At the same time, reverse migration from the West, as well as railroads and trade, notably in agricultural products, moved from west to east. Additionally, East and West each had ocean ports that made possible trade and diplomatic relations with other countries. And each had its emerging supercities, notably New York in the East and San Francisco in the West. The West dazzled itself by its new national importance.

Lincoln also contributed much to political philosophy. Although he was admittedly not a political philosopher, his ideas revolutionized American thinking, forcing the country to look forward to the world of the twentieth century. Like Thomas Jefferson, who defined assumptions regarding tyranny, democracy, and equality for early-nineteenth-century Americans, Lincoln redefined them for his own era. A number of historians agree that Lincoln's relatively brief, but huge influence brought about a second American Revolution, this time putting in place active state liberalism. Lincoln's leading concern was to keep government from interfering with individual liberty. According to historian Garry Wills, in his *Lincoln at Gettysburg*, Lincoln desired to restrain government, to reshape and "reconstitute" it in a way that would help citizens reach goals. In this process, liberal government would replace tyrannical government and would help people achieve freedom and rights. The U.S. Constitution would no longer be the national guide, for after all, the Constitution had protected black slavery by allowing the federal government to regulate slavery in the territories and in entering states. A "new" activist government would emphasize instead the modification of the Constitution through such amendments as the thirteenth, which altered the nation's stand on slavery. The new vision also broadened the nation's view of the Declaration of Independence, which could now be seen as offering the eventual expansion of rights to many groups, including Mexicans, Asians, mixed-heritage peoples, and white women.

Neither was force an issue for Lincoln, who, like many previous presidents, spoke against force, yet used it to protect what he deemed right for Americans. Thomas Jefferson considered employing force to maintain the boundaries of the Louisiana Purchase; Andrew Jackson made threat of force in his fight against John Calhoun's plan of nullification by South Carolina; and James Polk waged actual war against Mexico to protect American boundaries and add Texas to the Union. In time, Lincoln used it to end slavery, conclude the war, save the Union, and initiate Reconstruction. Along the way, he also used his powers to suspend such rights as habeas corpus and to direct military tribunals to hear cases involving civilians. Those who protested, and charged Lincoln with tyranny, missed his point; for him *what* was being protected was the central concern.

Naturally, Lincoln's thinking affected all regions of the country, but westerners, who believed themselves blessed with unusual freedom and democracy, took his ideas to heart. By the end of the nineteenth century, seventeen million American citizens—primarily white men and women—lived in the West. This figure did not count free blacks who were not yet citizens; Native Americans who could not, until 1924, become citizens; Europeans flowing in as workers and farmers who had to learn English and rudiments of American history for citizenship; and Asians coming to work on farms and sugar plantations and to help build the transcontinental railroad who were denied citizenship for a variety of reasons. These groups accounted for a huge number of people, now infused with the idea that they could aspire to equal civil rights. White women in the West obviously believed it, campaigning so hard and long that woman suffrage was first adopted in 1869 by the western state of Wyoming, followed in quick succession by Utah Territory. By the end of the century, Colorado, Utah (as a state), and Idaho had also enfranchised women.

Before and after Lincoln's death, his spirit hung large over the country, while his beliefs infected many areas, often moving from west to east. One usually overlooked legacy of Lincoln's was laid in the summer of 1864 as he guided the country through the last bloody battles of the Civil War. In spite of considerable and exhausting pressures upon him, he performed a generous and unprecedented act toward the American West. Even though the Lincolns themselves were unable to travel from the eastern end of the fulcrum of the United States in Washington, D.C., to the western end in California, the president had never let go of his hopes for the West. During the last grisly summer of war, he supported such optimism when, on June 30, 1864, he signed into law the Yosemite Land Grant Act, giving federal protection to California's Yosemite Valley, which lay in the central-eastern portion of the state and across part of the Sierra Nevada mountain chain. Lincoln set aside thirty-nine thousand acres for "public use, resort, and education," a provision he intended to "be inalienable for all time."

By preserving one of California's natural jewels, Lincoln contributed to the emergence of the national parks idea in the United States; many of these parks would be located on federal lands in the American West. Lincoln also established a

model for the emerging conservation movement and introduced a form of government that would foster and support conservationist goals and methods. At the
time, not everyone understood Lincoln's heritage. Years later, however, another
vigorous president—and one who was an enthusiastic Lincoln worshipper—would
take Lincoln's ideas and run with them. President Theodore Roosevelt would see
that there was no end to what President Abraham Lincoln, who came from the
older "frontier" of Kentucky, Indiana, and Illinois, and had helped develop the
newer "frontier" of the trans-Mississippi West, had done in opening possibility
after possibility for the nation's future.

FOR FURTHER READING

Arenson, Adam, and Andrew R. Graybill, eds. *Civil War Wests: Testing the Limits of the United States*. Oakland: University of California Press, 2015.

Basler, Roy P., et al., eds. *The Collected Works of Abraham Lincoln*. 9 vols. New Brunswick, NJ: Rutgers University Press, 1953, 1955.

Cottrell, Steve. *Civil War in the Indian Territory*. Gretna, LA: Pelican, 1995.

Dirck, Brian R. *Abraham Lincoln and White America*. Lawrence: University Press of Kansas, 2014.

Etulain, Richard W. *Lincoln and Oregon Country Politics in the Civil War Era*. Corvallis: Oregon State University Press, 2013.

Etulain, Richard W., ed. *Lincoln Looks West: From the Mississippi to the Pacific*. Carbondale: Southern Illinois University Press, 2010.

Flood, Charles Bracelen. *1864: Lincoln at the Gates of History*. New York: Simon & Schuster, 2009.

Foner, Eric, ed. *Our Lincoln: New Perspectives on Lincoln and His World*. New York: W. W. Norton, 2008.

Goodwin, Doris Kearns. *Team of Rivals: The Political Genius of Abraham Lincoln*. New York: Simon & Shuster Paperbacks, 2005.

McPherson, James M., *Abraham Lincoln*. New York: Oxford University Press, 2009.

———. *Tried by War: Abraham Lincoln as Commander in Chief*. New York: Penguin, 2008.

Nichols, David A. *Lincoln and the Indians: Civil War Policy and Politics*. Columbia: University of Missouri Press, 1978.

Oates, Stephen B. *Abraham Lincoln: The Man behind the Myths*. New York: New American Library, 1984.

———. *With Malice toward None: A Life of Abraham Lincoln*. New York: Harper Perennial 1994.

Scharff, Virginia, ed. *Empire and Liberty: The Civil War and the West*. Oakland: University of California Press, 2015.

Wills, Garry. *Lincoln at Gettysburg: The Words That Remade America*. New York: Simon and Schuster, 1992.

Zeitz, Josphua. *Lincoln's Boys: John Hay, John Nicolay, and the War for Lincoln's Image*. New York: Viking Penguin, 2014.

THEODORE ROOSEVELT, 1901–1909

LC-USZ62-13026

Chapter 5

THEODORE ROOSEVELT
SAVING THE AMERICAN WEST

During the closing decade of the nineteenth century, book buyers at home and abroad catapulted Theodore Roosevelt's multivolume work, *The Winning of the West,* to best-seller status. In his books, the man who would become the "conservationist" president revealed his love affair with the American West, which led to his crusade to save not only western lands and resources but those of the entire nation. Roosevelt the writer set his beliefs against the backdrop of the traditional, but skewed tale of the conquest of the West by intrepid white men and sometimes women.

Eventually totaling four volumes, Roosevelt's account offered a particular attraction. In other writings, he had demonstrated his meticulous research and engaging style; now he responded to critical reviewers by adding personal experience. In 1884, a family tragedy moved the twenty-four-year-old Roosevelt to relocate to Dakota Territory, where he purchased partnerships in two Badlands cattle ranches and threw himself into the demanding roles of the cowboy and, at the same time, of the owner-supervisor known as "the boss." Later Roosevelt stated, "This is where the romance of my life began."

The West was instrumental in forming Roosevelt's conservation ideas. He quickly came to understand the need to save the West before its physical and built environments disappeared, leaving a magnificently endowed region stripped of its riches. One observer remarked that Roosevelt's "first-hand experience of the West" led him to "a keen awareness of Resources." Another concluded that Roosevelt's conservationism was a "direct result" of witnessing destructive changes in the western environment.

Roosevelt claimed even more for his western experience, later maintaining that "I have always said I would not have been President had it not been for my experience in North Dakota." Certainly, he combined his conservationist philosophy with the presidency, creating five national parks, eighteen national monuments, five game preserves, and fifty-one bird refuges. Beside other achievements in the areas of progressive reform, social justice, and international relations, he bequeathed to the Northeast, the South, and particularly the West, a legacy of environmental awareness and action.

AN OYSTER BAY BOY

Theodore Roosevelt was born on October 27, 1858, in New York City, to Martha Bulloch Roosevelt, a southern belle, and Theodore Roosevelt Sr., a business entrepreneur and philanthropist. Theodore was the second child and first boy of four children, the only one who suffered from a chronic ailment, bronchial asthma, which caused him frequently to struggle for breath. Still, he preferred the outdoors, especially vacationing with his family in nearby Oyster Bay, Long Island.

Because Theodore was tutored at home rather than sent to school, where he would have encountered a larger world of boys and male adults, he was greatly influenced by several family members. On the female side was Theodore's mother, Martha, and her sister, Anna. Martha was a lovely, but sickly, woman who clung to her family's Southern, pro-slave, and Confederate sentiments, which she relayed to her son by telling family stories about heroic and influential Bullochs dating back to the American Revolution. She was especially mindful of, and very bitter about, her family's fall, including the destruction of their plantation by Sherman's troops during the Civil War. Her sister, Anna Bulloch, reinforced these stirring tales when she served as the Roosevelt children's first teacher.

On the male side stood Theodore's father and his father's brother, Robert B. Roosevelt, a lawyer, novelist, political reformer, and conservationist who passed on his interests to his nephew. There is no doubt that Theodore's father weighed in most heavily with the lad. Unlike his wife, he was pro-North and antislave, and strongly supported Abraham Lincoln and his brand of Republicanism. As Theodore Jr. grew up, he learned to admire free labor, stable banks, more colleges, and free land for homesteaders in the West. The boy also internalized tenets of the social gospel as he watched his father found museums and help fund facilities for the sick, mentally ill, and orphaned.

Young Theodore drew heavily from this quartet of strong personalities. He admired grand deeds and philanthropic causes, and held a Lincoln-style view of the American West. When in 1870, Roosevelt Sr. helped create the American Museum of Natural History, young Theodore established in his bedroom the "Roosevelt Museum of Natural History," consisting of birds he captured, stuffed, and mounted. On the negative side of these adult influences was Theodore's lack of understanding of black people and Native Americans, a limitation that he never fully overcame. As a Roosevelt biographer, Aida D. Donald, points out, young Theodore's father failed to model "either a personal connection with the poor or empathy" for them. Nor, Donald states, did Roosevelt Sr. realize that private philanthropy "could only ameliorate conditions." She adds that it would be years before Theodore Jr. would recognize that only a well-funded central government could wield the power and funds "to truly help the poor or that social and economic conditions themselves needed change." Thus, Theodore Jr., like his idol Abraham Lincoln, would be a prophet in his own time, even while somewhat lacking from a twenty-first-century perspective.

In other ways as well, Theodore's interests previewed his adult world. At age ten, when his family toured Europe, he kept a journal, including architectural and historical sites visited, and captured specimens for his "museum." At age twelve, he took seriously his father's injunction that "You have the mind but not the body. You must make your body." He worked out in the gym his father provided, developing muscles and skills that allowed him to take up rowing and boxing later at Harvard, and stood him in good stead when he settled in Dakota Territory. The next year, at age thirteen, Theodore received his first pair of eyeglasses, which brought ridicule down upon him. And at fourteen, the gift of a shotgun set off his hunting career.

While a student at Harvard, Theodore focused on natural history and political economy. When the senior Roosevelt died in 1878, at age forty-six, probably of stomach cancer, the Roosevelt clan fell into confusion at the sudden loss of its leader and role model. Theodore responded by pursuing his studies and activities with increased vigor. He felt he had fulfilled his father's wishes when he graduated magna cum laude and Phi Beta Kappa from Harvard. He entered Columbia Law School in 1880, but found law lacking in concerns of social justice, which he hoped to reestablish as a priority of the Republican Party. In 1882, Roosevelt, who already saw himself as a reformer, won a New York Assembly seat, and left law behind for writing and politics.

TRAGEDY

On his twenty-second birthday in 1880, Theodore had married Alice Hathaway Lee. In 1884, the couple hired an architect to design a twenty-two-room Queen Anne–style mansion in Oyster Bay. Tragically, when their first child, Alice, was born on December 2, 1884, the mother did not survive, dying a few hours after Theodore's own mother succumbed to typhoid fever.

For Theodore, these losses seemed too much to bear. He escaped to Dakota Territory, where he had invested in cattle. Once there, his fascination for the place and its life grew daily. Working with everyday cowboys, he learned to see people, animals, and land through new eyes. During long days in the saddle—one "day" once lasting twenty-six hours without a mount change—he improved his health, reshaped his body, and honed his character. In the evenings, he read and wrote about the West. Although he occasionally returned to the East for family and business matters, he became increasingly attached to the West, its values, its culture, and its meaning for American development.

In 1886, after two years in the Dakota Badlands, he moved back east to marry his childhood sweetheart, Edith Kermit Carow. In 1887, the couple moved into the Oyster Bay mansion, Sagamore Hills, where they produced a family of five, to which they added his daughter, Alice, from his first marriage. Yet Roosevelt never shed the western man from his personality and often visited the West.

THE WESTERN MAN BACK EAST

Besides being a devoted husband, a proud father, and a state politician, Theodore settled into writing. The success of his 1882 book, *The Naval War of 1812*, gave him hope that he could recoup funds lost in his western ventures, especially after the severe cattle-killing winter of 1887 wiped out most of his herds.

Accordingly, Roosevelt plunged into the most lucrative of his twenty books, *The Winning of the West*, of which the first two volumes appeared in 1889. Couched as a historical narrative, the volumes focus on the struggle between Native Americans and the white people who invaded their lands. Oddly enough, the author ignores the respect his hero, Lincoln, held for the Declaration of Independence and the equality of rights. Instead, like Thomas Jefferson, Roosevelt sees the two races at different stages of development, thus engendering conflict fated to end in white conquest. In an 1887 biography of Missouri politician Thomas Hart Benton, Roosevelt similarly had defended Manifest Destiny, labeling as "maudlin nonsense" any criticism of Texas frontiersmen who seized Indian lands. Biographer Aida Donald succinctly sums up his approach: "Ultimately, Roosevelt was a white man's historian."

Although Roosevelt accepted the decimation of Native peoples, he decried the damage that white invaders perpetrated on the environment and its wildlife. He declared that "The extermination of the buffalo has been a veritable tragedy of the animal world." Although an avid hunter, Roosevelt recognized that overhunting and the careless killing of buffalo, mule deer, elk, and other once-plentiful animals had to stop. He also delved into such ills as erosion, scarce water, intensive grazing, and destructive mining and logging practices.

Roosevelt came to believe that Americans must care for the surroundings that taught them about their past and instilled confidence for the present and future. He thought some areas and resources must be *preserved*, meaning kept in their pristine state without alteration, and others *conserved*, allowing careful usage without any permanent destruction.

Roosevelt's timing was superb, for the 1890s formed a decade of intense speculation regarding the West's future. On the basis of the 1890 census year, the U.S. Bureau of the Census declared the western frontier "closed," since the region now had a population average of two people per square mile. In the ensuing climate of uncertainty, and even panic, stood Roosevelt's *Winning of the West*, which warned about the loss of the western environment and history. A few years later, in 1893, historian Frederick Jackson Turner's bombshell essay, "The Significance of the Frontier in American History," asked what the disappearance of the frontier West might mean for democracy and the exceptionalism of the United States and its people. At the same time, spiraling urbanization and industrialization in the East aggravated worries regarding the decreasing quality of American life, whereas it became apparent that Native American–white American conflicts and sport hunting had taken an incredible toll on western people and wildlife.

As a result of the turmoil, Americans demonstrated great curiosity and equally great nostalgia for the "wild" West, including Indian-white wars, stagecoach and train robberies, and sharpshooters. Soon, entrepreneurs of all types fed the public what it seemed to want. Nebraskan William F. "Buffalo Bill" Cody mounted a wildly popular "exhibition" of Wild West history, replete with riders, shooters, and authentic Native Americans direct from reservations. Meanwhile, a new genre of fiction—sensationalist dime novels—chronicled highly romanticized versions of western events, and in 1903, a black-and-white film titled, *The Great Train Robbery,* became the first Western movie to gain popularity.

During these years, the fears Roosevelt raised, as well as his effective use of high drama, heroes and heroines, made him a successful author and western advocate. But he also tried to resuscitate his political career. He held a variety of positions, ranging from membership on the U.S. Civil Service Commission in 1895 to the governorship of New York in 1898, and culminating in election as vice president of the United States in 1900. In addition, in 1898, he became the ultimate model for American males aspiring to manliness when, during the Spanish-American War, he dashed up Kettle Hill, commonly called San Juan Hill, in Cuba with his Rough Riders.

Despite his frenetic life, Roosevelt never lost sight of his conservation goals. During the late 1880s and 1890s, he laid groundwork and made contacts that would serve him well during his presidency. In 1887, Roosevelt and his friend, supporter, and advisor, George Bird Grinnell, organized the Boone and Crockett Club, which began operation the following year. The group recruited wealthy, influential, and learned men, who were also hunters, to help stop animal slaughter, especially in the West, and to advocate responsible hunting practices.

Roosevelt took an active part, serving as the club's first president, participating in committees, giving speeches, and identifying conservation advocates, even drawing a few to his side as supporters and advisors. In 1895, he and Grinnell edited and published the club's first book, *Big Game Hunting*, presenting members' memoirs of their hunting adventures. Although Roosevelt's participation lessened as his political career accelerated, he gained invaluable support, learned about conservation issues, and spread his reputation among early conservationists.

During this period, Roosevelt had also formed close alliances with influential men. In a campaign to restore bison, or buffalo, he helped lobby Congress for the passage of the National Park Protection Act of 1894. Also known as the Lacey Act, named for member of Congress, John F. Lacey, who sponsored the legislation, the act sought to stop damage to Yellowstone and to protect the park's last two hundred buffalo and save the species. In the process, Roosevelt gained in Lacey a political colleague who would prove invaluable during his presidency.

Through the Boone and Crockett Club, Roosevelt also became acquainted with Gifford Pinchot, the first professional forester in the nation, who later became his advisor, especially relating to forest management. Early in the 1890s, Pinchot had despaired that the usual description of American forests employed the term "inexhaustible," which he believed was patently inaccurate. In his view, far too many unregulated loggers operated in western forests, while large companies cleared tracts for mines, quarries, or sale. Pinchot championed a new idea, the establishment of a central agency on the federal level to implement scientific management of the nation's timberland. This approach appealed to Roosevelt, who was beginning to recognize that a problem of such huge dimensions demanded equally huge solutions. In 1891, Congress adopted the Forest Reserve Act, which provided for reserves managed by the Department of the Interior. Five years later,

Pinchot joined the U.S. National Forest Commission, which scouted the West for possible forest reserves. In 1898, he became chief of the Division of Forestry, later renamed the Forest Service. In 1900, he was the primary founder of the Society of American Foresters. Pinchot was educated, experienced, and ideally placed to be President Roosevelt's main aide in the regulation and management of American forests.

THE CONSERVATIONIST PRESIDENT

In 1900, the Republican Party nominated Roosevelt as William McKinley's running mate in the presidential race. Roosevelt's enemies hoped that he would flounder in the vice presidency, while disgruntled colleagues at home said they would be happy to see him leave New York state. As usual, Roosevelt threw himself into the challenge, conducting a vigorous whistle-stop tour in western states. The McKinley-Roosevelt ticket proved victorious, but on September 6, 1901, President McKinley fell to an assassin's bullet, and Roosevelt was inaugurated as the twenty-sixth president of the United States.

At age forty-two, Roosevelt, the youngest man to hold the presidency, now had the position, power, and prestige to implement his complex agenda of reforms. If he was at all overwhelmed, that condition lasted just a minute before he dove, with his usual boundless energy and enthusiasm, into plans that would force under federal control such industries as meatpacking, railroads, and utilities and would lead to his nickname, the "Regulatory President." Along with the congressional leader from Wisconsin, Robert M. La Follette, Roosevelt was increasingly convinced that progressive reforms could be achieved and regulated only by the federal government. He promised that such programs would provide a "Square Deal" for average Americans.

Theodore Roosevelt was also dubbed the "Conservationist President." In 1901, industrialist Mark Hanna complained, "That damned cowboy is president now." Well might Hanna have worried, because Roosevelt had repeatedly stated that water and forest management were "the most vital internal problems of the United States."

Still, the concept of conservation was hardly novel when Roosevelt came to the presidency. Congress had set aside twenty-six million acres of land, yet federal administration and regulation were weak. What Roosevelt did was to move conservation to a top position on the federal agenda. His concern, and his devotion to the conservation cause, would also affect state and local levels; the East and the North as well as the West; people of all races and creeds; and men, women, and children. One example was the rush of women's clubs, white and black, to support his innovations. Roosevelt identified a growing need in the United States and caused a sea change by filling it.

As president, Roosevelt took action. He immediately started working on water for the West, declaring in his 1901 address to Congress that reclamation of neglected, denuded, or land too dry to farm was high on his to-do list. He had seen the destructive results of aridity during his time in Dakota Territory, and had written home about the difficulty of people, crops, and livestock to survive with only scarce or brackish water. Now he stated that "the sound and steady development of the West" depended upon the establishment of homes and farms, and that water in western rivers went to waste unless it was diverted to help homesteaders and farm families who needed it to succeed, especially after 1890, when good land was hard to find and water sources were increasingly limited.

President Roosevelt encouraged Congress to adopt the reclamation act that Nevada Democratic representative Francis G. Newlands had introduced. The bill stipulated that income from the sale of public lands in western states be invested in a "reclamation fund" to pay for "irrigation works for the storage, diversion, and development of waters," especially in the Far West, but administered on the federal level by the secretary of the interior. The president signed the Newlands Reclamation Act on June 17, 1902.

During the first year alone, five projects were authorized under the Newlands Act, the first being the Salt River Project, later renamed the Theodore Roosevelt Dam. The Bureau of Reclamation chose a site in Arizona seventy-six miles east of Phoenix, originally called "The Crossing" by Native Americans, settlers, traders, and other travelers who forded the Salt River. A photograph shows a deep, ragged crevice with rough, steep hills on each side. No individuals or companies had harnessed the site; as Roosevelt maintained, it took the weight and wealth of the federal government to do so.

Despite several disastrous floods that stopped progress temporarily, the resulting dam opened in 1911. On March 18, President Roosevelt dedicated the dam, explaining that because New Mexico and Arizona lacked representation in Congress, he had acted as their advocate. He later said that the Roosevelt Dam and the Panama Canal were the two greatest achievements of his presidency.

Naturally, not everyone accepted Roosevelt's approach. A fierce opponent was California environmentalist John Muir, who, in 1892, had founded the Sierra Club, which was dedicated to saving America's wilderness areas and their riches. Muir believed that conservation was not enough; precious resources needed absolute preservation from use and possible destruction. Through the decade, Muir grew stronger in his opposition to conservation, moving from willingness to compromise to opposition. In 1903, he invited Roosevelt to the Yosemite Valley to discuss their ideas of wilderness salvation. Although the debates fired Roosevelt's vision, it was obvious that the two men differed. To Muir, conservation was a flawed concept because it saw the natural world as a source of economic production, which would eventually lead to the erosion of irreplaceable natural gifts. Although Roosevelt agreed in certain cases, he held that many resources could be "managed"; that is, he wanted to allow regulated usage as long as no irremediable damage occurred.

In 1906, these philosophies clashed in a vitriolic argument over the possibility of damming Hetch Hetchy Valley, fed primarily by the Tuolumne River and located in Yosemite National Park. San Francisco officials had long looked at Hetch Hetchy as a possible reservoir site, but a devastating earthquake and fire that nearly leveled the city now made it mandatory that the city's water supply be supplemented. Because the proposed dam site was in a national park, the project required congressional approval. For seven years, preservationists clashed with conservationists. In 1912, John Muir pointed out that "everyone needs beauty as well as bread, places to play in and pray in, where Nature may heal and give strength in body and soul alike." Although not without followers, in 1913 Muir lost to what he called "temple destroyers" and "devotees of ravaging commercialism" when Congress approved the Hetch Hetchy project.

In the meantime, President Roosevelt applied the idea of scientific management to national forests, another goal he had stated in his 1901 address to Congress. In 1905, he designated the Forest Service as a division of the U.S. Department of Agriculture; the new agency would protect and develop national forests and grasslands, all now under Gifford Pinchot's purview. Roosevelt heartily agreed with Pinchot that forests should "produce the largest amount of whatever crop or service will be most useful, and keep on producing it for generation after generation of men and trees." This policy riled commercial interests, who wanted quicker turnover in timber-cutting and thus more profit. Congress concurred. In 1907, it prohibited setting aside new protected forests in western states. In rebellion, just before midnight on the day before the provision was to take effect, Roosevelt designated sixteen million acres for new forests, which became known as the "Midnight Forests."

In the middle of these crusades and controversies, not only for water and wood, but for control of trusts, railroads, and big industry, Roosevelt had to take into account his political future. He always had campaigning and the hope of reelection to a second term on his mind—and on his schedule. In 1903, he became the first successful presidential candidate to campaign in the West. On May 4, he enjoyed a parade held in his honor in Denver, Colorado. In Hugo, Colorado, he joined a group of cowboys for a roundup and chuck-wagon meal. In mid-May, he visited Portland, Oregon, and later in the month made his famous camping trip to Yosemite with California preservationist John Muir. On May 30, in response to an invitation from the University of Wyoming, he visited Laramie, where he was feted and presented with an exceptional horse and an engraved silver saddle. Instead of taking the train sixty-five miles to Cheyenne, his next stop, Roosevelt decided to ride his gift horse—ten hours in the saddle across the Continental Divide alone. Once back in the capital, the horse, renamed Wyoming, became his favorite mount.

Although Roosevelt maintained his cowboy persona throughout the campaign, he also espoused Progressivism. To him, this meant three things. First, he was a committed reformer, ferreting out corruption, cheating, and unfairness at every level. As a former deputy sheriff in the Dakota Badlands and police commissioner of New York City, he knew the methods and the stance needed to be effective. Second, he shared the era's growing reliance on science, social sciences, engineering, and technology to resolve society's problems. He was not beyond reminding people that he was trained in the natural sciences and was a biologist of sorts, thus an integral member of the scientific movement. And finally, he advocated the need for the president to serve as "the steward of the public welfare," with federal agencies acting as his deputies. These ideas were more acceptable than they would be today because, as historian Hal K. Rothman explains in *Preserving Different Pasts,* they gave people hope and expectations of order in a society battered by incredible changes.

Roosevelt's presidential campaign proved so effective that a landslide swept him into the White House in his own right. Now assured of public support and free of the campaigning he so obviously enjoyed, but which drained time and energy from his presidential endeavors, he attacked the conservation-related issue of national parks. These had come into being during the time of President George Washington and the Continental Congress, and during the ensuing century, a number of battlefields, national monuments, and natural areas had been added to the list of areas set aside for the public. But President Roosevelt believed that Americans paid too little attention to saving the natural riches as well as physical evidence of the nation's development. Only five national parks existed, the first being Yellowstone, which Congress designated "a public park or pleasuring ground for the benefit and enjoyment of the people." Because Roosevelt believed that the United States would be far poorer for the loss of such environmental riches and historical landmarks, he decided to designate many worthy areas before they disappeared or were destroyed.

Given the numerous natural and historic areas in the nation, many in the West that Roosevelt had seen or knew about, he found the congressional procedure painfully slow. He did sign bills creating five new national parks: Crater Lake in Oregon; Wind Cave in South Dakota; Sullys Hill in North Dakota (later a game preserve); Mesa Verde in Colorado; and Platt in Oklahoma (later to become a part of Chickasaw National Recreation Area). Still, Roosevelt chafed at the number of places yet to be saved.

The president was especially distraught when news reports and exposés crossed his desk describing vandalism occurring on unprotected federal lands. Looters robbed cliff dwellings, pueblos, and missions in the West and Southwest. From places like Chaco Canyon in New Mexico and Mesa Verde in Colorado, thieves took Native American pots, tools, weapons, religious items, building stones, roof beams, and even human remains. In turn, they sold these at enormous profits to private collectors in the United States, Europe, and Asia. Even museum officials and people claiming to be archeologists sometimes participated in the illegal sales, which could involve millions of dollars. And the problem never abated because each drought, dust storm, flood, fire, or other natural disaster brought to the surface another cache of goods to be exploited.

Although ranchers and other local interests tried to protect resources, it was an impossible situation because of the distances involved. During the 1880s, 1890s, and early 1900s, the problem became public knowledge, and an outcry for federal intervention came from concerned citizens, scholars, and government officials—first in Boston, then gradually spreading down the coast to Washington, D.C. Various bills were introduced in Congress, sparking debates, but no legislation resulted. Then, in 1902, Iowa representative John F. Lacey, chair of the House Committee on the Public Lands, traveled to the Southwest to investigate the pot-hunter scandal and assess the damages. Roosevelt was delighted that his longtime friend and associate from the early days of the Boone and Crockett Club had entered the fray. Lacey was well known for his conservation efforts, notably the Lacey Act of 1900, which protected wild birds. He was also a savvy politician who often used his clout on behalf of conservation issues.

In New Mexico, Lacey enlisted the aid of archaeologist Edgar Lee Hewett, who investigated Pueblo cultures in Frijoles Canyon near Santa Fe, which later formed part of Bandelier National Park. After touring sites together, Hewitt prepared a massive report to Congress, while Lacey submitted his own findings. Hewitt and

Lacey subsequently spent two years shepherding legislation through Congress. The bill's most controversial feature allowed a president to proclaim a national monument, thus reducing congressional power and—some pointed out—upsetting the separation of powers established in the Constitution. Somehow, the experienced Lacey convinced Congress to pass the bill in 1906.

The Antiquities Act was short and to the point. Section 1 established fines of not more than five hundred dollars or imprisonment of ninety days, or both, for people who entered a site without a permit from the secretary of the interior, war, or agriculture, depending on which department oversaw the property, and excavated, removed, or injured government holdings. Section II, however, was crucial, authorizing the president—in this case, Theodore Roosevelt—to publicly proclaim "historic landmarks, historic and prehistoric structures, and other objects of historic or scientific interest" located on public lands as "national monuments," as well as areas around it. This provision would enable the executive to "save" key areas without long, and sometimes fruitless, congressional investigations and debates.

On June 8, 1906, Roosevelt exuberantly signed into law the Antiquities Act. During the rest of his second term, he proclaimed a total of 1.2 million acres worth of national monuments at Devils Tower, El Morro, Montezuma Castle, Petrified Forest, Chaco Canyon, Cinder Cone, Lassen Peak, Gila Cliff Dwelling, Tonto, Muir Woods, Grand Canyon, Pinnacles, Jewel Cave, Natural Bridges, Lewis and Clark Cavern, Tumacácori, Wheeler Geologic Area, and Mount Olympus, thus establishing a precedent for successive presidents.

There were other gains that Roosevelt had not anticipated. The Antiquities Act saved a good deal of the West by setting a standard for the assessment and handling of cultural resources, ranging from artifacts and buildings to landscapes and battlefields. By requiring that qualified individuals from such organizations as museums and universities obtain federal permits to excavate, the act accelerated the growth of graduate archeology programs, as well as the professionalization of young archaeologists. It also opened for viewing parts of natural and historic areas to thousands of Americans who had reasonable incomes and mobility, although for the nation's poor, white and of color, who remained trapped by poverty in urban slums or on hardscrabble farms, the creation of these public spaces was essentially a nonhappening.

There were also problems that Roosevelt did not expect. Native American leaders objected that the Antiquities Act separated them from control of their artifacts and the interpretation of their past. Instead, archaeologists and other scholars would decide how to present Indian cultures to the non-Indian public.

And because of the permit system, "unqualified" Native Americans would be excluded from excavating their ancestral lands, homes, and material legacies.

To these critics, such treatment mirrored events that had occurred before Roosevelt's time. In 1879, for example, dispossession of Native Americans from nationally held lands began when Indian removal at Yellowstone separated an indigenous population from its roots. In Yellowstone during the 1870s, there were reports of Indian "attacks" on tourists. Later, accounts circulated concerning Nez Perce, Bannocks, and Crows in Yellowstone. Even though there was much arable and hunting land in the far reaches of the park, away from visitors, politicians and administrators maintained that Indians would be more comfortable on reservations than in a land of fire pits, geysers, and brimstone.

If President Roosevelt knew of these developments, he avoided mentioning them. Generally, he spoke little of Native Americans. Like Thomas Jefferson, he had long thought it inevitable that a more highly developed society of white Americans would take over a lesser one like that of Native Americans. Perhaps his most telling statement was that "I don't say the only good Indian is a dead Indian but it is probably true of nine out of ten, and I don't care to examine too carefully the tenth."

EUGENICS

In many ways, President Roosevelt's attitudes reflected his era, when Social Darwinism was widely supported and "scientific racism" was in vogue in some circles. Darwinism put forth the concept of the survival of the fittest, whereas "scientific racism" identified characteristics of white people as making their race fitter and predicted that races not having these characteristics would eventually lose the struggle to survive. Some even argued that the fittest *should* survive. Of the latter persuasion was lawyer Madison Grant, a friend and associate of Roosevelt's since the two men had met in the Boone and Crockett Club after Grant joined in 1893. In following years, Grant excelled as a conservationist, notably in saving giant redwoods. More controversial were Grant's contributions to the science of eugenics, which maintained that the fittest must protect themselves from being overwhelmed by growing numbers of the unfit, ranging from the poor to the mentally unstable. Grant recommended to Roosevelt that the United States limit immigration to the (white) Nordic races and sterilize members of the unfit so that they could not reproduce.

President Roosevelt vacillated between many theorists' statements concerning scientific racism, including those of Grant, at times supporting ideas that today are very unpopular. For instance, in 1911, Roosevelt wrote to the sociologist Edward

Alsworth Ross at the University of Wisconsin, saying he agreed with Ross's support of Chinese exclusion because Asians would "inevitably clash" with whites on the Pacific coast. At the same time, he had regular physical workouts with Japanese wrestlers, and he described the Japanese as "a wonderful people."

Roosevelt demonstrated similar ambivalence toward black Americans, including in the West where such actions as lynching were used to control black men and women. Although he occasionally declared that blacks should be treated as individuals rather than in a prejudiced and dismissive way as "Negroes," other of his views did not promise blacks a bright future. He publicly declared that black people belonged to a "backward" and even "savage" race, and he adopted the widespread belief that lynching could be justified as punishment of black men who had defiled white women. What he failed to address was the fact that black women who "stepped out of their place" by achieving some success—perhaps by owning property and thereby gaining enough independence to frighten whites—were also often the victims of "lynch parties."

Unsurprisingly, Roosevelt's encounters with black men and women were mixed. One example is found in his presidential appointments. Although Roosevelt maintained that he believed in putting qualified blacks into office, between 1901 and 1909 black appointments actually declined. Another example occurred in Texas, part of the trans-Mississippi West. In 1906, an incident in Brownsville resulted in an outpouring of nationwide criticism of the president's actions. After locals accused black troops of "shooting up" the town on two summer nights, President Roosevelt released the men from their army commitment; in other words, he fired them without a hearing or trial. Nor, despite the criticism, did he rescind his judgment.

Because of his ambivalence, President Roosevelt did little to resolve racial conflicts, including those occurring in the West. In 1905, the president urged white leaders to "proceed slowly" and to avoid radical changes in government policy. He preferred that white Americans gradually adjust their attitude regarding blacks. After all, he maintained, white Americans were the "forward race" who must preserve their culture by training "backward" people in the white work ethic, in politics, and in morality. Roosevelt held, and often preached, a passive, long-term view of race relations.

THE STRUGGLE OVER PANAMA

Another instance in which President Roosevelt showed his mistrust of peoples of color occurred over a western-related improvement, the oft-proposed Panama Canal, which could potentially revolutionize the West's commerce and communication with the rest of the world. As president, he recognized that an improved passage across the Columbian-held Panama isthmus in Central America would ease trade, travel, and protection for the American West and thus for the entire nation. Unfortunately, he had no respect for the people he would have to deal with. In *Theodore Roosevelt and the Idea of Race,* Thomas G. Dyer states that the president held "negative opinions about the principal victims of American imperialism, Filipinos and Latin Americans," once describing Columbians as "a corrupt pithecoid community."

Roosevelt decided to plunge into the huge, complicated issue with his "big stick" mentality in full force. He discovered that, in 1881, a French company and engineer had unsuccessfully attempted to dig a canal at land level through the Isthmus of Panama, which would join the Atlantic and Pacific Oceans and save ships the arduous, more-than-twelve thousand-mile trip from New York around the treacherous Cape Horn at the southernmost end of South America. For travelers, there was available a rudimentary and dangerous rail trip across Panama to a port where California-bound ships waited, but as gold-rush travel had shown, it was fraught with difficulties, not the least of which was malaria. Dismissive of vast cultural and language differences, Theodore Roosevelt decided to resolve the issue his own way. In 1903, he made his intentions clear to Congress, stating that "no single great material work . . . on this Continent is of such consequence to the American people," especially those in the West.

The struggle was already ongoing. The United States had offered up to $40 million for the property and equipment the French company still held on the isthmus; the company seemed inclined to accept the offer. The real crux of the controversy, however, lay in land and permit negotiations with "hostile" Columbian representatives. As Roosevelt saw it, the Columbians were "excitable" and showed a lack of good sense and rational decision making in their response. The result was that U.S. officials quietly undermined Columbian officials by encouraging Panama to declare independence, which was not difficult, given the confused state of affairs there. Almost immediately after Panamanian independence was declared, the United States purchased a six-mile-wide strip of land, which ended any need for further negotiations.

In 1904, the United States finally ordered Americans into Panama, but little prior planning had been done to counter work conditions in a tropical, poor, and often unfriendly country. Few preparations had been made to provide such necessities as clean water and food, and to defeat the malaria-bearing mosquitos. Three out of four American workers soon left the job, and the project collapsed again. But President Roosevelt was not about to accept defeat. He appointed a new engineer, John F. Stevens, who had built the Great Northern Railroad across the demanding Pacific Northwest. Unlike his predecessor, Stevens began by having workers drain swamps, build homes, install plumbing, and put up such public buildings as schools and churches. As for the mighty mosquito, Dr. William Gorgas, who had defeated yellow fever in Havana, hired on to oversee sanitation work. By late 1905, malaria was largely under control.

In 1906, Roosevelt was so pleased with the progress of the canal that he became the first sitting president to leave the country. He visited Panama, where he marveled at the achievements and minimized the setbacks. Photographs of the president sitting at the wheel of a mammoth Bucyrus steam shovel appeared in U.S. papers, assuring the folks back home. After Roosevelt returned to Washington, D.C., however, a discouraged Stevens resigned. This time the president found an army engineer, Colonel George Washington Goethals, who had experience constructing the type of canal Roosevelt wanted and for which he had created a specific design. This was a lake-and-lock canal in which a series of locks would lift ships on the Atlantic side to a lake crossing, after which other locks would lower them to the Pacific, or vice versa.

Unfortunately for Roosevelt, he was out of office when the Panama Canal reached completion in 1913, and a series of tests proved the lake-and-lock system every bit as efficient as Roosevelt had predicted. When the canal opened in August 1914, Roosevelt must have celebrated the completion of the great engineering project that he had initiated, which would soon provide unbelievable benefits to his beloved American West. The canal reduced travel time between New York and San Francisco from months to mere weeks. Naval protection was also assured, since the U.S. Navy could move from the Atlantic side of the country, or the reverse, in three weeks rather than two or three months. Ignoring the rupture in trust between the United States and Central America, Roosevelt claimed the canal as one of the greatest achievements of his presidency.

CLOSING OUT THE PRESIDENCY

Roosevelt's concern for the conservation of the American West never lessened. During the last year of his presidency, March 1908 to March 1909, he pursued reform as actively as ever, challenging railroads and other big businesses at every opportunity. He and Gifford Pinchot also mounted a vigorous campaign to broaden the scope of support for their conservation programs. More specifically, they involved a variety of people as well as institutionalizing their concerns through a series of annual conferences and committees that they hoped would exert pressure on future presidents and Congresses.

One of the most important was the first Conference of Governors, convened at the White House early in 1908. The president's opening address set the theme: "Conservation as a National Duty." Because making conservation an element of citizenship had wide appeal, the conference stirred public interest, as well as stimulating individual and state conservation initiatives.

In June, Roosevelt followed up by appointing the National Conservation Commission made up of congressional members and agency administrators, with Gifford Pinchot as chair. A three-volume report reached Congress in 1909, recommending Pinchot's concept of scientific management and presenting an inventory of the nation's natural resources.

Also in 1908, Roosevelt created the Commission on Rural Life, again with Pinchot in a prominent role. The group's charge was to identify problems of rural life in an increasingly industrialized nation and to suggest solutions. The commission published its report in 1909, bolstering the emerging Country Life Movement and reinforcing Roosevelt's land and water reclamation and timber initiatives.

In 1909, the president took an even broader action to shore up the conservation ethic. He called the North American Conservation Conference, involving representatives from the United States, Mexico, Canada, and Newfoundland. Although no definitive action resulted, the conference highlighted the international nature of destructive environmental practices. In 1909, a disgruntled Congress refused any further funding for the National Conservation Commission. Roosevelt thought Congress argumentative and poky in conservation legislation, whereas many members of Congress perceived Roosevelt as controlling. They may have had a point. Besides creating new conservation groups, Roosevelt had been especially active in 1908 in issuing presidential proclamations designating national monuments at Muir Woods and at Pinnacles in California, Grand Canyon in Arizona, Jewel Cave in South Dakota, Natural Bridges in Utah, Lewis and Clark Cavern in Montana, and Wheeler Geologic Area in Colorado. His last proclamation established Mount Olympus National Monument in Washington State.

"THE OLD LION IS DEAD"

When Roosevelt left the presidency, he made a wise move for himself, and for the nation, by leaving behind the political scene, at least temporarily. In March 1909, he and his son Kermit departed for a one-year safari in East Africa. After landing at the coastal city of Mombasa in Kenya, they boarded the Uganda railroad, heading east for the game preserves and national parks of the interior. One year later, in March 1910, Theodore met up with Edith and proceeded on a triumphant tour of Europe during which he received an honorary degree from Cambridge University, and presented the prestigious Romanes Lecture at Oxford University.

Back in the United States, Roosevelt learned that President William H. Taft appeared ineffective and, worse yet, gave little credence to conservation efforts. In 1910, Roosevelt reentered politics with a stinging speech delivered in Osawatomie, Kansas, which espoused a program called the New Nationalism, and declared that "the object of government is the welfare of the people." This speech launched Roosevelt on a political odyssey—he left the Republican Party for the new Progressive Party and ran unsuccessfully as its presidential candidate in 1912. He was later to contract malaria on a junket to Brazil and witness the coming of World War I, which eventually took his youngest son, Quentin, from him. By 1916, he had left the Progressive Party behind; in 1918, he expressed doubts about the Treaty of Versailles and the League of Nations.

On January 16, 1919, Theodore Roosevelt died in his sleep at his beloved Sagamore Hill home. His son Archie reported to his brothers, "The old lion is dead."

ROOSEVELT'S WESTERN LEGACY

Since Theodore Roosevelt's death, scholars, journalists, and others have tried to assess his legacy, which was vast and varied, particularly for the American West. Of course, Roosevelt's Progressive reforms, including those concerning banking, workers' rights, food and drug control, and the regulation of large business, touched all regions, but some of them had particular impact on the West. Making railroads reasonable and accessible, as in the 1902 Elkins Act, which prohibited rebates, and the 1906 Hepburn Act, which reinforced other regulations, brought tremendous gains to a region that lay far from markets and major ports, and produced heavyweight agricultural products and raw materials that northeastern cities and its factories so badly needed. The railroads aided two of the West's largest industries by simplifying the transportation of beef on the hoof and the shipping of tons of partially refined blister copper. States such as Arizona, Utah, New Mexico, Nevada, and Montana were able to develop copper mining largely because of railroads.

But Roosevelt recognized that railroads could not operate without oversight, for such practices as short- and long-haul charges and far-flung railheads would seriously hurt western farmers, ranchers, and miners. His railroad reforms enabled the West to become the premier agricultural center of the United States, as well as an important mining center. Similarly, Roosevelt's controls on banking and specie kept inflation down and prices stable, so that small entrepreneurs in the West had a chance not only to compete in the nation's expanding capitalist economy, but to become an important cog in its development.

Another type of transportation revolution resulted when Roosevelt initiated the building of the Panama Canal and provided the necessary badgering to keep the project alive. When the canal opened in 1914, it gave the West relatively quick water access to the Northeast and South and to Asian trade. The canal also made possible an increase in the size and mobility of the U.S. Navy, which could reach western ports in incredibly fast time. This lake-and-lock canal, thus far the most creative and expensive of public works in the United States, facilitated the integration of the West into the rest of the world.

Another huge change that Roosevelt implemented was his broadening of the U.S. presidency, giving it powers that helped integrate the West into national affairs. Numerous scholars describe Roosevelt as the first "modern" president of the country in that he vowed to empower the office—and succeeded in doing it. He believed that the executive had the right to exercise all powers not specifically denied him, to regulate big business for the welfare of the people, to put into effect efficacious reforms, and to provide a strong U.S. presence in foreign affairs. He was unusually open, introducing the daily press conference and regular interviews. Roosevelt even encouraged writers whom he had first labeled "muckrakers," yet soon came to appreciate for their contributions to his reform crusades. For example, in 1904, an influential muckraker, Lincoln Steffens, published *The Shame of the Cities* in which he criticized Minneapolis and other cities for political corruption. Roosevelt was thankful to him for definitive evidence that helped the president make possible regulatory legislation for western cities outside of his immediate purview.

Although Roosevelt's personal appeal and ebullient manner were like tasty frosting on a cake, making his ideas more palatable, many westerners were displeased with his type of executive, especially one who operated thousands of miles from their home bases. Numerous ranchers, timber and mining interests, and railroad magnates had historically opposed what they thought of as too much federal involvement in their local affairs, and they found distasteful Roosevelt's segue from emphasizing individual rights to emphasizing community rights. When the president candidly stated that his programs meant increased "governmental intervention" and pushed federal oversight by regulating unemployment, medical issues, and retirement, these westerners feared what his precedents might mean for future presidents. They probably suspected just what *did* happen. Roosevelt's progressivism, expressed in his Square Deal and New Nationalism, set the stage for Franklin Delano Roosevelt's New Deal, Harry S. Truman's Fair Deal, John F. Kennedy's New Frontier, Lyndon B. Johnson's Great Society, and perhaps even Barack Obama's Affordable Care Act. Like industrialist Mark Hanna, many lamented that the "cowboy" had ever come to the White House.

Yet Roosevelt's cowboy ways were one more of his contributions to the West. To the nation's men in general, many of whom felt diminished after the erosion of their roles by industrialism, or the defeat of the white male Confederacy in the Civil War, Roosevelt expanded the western cowboy into a cowboy/soldier/hero who was a "real" man—strong, courageous, individualistic, tough—and western. Almost single-handedly, with his author's pen and his charisma, he made the West and its manhood a national standard. General Arthur MacArthur Jr. summed it up well when he said that at last he had a president who could review troops on horseback.

It should be noted that Roosevelt's western ideal was also white, thus giving white men a sense of belonging to a group that was more threatened each day by people of color and by "New Women." A bevy of these white, would-be cowboys thronged to Wild West arenas to watch, and to live vicariously through, white male performers who always defeated their Indian adversaries. Although there were black, Mexican, and even female cowboys in the real West, no blacks, no Mexicans, and very few women appeared in the Wild West arena at this time. Rather, that arena reflected Roosevelt's vision—and his hesitancy to act for racial change. As a result of his view of Indians, blacks, and Asians, he did not take an active part in sorting out the West's intercultural conflict.

Many scholars and other commentators state that one of Roosevelt's greatest legacies, or perhaps *the* greatest, was his conservation programs. Certainly for the West, Roosevelt's conservationism had lasting effect. In addition to national parks and monuments, game preserves, and bird refuges, he increased 42 million acres of protected land to 172 million. Of the eighteen national monuments that he personally proclaimed under the Antiquities Act, all were in the West, ranging from Devils Tower in Wyoming in 1906 and Montezuma Castle in Arizona later that year, to Natural Bridges in Utah in 1908 and Mount Olympus in Washington State in 1909. In combination with railroads, this proliferation of public spaces helped western tourism blossom and a flood of dollars enter the region. Railroads advertised their western ventures widely, while entrepreneur Fred Harvey established railroad stops with restaurants, gift shops, and hotels, ensuring a safe and comfortable trip for young people, single women, and families.

In addition, Roosevelt's advocacy of an outdoor "strenuous life," encouraged a bevy of writers to describe nature and such outdoor activities as camping and hiking, which made men and women hunger to see the West and experience its delights. One extremely popular adventure writer of the time, James Oliver Curwood, wrote stories that championed endangered animals, giving the animals' point of view and begging for their protection. Eventually, men and women who engaged in agriculture, and worked outdoors every day of their lives, also came to consider camping and hiking a respite from cultivating the land.

Roosevelt's programs regarding environmental reform influenced the West even more deeply. His 1907 message to Congress particularly illustrated how central the West was to his thinking and ethical center. He stated that reclamation and irrigation were more important to the West "than any other region of the country" because such improvements opened land to "permanent home-makers," who would help the region grow and prosper. Notably, the 1902 Newlands Act had established the precedent of utilizing funds from the sale of public lands in the West that, in turn, had made numerous reclamation plans possible and more land available to "home-makers." In fact, some experts maintain that Roosevelt's reclamation legislation was second only to Lincoln's Homestead Act in the amount of settlers it lured west.

In 1907, Roosevelt also mentioned another concern: land unfit for cultivation that was currently used for public grazing. He disliked the fences that individuals built, keeping others from public land. He declared that "unlawful fencing of public lands for private use must be stopped." According to the president, these lands had to be regulated to stop overgrazing. Subsequently, he introduced the use of federal fencing, permits, and leasing. Although cattle and sheep interests resisted, his policies often proved fair to people and to the land.

In retrospect, it is apparent that President Theodore Roosevelt upset a number of western individuals and groups by introducing a new form of land and resource management. With Gifford Pinchot's help, Roosevelt replaced laissez-faire with modern scientific management. Some people complained because they lost favors they had gained under the old system, while others felt an unintentional sting from the new provisions. For example, when impecunious homesteaders who needed timber for homes and outbuildings cut trees, they might now be committing a crime. Similarly, when hungry people hunted game to eat, they were most likely poaching. Logging and hunting had been long-term practices in the West and part of its bounty for settlers, but, in an odd twist, Roosevelt's conservation laws sometimes hurt the very homemakers he wanted to settle the region.

Still, Roosevelt never backpedaled. In 1910, he declared that "Wasting resources is robbing future generations." To him, only the country's "preservation of its existence in a great war" could be more important. In 1914, he witnessed just that, a "great war" developing in Europe, and three years later involving the United States. He was disappointed when his offer to raise and lead a special troop at the front was refused; he was then fifty-nine years old.

When Theodore Roosevelt died in 1919, he left behind far more than it seems any one person could. From the West's perspective, he was especially a successful writer who deified the old West in prose. Biographer Aida Donald reminds us that "all the volumes of *The Winning of the West* are still in print today, and they remain among the great classics on the American West." Also, he was the consummate conservationist. As Progressive Republican senator Robert La Follette of Wisconsin bluntly stated, "The Conservation of our Resources . . . is probably the greatest thing Roosevelt did, undoubtedly." And to many westerners he was one of them, their kind of hero. One summed it up by saying that Roosevelt was "part western" and that he "carried the West" in his heart until his death. Undoubtedly.

FOR FURTHER READING

Brinkley, Douglas. *The Wilderness Warrior: Theodore Roosevelt and the Crusade for America.* New York: Harper Perennial, 2009.

Dalton, Kathleen. *Theodore Roosevelt: A Strenuous Life.* New York: Alfred A. Knopf, 2002.

Di Silvestro, Roger L. *Theodore Roosevelt in the Badlands: A Young Politician's Quest for Recovery in the American West.* New York: Roger & Co., 2011.

Donald, Aida D. *Lion in the White House: A Life of Theodore Roosevelt.* New York: Basic Books, 2007.

Dorsey, Leroy G. *We Are All Americans, Pure and Simple: Theodore Roosevelt and the Myth of Americanism.* Tuscaloosa: University of Alabama Press, 2007.

Dyer, Thomas G. *Theodore Roosevelt and the Idea of Race.* Baton Rouge: Louisiana State University Press, 1980.

Fromkin, David. *The King and the Cowboy: Theodore Roosevelt and Edward the Seventh, Secret Partners.* New York: Penguin Press, 2008.

Goodwin, Doris Kearns. *The Bully Pulpit: Theodore Roosevelt, William Howard Taft, and the Golden Age of Journalism.* New York: Simon & Shuster, 2013.

Grant, George. *The Courage and Character of Theodore Roosevelt: A Hero among Leaders.* Nashville, TN: Cumberland House, 1996.

Haley, Joshua David. *Theodore Roosevelt: Preacher of Righteousness*. New Haven: Yale University Press, 2008.

Harmon, David, Francis P. Manamon, and Dwight T. Pitcaithley, eds. *The Antiquities Act: A Century of American Archaeology, Historic Preservation*. Tucson: University of Arizona Press, 2006.

Hilpert, John M. *American Cyclone: Theodore Roosevelt and His Whistle-Stop Campaign of 1900*. Oxford: University of Mississippi Press, 2015.

Morris, Edmund. *The Rise of Theodore Roosevelt*. New York: Modern Library, 1979.

Riley, Glenda. *Women and Nature: Saving the "Wild" West*. Lincoln: University of Nebraska Press, 1999.

Rothman, Hal. *Preserving Different Pasts: The American National Monuments*. Urbana: University of Illinois Press, 1989.

Spence, Mark David. *Dispossessing the Wilderness: Indian Removal and the Making of the National Parks*. New York: Oxford University Press, 1999.

Franklin D. Roosevelt, 1933–1945

LC-USZ62-26759

Chapter 6

FRANKLIN D. ROOSEVELT
MOLDING UNCLE SAM'S WEST

It was the end of September 1937 in northwestern Oregon. President Franklin D. Roosevelt was there near the top of the world—far up on the slopes of Mount Hood, the highest place in Oregon. Roosevelt had come west to dedicate the nearly completed Timberline Lodge on Mount Hood. A large stone-and-timber building, the lodge was, as Roosevelt put it, "a venture that was made possible by W. P. A. [Works Progress Administration], emergency relief work . . . installed by the Government itself and operated under its capable control."

But Timberline Lodge was much more. It was a revealing symbol of Franklin D. Roosevelt and his New Deal bounding across the country to the Far West. Whether in programs for farmers, laborers, families, war workers, or any of numerous other groups, Roosevelt's presidency from 1933 to 1945 clearly shaped the history of the American West. Nearly all of these New Deal policies had a notable impact on the West—saving farms and helping farmers, developing and protecting landscapes, and rescuing the needy, poverty-stricken, and nearly destitute. So moving and long lasting were these transformations that more than one historian has dubbed the region that resulted from Roosevelt's precedent-setting presidency "Uncle Sam's West."

There were, however, other, negative measures and actions. Chief among these was Roosevelt's issuing Executive Order 9066 in February 1942. Relocating inland about a hundred thousand Americans of Japanese heritage, the president brought on a tragedy. Nor did Roosevelt's New Deal, despite its many clear achievements, lift the West out of a horrendous depression by the end of the 1930s. It would take a booming war economy, also obviously linked to Roosevelt, to achieve that.

BEFORE THE PRESIDENCY

Roosevelt's long-lasting links to the American West are all the more unusual because his background would not have predicted such important connections.

Born on January 30, 1882, in Hyde Park in upstate New York, Franklin Delano Roosevelt descended from elite, northeastern sociocultural backgrounds. Educated at Harvard and Columbia Law School, Roosevelt represented his New York and Atlantic seaboard ancestors (including his distant cousin, President Theodore Roosevelt), who were far removed from the trans-Mississippi West. On March 17, 1905, Roosevelt married another distant cousin, Anna Eleanor Roosevelt, a wife who proved to be a strong, immensely important partner despite some rocky times in their marriage. Throughout Roosevelt's long presidency, Eleanor was increasingly an invaluable advisor at her husband's shoulder, giving suggestions and advice, and also traveling throughout the country, serving as his eyes and ears. No First Lady had more influence on her husband's policies than did Eleanor Roosevelt.

Franklin Roosevelt, after briefly practicing law in New York City, was elected a New York Democratic state senator (1911–13). Later, he was named assistant secretary of the navy (1913–20) in the Woodrow Wilson administration. In 1921, tragedy intervened: Roosevelt was stricken with infantile paralysis (polio). Courageously fighting back, and recovering partial use of his legs, he again became politically active and was elected governor of New York in 1928. His strong leadership and outgoing personality led to his reelection as New York governor in 1930, and his successes as governor made him an obvious candidate for the presidency in 1932. He easily defeated Herbert Hoover, a westerner by birth and heritage.

When Roosevelt came to the White House in March 1933, he knew very little about the American West. His experiences came from the Northeast and Washington, D.C., and he looked more to Europe than to the West. But once president, the energetic and farseeing Roosevelt desired to know about—and understand—the West. In turn, the region forced itself, in elections and in reactions to his policies, on an enthusiastic and insightful leader who wanted to serve all Americans. Before his death in 1945, Roosevelt, more than any other recent president—perhaps more than all presidents—molded the trans-Mississippi American West.

Roosevelt's temperament and ideology powerfully shaped his presidential leadership and policies. Roosevelt was a risk taker. In his prepresidential years, especially in his gubernatorial leadership of New York State, he proved to be an able leader willing to experiment with new approaches, such as direct governmental relief, to solve problems. His willingness to listen to diverse opinions also gained him a reputation as a consensus builder, not a stubborn ideologue as many found his predecessor, Herbert Hoover.

Roosevelt was a progressive Democrat committed to the idea of a strong central government directly involved in the lives of its citizens. He much preferred that stance to the Jeffersonian ideal: a government that governed least was the best form of government. FDR was much more attracted to the New Nationalism of his distant relative, Theodore Roosevelt—standing for a central government strong enough to control large trusts—than to the New Freedom of Woodrow Wilson, who would break up large conglomerates and return the country to a nation of farmers, workers, and small shopkeepers.

In both his political preferences and in his outlook on political life, President Roosevelt followed paths clearly divergent from those of Republican leaders of the preceding dozen years. Warren G. Harding (1921–23), Calvin Coolidge (1923–29), and Herbert Hoover (1929–33) were cautious conservatives. Harding frequently left decisions in the hands of his cabinet and other undependable leaders, and they often betrayed him. Coolidge was "a real conservative," his successor, Herbert Hoover, declared, who preferred small government and strong individual initiative. Hoover followed primarily in these tracks away from an active central government directing the country, and he paid little or no attention to the West, despite his being a westerner by birth. To Hoover's credit—and because he was forced to do something after the Great Depression fell on the country like a huge, heavy blanket in 1929—toward the end of his presidency he experimented with government policies to help counter the Depression. These efforts, including those of the Reconstruction Finance Corporation and the Federal Farm Board were too little, too late, like trying to dam up an out-of-control flood.

From his political beginnings, Roosevelt signaled that he would be an energetic administrator. Even before taking up the country's reins, Roosevelt hinted at his activism. In July 1932, he broke tradition by flying to Chicago to accept the Democratic presidential nomination, telling the convention's delegates that he pledged himself "to a new deal for the American people." These two words, "New Deal," became the catchphrase signifier of his administration in the 1930s—and the caption for the body of legislation that would be passed in the "Hundred Days" during the late winter and spring of 1933.

Campaigning in September 1932, in a speech before the Commonwealth Club of San Francisco, Roosevelt hinted at some of the avenues he might follow if elected president. While in the West, he told his listeners that the explosive expansion of giant corporations, large plants, and spreading railroad webs "is over." Now, the role of government was not expansion but "adjusting resources and plants already at hand" and finding a balance between production and consumption. In addition, Roosevelt mentioned his expanding views of the West. Although he had traveled a good deal, he had never felt "the arresting thought of the change and development" of community "more than here." He was driven to reflect more deeply and broadly "when he . . . [stood] in this community" of San Francisco.

In March 1933, having been elected, Roosevelt had, as yet, no well-organized, coherent plan to turn the country around. His mind and decisions, instead, were like a kaleidoscope; when new events, persons, and ideas came on the scene to give a sharp twist to his thinking, fresh ideas and policies came into focus. When someone asked him what his working philosophy was, Roosevelt replied, "Philosophy? Philosophy? I am a Christian and a Democrat—that's all." In his *After Seven Years*, Raymond Moley, a close advisor of Roosevelt's, later provided a revealing description of the president's ideas and actions. "To look upon these policies as the result of a unified plan," Moley wrote, "was to believe that the accumulation of stuffed snakes, baseball pictures, school flags, old tennis shoes, carpenter's tools, geometry books, and chemistry sets in a boy's bedroom could have been put there by an interior decorator."

Some have suggested there was an "ideological innocence" about the way Roosevelt approached governing and leadership. Perhaps so, but he gave several hints of what he was thinking before and just after he entered the White House. A few weeks before his inauguration, Roosevelt made clear that, because the country was in deep trouble, the president, Congress, and the country must move. What was needed was "action, action." Indeed, action—and much of it—was soon emerging out of Washington and fanning across the country. In the next Hundred Days, Roosevelt sent more than a dozen presidential messages to Congress and placed his signature on fifteen bills.

Another hint came a bit later when Roosevelt pointed out that the imbalance between industrialists and farmers was a major reason for the Depression. It was the "continued lack of adequate purchasing power on the part of the farmer" that had to be revised. The needy agriculturists, spread across the country, included hog farmers in Iowa, wheat raisers in the Dakotas and Pacific Northwest, huge-market farmers in California's interior valleys, and cattle and sheep ranchers all over the West. Roosevelt would take action, and his subsequent actions illustrated what he had pointed out in San Francisco: the imbalance between overproduction, underconsumption, and excessively low prices must be readjusted. In the same month as his San Francisco speech, Roosevelt informed an audience in Topeka, Kansas, that he stood for "national planning in agriculture."

In short, when Roosevelt entered the White house in March 1933, he was primed, by both his experience and his pragmatic outlook, to launch what became known as the New Deal. He was, himself, a new deal in the White House. But what direction Roosevelt's dramatic moves would take and where he was headed were still unclear in the first months of his presidency.

IN THE WHITE HOUSE

In his first week in office, Roosevelt exuded energy. Even before he called Congress into special session, he acted. To stabilize an increasingly shaky national banking system and to stem the outgoing tide of depositor withdrawals, Roosevelt declared a national bank holiday. When Congress met on Thursday, March 9, a hastily thrown together bank bill awaited them. The legislation would allow the government to shore up unstable private banks, give the president control over gold circulation, issue new Federal Reserve notes, and reorganize banks that needed such before they reopened. Congress passed the bill, and the president signed it soon after 8 p.m. At first, Roosevelt thought of limiting his admonitions to Congress to the banking issue, but when he saw that they had a desire to move, he turned to unemployment and agricultural issues—along with several other measures.

All these activities, of course, would have direct, lasting impact on the American West. A. P. Giannini, president of the Bank of America and one of the West's leading bankers, applauded Roosevelt's bank holiday policy. Granted, Giannini's Bank of America stood to benefit from the president's banking measures, but those policies also stabilized banks throughout the West. For the most part, Giannini and another leading western banker, Marriner Eccles (later chairman of the Federal Reserve Board), agreed with Roosevelt's banking guidelines because they thought he helped western banks to escape from under the lion's paw of the dominating banks in the East and to stand on their own. Ironically, like so many other New Deal policies, FDR's banking legislation provided more evidence of the encroaching power of Uncle Sam's West, although that mushrooming power was not yet evident in 1933.

Two weeks later, President Roosevelt sent another bill to Congress. This bill, writes FDR biographer H. W. Brands, was "the New Deal report . . . closest to his heart." In what became the Civilian Conservation Corps (CCC), Roosevelt sought to get unemployed young men out of eastern cities and into the nation's forests and parks, working on worthy projects. Their efforts would not conflict with other public works underway, and, for Roosevelt, the open spaces and forested places of the West were ideal settings in which to place urban youth; they would experience pristine settings, do valuable conservation work, and reenergize themselves. His plan called for 250,000 young men to be paid a dollar a day for their conservation, reforestation, road-building, flood-control, and erosion-checking projects. Congress passed a bill authorizing the CCC on March 31, and the president expressed his immense satisfaction with legislation that helped the unemployed with direct relief and sent them west out of urban environments.

The CCC was extraordinarily popular in the West, where most of its work took place. Corpsmen planted shelterbelts of trees from Texas to the Dakotas, helped eradicate tree fungus problems in numerous forests, planted grasses in the Dakotas, built miles and miles of mountain trails, and erected needed buildings in national parks. Since these projects focused on public lands, the West received the lion's share of the relief work and direct aid. Per capita expenditures in the West—twenty-eight dollars per person in the coastal states and eighty-five dollars in the mountain states—exceeded the national average of nineteen dollars per person. In addition, the popularity of this direct-relief measure added to Roosevelt's political strength in the West.

In May 1933, the president turned to the problem that mattered most to westerners, relief for the unemployed and indigent. Roosevelt urged Congress to create (which it did) the Federal Emergency Relief Administration (FERA) to provide direct economic relief. A sum of $500 million would be allotted for the program, half going directly to the states and the remaining half also to the states if they provided a three-to-one match for the federal dollars. These efforts moved well beyond Herbert Hoover's attempts at direct economic relief; in fact, for the most part, Hoover had refused to back such relief efforts. These measures of direct relief flew in the face, too, of the hegemonic "western myth" that touted westerners as independent, freedom-loving, and two-fisted men and women who would not accept a handout from anyone, private or governmental.

Revealingly, when economic need ran headlong into the questionable truisms of this western myth, necessity won out. All over the West, residents embraced the program. State officials might look askance at the FERA and think of it as a symbol of the central government bulling its way into state affairs, but most westerners did not arrive at that conclusion. Instead, they lined up to take relief checks and participate in job-providing programs. There were some exceptions, however. For example, when the Colorado state legislature refused to raise funds to meet the financial demands of the three-to-one match, rowdy residents of Denver invaded the legislative chambers and threatened violence and spoke of breaking into grocery stories for needed food. The Colorado legislators relented, raising some taxes and reallocating other funds to secure the needed match.

On the same day that the FERA was launched, Congress passed the Agricultural Adjustment Act (AAA). No area was of more economic concern in the West than agricultural matters. Farming and ranching were the region's most important occupations. More than most other Americans, agriculturists in the West (and farmers elsewhere, as well) had suffered throughout the 1920s, beginning with the collapse of food demands at the end of World War I. Farming interests, bewildered with falling prices and growing stockpiles of products, had gained congressional support in the 1920s through two McNary-Haugen bills to dump overproduced farm products on foreign markets. They were angered to hear that President Coolidge had vetoed both measures. President Hoover did a bit more than Coolidge did to help farmers, but he strongly opposed any direct government relief for agriculturists.

When FDR assumed the presidency, he acted like a good broker for many American interests. He looked at the varied segments of the American economy and society and tried to produce legislation tailored to fit these diverse needs. The president did not have to look far to see the dire needs of western agriculturists. Overproduction and shrinking markets were besieging farmers. The AAA of May 1933 aimed to readjust those imbalances. Production would be controlled so that surpluses could be reduced and prices raised. To achieve this goal, the government would pay farmers to produce less. FDR, serving as a broker for farmers, moved into new territory: as the CCC had already begun to do, this new legislative measure out of Congress would provide direct relief to farmers who followed the AAA guidelines.

Another major piece of New Deal legislation, the National Industrial Recovery Act (NIRA), passed Congress on June 16, the final day of the special session. The act contained three major parts: Section 7(a) allowed workers to "bargain collectively," thus encouraging unionization; a second part established the National Recovery Administration (NRA), which would control prices, wages, and production in businesses and industries; and a third section organized a Public Works Administration (PWA) to construct hundreds of public works projects. The NIRA and NRA had less impact on the West than elsewhere in the United States because, in the early 1930s, manufacturing and industry beyond the Mississippi still lagged behind that of other regions. Also, codes set up to control production in the lumber and oil industries, for instance, did not function well in the West. But the PWA, working with the Bureau of Reclamation, built dams and other reclamation projects across the West, including the completion of Boulder (Hoover) Dam on the Colorado River, the Grand Coulee Dam on the Columbia River, and the Central Valley Project in California. These huge projects put hundreds of thousands of laborers to work, achieving one of Roosevelt's major goals of providing salaries for workers so they could, in turn, spend their wages and thereby help revive the country's lagging economy.

In the next two years, the Roosevelt administration launched a "Second New Deal," building on previous legislation and initiating new measures. Some of these presidential and congressional decisions clearly augmented earlier bills. Several acts helped farmers to refinance loans, provide loans for crops, and forestall farm bankruptcies. Even more significant for western ranchers was the Taylor Grazing Act. This legislation, issuing out of Congress in 1934, attempted to bring order from the chaos of grazing competitions and conflicts in the West. Reversing previous trends, Roosevelt pushed for the withdrawal from sale of all remaining public lands (almost all in the West), the implementation of conservation measures, and close watch on grazing practices. The act, not always popular with aggressive western stockmen, nonetheless won eventual approval, especially from the large ranchers who succeeded in being named to local decision-making boards.

Perhaps even more game changing for a wider swath of westerners was the establishment of the Rural Electrification Administration (REA) in 1935. Most western farms lacked electricity. Once it arrived, electricity transformed the lives of many ruralites. As historian William E. Leuchtenburg points out in his classic study, *Franklin Roosevelt and the New Deal* (1963), "The REA revolutionized rural life." Some rural people saw electric lights for the first time. And power lines strung out to remote areas allowed agriculturists and their families to enjoy electric-powered machines and electric stoves, refrigerators, and washing machines. Across the West, the REA, by extending electricity throughout the region, symbolized the extensive reach of the New Deal, demonstrating again the spread of Roosevelt's powerful new central government at work in lands beyond the Mississippi.

A SECOND NEW DEAL

Some Second New Deal legislation expanded what was already on the books. The Works Progress (later Projects) Administration (WPA) moved beyond what earlier relief programs had done, this time bypassing states and providing direct federal relief. Western rural and urban areas benefitted from hundreds of road-building and airport-construction projects, with western towns and cities receiving relief funds to build schools, hospitals, courthouses, and even sewage systems. The Federal Art Project and the Federal Writers' Project (both part of the WPA) generally encouraged western cultural regionalism, as did similar efforts in the

South. The FAP helped well-known western artists such as Jackson Pollock of Wyoming, and the FWP helped writers like Vardis Fisher of Idaho, to complete artistic and literary works. Artists prepared murals for city halls, public libraries, and courthouses, and Fisher's *Idaho Guide* became a model for the guidebooks emanating from all other states. Similarly, the National Youth Administration (NYA) mimicked the CCC in funding youth with part-time jobs, thereby keeping them in school and off the job market.

More pathbreaking was the Social Security Act. Responding to the challenges of advocates such as Francis Townsend of California and to the clear needs of seniors, Roosevelt pushed for—and Congress passed—the landmark act in August 1935. The new program provided federally funded retirement-pension benefits for retired persons, to be funded by earlier payroll deductions. It also furnished funds to states to support those challenged with physical, mental, or psychological disabilities that kept them unemployed. To this day, the varied Social Security benefits are a major influence in the West, as they are in the rest of the country.

Although hesitancy, disagreements, and even outright hatred in the West marked some regional reactions to FDR's unfolding New Deal, most westerners supported these tipping-point actions. The hesitancies came largely from conservatives, Democrats and especially Republicans, who disagreed with the increasingly large federal government—and its spreading power—that Roosevelt had created. The election of 1936 provided a test case for the president's popularity in the West, and the outcome was nearly a blank-check endorsement. Every western state, as in 1932, voted a clear majority for FDR in 1936. Western states also helped the president's Democratic Party to pack the Congress with its political partisans in greatly expanding numbers. The Democrats enjoyed a 334 to 88 margin in the House, and a 76 to 16 margin in the Senate. Clearly, these outcomes indicated that FDR had strengthened his control of the American political scene. He had attracted, retained, and enlarged his hold on American politics, and his support in the West.

If a majority of westerners voted their support for Roosevelt at the polls in 1936, more than a few well-known leaders of the West had also become clear advocates of the president in the first years of his administration. Chief among these were a number of western governors, including Culbert Olson (D) of California, Charles Bryan (D) of Nebraska, and Payne Ratner (R) of Kansas. Like other state leaders, these governors knew that Roosevelt and Washington, D.C., were sources of needed funds; all three were friendly and supportive of Roosevelt. Other governors or senators were even more pragmatic; Dennis Chavez (D), senator from New Mexico, and Alf Landon, governor of Kansas (who later was FDR's Republican opponent in the election of 1936), would support the president and take his funding—but for their own purposes. Chavez funneled as much funding as he could toward CCC and NYA programs, which he favored above all other New Deal measures, whereas Landon criticized FDR for being antibusiness and guilty of corruption. Two Texans, first John Nance Garner and then Sam Rayburn, were also supportive. Both the gruff and partly educated Garner, FDR's vice president from 1933 to 1941 and previously Speaker of the House, and Rayburn, congressman and later also Speaker of the House, were helpful in moving New Deal legislation through Congress—Garner from the executive branch, Rayburn from the House floor.

A more unusual group of supporters was a coterie of progressive Republican senators who bolted their own party on domestic issues to back Roosevelt's New Deal. These included westerners such as Hiram Johnson of California, William Borah of Idaho, Gerald Nye and Lynn Frazier of North Dakota, and Bronson Cutting of New Mexico. Nearly all these senators were isolationists in foreign affairs; in fact, they were "irreconcilables" in events leading up to and through World War I. And they would later oppose some of FDR's moves away from neutrality on the eve of and in the early years of World War II. On his New Deal policies, however, they were a band of brothers. In fact, on a few occasions Roosevelt even turned his boat in their direction to keep them happily onboard and avoid any conflicts over foreign affairs. As Robert Dallek has written in *Franklin D. Roosevelt and American Foreign Policy, 1932–1945*, "A struggle with his progressive Republican friends for minor foreign policy goals at the likely expense of domestic advance was something he would not do."

In the years following Roosevelt's smashing victory at the polls in 1936, attitudes began to change more than a little. Part of the shift toward negativity came from the country's faltering economy and expanding needs, and other parts derived from Roosevelt's poor decisions. The era of good feelings, so evident in Roosevelt's first administration, began to sour from 1937 forward. Indeed, some of the negative reactions were building in the West even before the president's landslide win in 1936.

An illuminating symbol of the growing discontent was the rise of the Townsend movement in California. Francis E. Townsend, a sixty-six-year-old doctor concerned about his own status and that of aging citizens in the United States, began to promote a new idea. The Townsend plan called for a monthly two-hundred-dollar payment to elderly citizens, who would agree to retire and spend the money within the month it was received. These pension payments would be funded by a 2 percent tax on the processing of goods moving to markets. Critics pointed to the shaky financial formulations behind Townsend's plan—it would double the nation's taxes and shift the country from youthful earnings to senior spending. And the huge program would focus on only 9 percent of the country's citizens. Despite the wacky, unworkable funding details of the Townsend plan, it quickly gained supporters and was formally organized as the Old Age Revolving Pensions, Ltd. By 1935–36, perhaps as many as twenty-five million Americans had indicated, in writing, their interest in the plan.

Another disturber of Roosevelt's peace and a challenger of the New Deal was Californian Upton Sinclair. A well-known muckraker of the Progressive Era, author of *The Jungle* (1906), and a lifelong Socialist, Sinclair moved to California during World War I and quickly entered the state's political contests. A Socialist candidate for governor in 1926 and 1930, Sinclair published in 1933 his *I, Governor of California, and How I Ended Poverty*, which sold one hundred thousand copies and helped launch his EPIC (End Poverty in California) program. EPIC was formulated so as to push reform farther left by establishing communal farms, having the government operate reopened plants, and providing welfare support for the old and the needy. Running again in 1934, Sinclair won the Democratic Party nomination but could not gain the support of President Roosevelt, who chose to stand back, allowing Sinclair to lose—even though he won nearly one million votes in California.

Townsend and Sinclair never joined hands to challenge Roosevelt. Nor did the "Ham and Eggs" crusade, another liberal/progressive western cause promoting pensions for persons over sixty, seek his endorsement. Rather, these movements supplied evidence of disagreements with Roosevelt that were emerging at the end of his first administration, protests calling for more benefits, particularly for seniors. These movements stood for some of the issues that made their way into the Social Security Act of 1935.

Other disgruntled spokesmen, what one historian labels the "voices of protest," sounded their "barbaric yawp" across the country by taking issue with Roosevelt and his New Deal. Huey Long, the self-absorbed dictator of Louisiana, launched his Share Our Wealth Program in 1934. In promising to make "every man a king," the Kingfish planned to capture the huge assets of the rich, raise tax rates on the wealthy, and give every family a "$5,000 gift and promise . . . an annual income of at least $2,500." A second voice of protest came from an unusual source, a Catholic priest, the Reverend Charles E. Coughlin, a pastor in Detroit. He organized the National Union for Social Justice, lashing out at Roosevelt and his New Deal for not doing more, especially for not denouncing the Jewish bankers he thought had misled the United States into the Depression. Coughlin joined Long, Francis Townsend, and Upton Sinclair as well, in calling for much more than merely reforming the United States; they wanted, quite simply, a redistribution of the country's wealth.

In the election of 1936, the new Union Party attempted to pull together a loosely organized political organization drawing on these protest movements. Although Huey Long (before his assassination in September 1935) and Father Coughlin were the most charismatic leaders among the dissenters, the Union Party, in an attempt to find unity among the individualists, selected William Lemke, a congressman from North Dakota, to be their standard-bearer. Earlier, the party leaders had thought of Senator Burton K. Wheeler of Montana or William Borah of Idaho as their presidential candidate. The Unionists, drawing less than a million votes, or about 2 percent of the populace, proved to be more raucous than vibrant. The party did well in sections of the West, especially in Minnesota, Washington, Oregon, and South Dakota, but twice as well in North Dakota, Lemke's home state. Despite their low numbers, the discordant voices demonstrated that not all the country, westerners included, had chosen FDR as their Pied Piper of politics.

Probably an unwise action by FDR himself following the election of 1936 did more to undermine his leadership and popularity than the disruptions from his opponents. The president wrongheadedly decided to take on the Supreme Court. Upset with Court decisions declaring New Deal legislation unconstitutional, he proposed a law to Congress that would allow the president to add other members to the Court when judges of "retirement age . . . do not choose to retire or to resign." New nominees could raise the number of Supreme Court justices from nine to a maximum of fifteen. Strongly negative reactions quickly followed FDR's announcement of what opponents immediately labeled the "Court-packing plan."

The Court expansion idea was not popular in many parts of the West, even though one year earlier the region had overwhelmingly voted for Roosevelt. The *Los Angeles Times* denounced Roosevelt's plan as one of "almost devilish ingenuity." To the north, the *San Francisco Chronicle* described the president's idea as "an open declaration of war on the Supreme Court." Vice President Garner, former Roosevelt supporter Burton Wheeler, and Senator Edward Burke of Nebraska joined the growing chorus of negative reactions to Roosevelt's Court plan.

Then, an unexpected Court turnabout occurred. After declaring portions of the NRA and AAA unconstitutional in 1935–36 and seemingly turning a jaundiced eye toward other New Deal legislation, the Court moved in a new direction. In

March 1937, in a Washington State case dealing with a minimum wage law, the Court voted five to four for the worker and against the company, the opposite of a Court vote on a similar case in the previous session. Justice Owen Roberts, a swing voter on the Court, now sided with the more-liberal justices supporting Roosevelt's New Deal. In the months to come, the Court stayed on the new track, and Roosevelt dropped his Court-expanding plan.

More importantly in the long run, the engine of the New Deal seemed to sputter after 1936–37. True, the relief programs under the PWA and WPA continued to operate, Social Security was now in place, and revised programs much like the scrapped NRA and AAA were passed. Yet westerners and other Americans seemed less willing to give Roosevelt a blank check for new reforms. Conservative Charles Martin, governor of Oregon, found much to criticize in Roosevelt's New Deal. The governors of Utah (George Dern), Wyoming (Leslie A. Miller), and Colorado (Edwin C. Johnson) demonstrated more than a little hostility toward Roosevelt's ideas and leadership, largely because they were more conservative than Roosevelt and the New Deal and detested having to raise matching state taxes to qualify for federal funds. Plus, Roosevelt himself seemed satisfied to continue programs begun earlier rather than to launch new ones.

Roosevelt's New Deal not only impacted western economic and political life, it also clearly shaped social life in the West. Even though New Deal measures were aimed at economic inequities in the United States, most of the president's reform and relief programs also had class implications, looking to relieve the joblessness and poverty of the needy. Most these programs did not include explicit stipulations to deal with minority peoples, but a few did. The most significant of Roosevelt's New Deal programs focused specifically on western minority groups was the Wheeler-Howard, or Indian Reorganization, Act (IRA) of 1934. Pushed energetically forward by the presidentially appointed commissioner of Indian affairs, John Collier, the act tried to address several of the huge, enduring problems facing Indians in the United States. Collier, driving hard to reverse the earlier allotment system that broke up reservations and gave land out to individual tribal members, pushed in controversial new directions. Moving away from previous efforts to turn Indians into acculturated farmers, Collier encouraged, instead, a revival of ethnic identity, communal economic organization, and self-determination. Leading politicians and some Indian groups themselves opposed the IRA because they thought it undermined Indian self-determination and called for too many cultural changes. They were able to gain large revisions in the bill before Congress passed it in 1934.

Roosevelt spoke out for the IRA, asserting that "the continued application of allotment laws . . . must be terminated." Others resisted Collier's idealistic cultural revitalization programs. Senator Clarence C. Dill of Washington State led the IRA opponents in Congress. Even though substantive changes were made in the so-called Indian New Deal bill, Roosevelt endorsed it as "a measure of justice that is long overdue." The allotment system, in place since the 1880s, was overthrown under the charismatic, if controversial, leadership of John Collier and with the backing of President Roosevelt. Many of the IRA features remain in place more than eighty years later.

On the other hand, Roosevelt paid minor attention to other American racial groups, including most Hispanics and Asians living in the West, even though several of the New Deal programs benefitted western minorities. For example, Indians and Hispanics worked for the CCC, the Farm Security Administration set up migrant camps, and the WPA hired both groups to work on large dam, road, and municipal building projects. Although the National Youth Administration, under the able and courageous leadership of a young Lyndon B. Johnson in Texas, did not integrate black and white workers—Johnson argued that he would have been "run out of Texas" if he did that—he did work directly with black leaders to bring black youth into the NYA programs. Blacks praised his efforts in this regard.

When charges of discrimination surfaced in several New Deal relief programs, FDR and his lieutenants did little to address this clear mistreatment. Beyond the IRA and a few other lesser efforts, Roosevelt, like many (perhaps most) Americans, did not see the need for launching specific programs to help minority groups. Although he had promised to look after "the forgotten man" in his New Deal policies, Roosevelt did not do much to deal with minority needs. Those efforts would begin in earnest with President Lyndon B. Johnson's Great Society in the 1960s.

ROOSEVELT, WORLD WAR II, AND THE WEST

The surprise Japanese attack on Pearl Harbor on Sunday, December 7, 1941, thrust Franklin D. Roosevelt into the second stage of his presidency. If the first eight years of his administration utilized his New Deal policies to focus on domestic needs, the final four years of his White House stay concentrated on World War II and the national and international efforts needed to defeat the nation's opponents. Historians frequently and explicitly depict Roosevelt at the throttle of changes that transformed the West during the 1930s. Revealingly, some of the same scholars less often point to how much Roosevelt's plans during World War II even more

extensively shaped the West. It is as if these scholars thought the country's transformation occurred on its own, with no one behind the high-velocity engine of
change. This oversight underestimates how much Roosevelt transformed the West
in wartime. During the international conflict, Roosevelt as Dr. Win the War did
more to alter the West than he did as Dr. New Deal during the Depression years.
These metamorphoses were everywhere evident in economic and social matters,
if a bit less clear in political and cultural arenas.

In the weeks following the smash attack in Hawaii, Roosevelt, his advisors, and
perhaps most Americans had to change their point of view: the conflagration would
be a two-theater war. Roosevelt, like most of his country, viewed the mounting
international tensions as Europe-centered. That was *the* important theater. Still,
very slowly, Roosevelt and Americans, generally, began to realize that Japan and
its expanding new empire were also a major threat that demanded more attention. Roosevelt's largest blindness, writes historian David M. Kennedy, "was his
inattentiveness to Asian matters and his unwillingness to be seen as 'appeasing'
Japan, when in fact a little appeasement—another name for diplomacy—might
have yielded rich rewards." Roosevelt's late, inadequate efforts at diplomacy in the
Far East, continues Kennedy, may have been his "deepest failure."

When war came, a quickly launched plan of war preparedness revolutionized
the American West. Economic decisions, like a series of transfusions, transformed
most subregions of the West. President Roosevelt's decision to scatter shipyards,
plane factories, and military complexes meant that several sections of the West
immediately felt the economic transformations that came their way. Roosevelt
also thought, for strategic purposes and national safety, that air, naval, army,
and marine bases should be spread across the West so that any possible enemy
attacks would be less destructive. The president viewed the West as a place ready
for quick expansion.

Roosevelt and his planners sent more than $70 billion west during the hectic
years between 1941 and 1945. A lion's share of the funding was earmarked for
the construction of planes and ships and the erection and support of military
installations. Shipyards, particularly along the Pacific coast, sprouted like a string
of newly fertilized plants from Los Angeles to the Bay Area and on to the Pacific
Northwest. Aircraft factories, scattered from Southern California to Seattle, paral-
leled shipyards on the coast.

Two westerners played pivotal roles in the explosive war machine rising in
the West. Henry J. Kaiser, an experienced engineer from Oakland, California,
who had constructed large dams and roads, became one of Roosevelt's favorite

builders of ships—and later of steel plants. A man of immense energies and valuable construction experience, Kaiser was also an extraordinarily hard-working and brusque person. In a few months, he gained huge government grants and immediately began to build a new fleet of ships. Employing as many as 250,000 men and women in around-the-clock shifts, Kaiser turned out ships in a few weeks that took up to a year to build in eastern plants. By also providing health benefits, child care, and housing, Kaiser appealed to, and hired, huge numbers of women in his plants. In fact, women, working in unprecedented numbers in Kaiser's and other war-related industries, became widely known and touted as "Rosie the Riveter."

Banker A. P. Giannini also filled a critical financial gap in the economic development of the wartime West. Expanding his mushrooming banking and investing empire in the 1930s, Giannini, the son of immigrant parents, had become the West's leading banker by 1941. As president of the Bank of America and in partnering with the Roosevelt administration, he secured funding for contractors and builders to participate in government-sponsored projects otherwise well beyond their means. When Giannini wrote a strong supportive letter about FDR's banking policies, stating "that business in the Far West" had returned to pre-Depression stability, the grateful president wrote him a warm letter of thanks.

The ship- and airplane-building plants, as well as the military bases dotting the western landscape, were crucial in turning lands beyond the Mississippi into Uncle Sam's West. The military-industrial complex that Roosevelt was erecting invaded and captured the region. Gerald D. Nash, the leading historian of the World War II West, captures the essence of this memorable shift in two succinct sentences in his book, *The American West Transformed*: "In four short years [1941 to 1945] the war brought a maturation to the West that in peacetime might have taken generations to accomplish. It transformed an area with a self-image that emphasized colonialism into one boosting self-sufficiency and innovation." The economic transformation also opened the floodgates for new populations of men, women, and children flowing west.

Workers and their families deluged the West from early 1942 on, searching for the Holy Grail of new, good-paying jobs. Most did not have to go far. One young woman coming to the West Coast from Texas experienced what hundreds of thousands of others discovered. "All hell broke loose on the 7th of December," she wrote; she did not have to search for a job. Instead, "people were coming to me with jobs. Not just me, but everyone. They were recruiting workers and they didn't care whether you were Black, white, young, old." War plants "were begging for workers." The rush west was on; nothing like this explosion of incoming migrants had occurred since a century earlier, when the California gold rush served as a giant magnet pulling people west.

In the 1940s, in excess of eight million people moved west of the Mississippi, most of them as a result of Roosevelt's programs. The largest portion of the new-comers had arrived by 1945. More than 3.6 million alone moved to California, sending its population to 10.5 million in 1950. A giant "westward tilt" was underway, with most of the newcomers flocking to western cities and towns. Urban spots on the demographer's map from Seattle to San Diego and on to San Antonio and Houston darkened and enlarged. Inland cities like Albuquerque, Denver, Dallas, and Phoenix also boomed. The American West was making giant strides toward becoming the country's most urban region.

The incoming population greatly diversified the West's sociocultural mixes. Increasing numbers of Native Americans moved off reservations and into cities; many Indian soldiers served in the war and returned with enlarged worldviews. Hispanics also felt the impact of the war. Mexican Americans, as well as recent immigrants from Mexico, found jobs on farms and fields and in a variety of skilled and unskilled jobs in war industries. Perhaps as many as five hundred thousand of the country's three million Mexican Americans served in the war. Casualties were extraordinarily high among Hispanics, including during the horrendous Bataan Death March in the Philippines, where one in four deaths were of Hispanic soldiers. African American numbers in the West likewise rapidly expanded, from 1.3 million in 1940 to 1.7 million in 1950. Although the black population remained largest in Texas in the 1940s, the flood of newcomers pushed even farther west, especially into California. African American men and women, previously limited to field and menial domestic work, now found new opportunities in the service and in war-related factories. Discrimination and racism continued, certainly; but also new economic and social opportunities in the West expanded well beyond such opportunities in prewar days.

Even though President Roosevelt's war production plans were the major catalyst that brought about these spectacular shifts, he often paid scant attention to the momentous outcomes—either nationally or in the West. In fact, an unfortunate action of his added to the dilemmas of one group. In February 1942, Roosevelt issued Executive Order 9066, allowing the U.S. military to move out of military-challenged areas any persons they considered suspect. The controversial order did not mention Japanese Americans, but its purpose was clear: remove Japanese Americans from the Pacific coast and place them in inland detention centers.

During the next three years about one hundred thousand persons of Japanese ancestry were relocated to camps, most of which were east of the Pacific coast states. Roosevelt was following the advice of political and military leaders in issuing the executive order. Although the president was never guilty of condemning Japanese Americans, as were many other Americans, neither did he ever show remorse for the tragic act.

The controversies surrounding the relocation of the Japanese cast light on the difficult role that Eleanor Roosevelt sometimes faced. An important lobbyist for women's rights and benefits in New Deal programs, working conditions, and job opportunities, she also spoke out for minority rights, particularly for African Americans. On the relocation issue, the negative outcomes quickly became apparent to her. Before the appearance of Executive Order 9066, Eleanor praised Japanese Americans as loyal and hardworking and blasted their critics as racists guilty of "unreasonable hatred." Once the plan for relocation came on scene, she denounced it as "absurd" and "vicious" and told the president that relocation would be mistreating the Japanese. But when FDR signed the executive order, Eleanor stopped her public comments. Had her husband asked her to be silent? Perhaps. What remains clear is that Eleanor was right and her husband wrong, tragically wrong, in relocating the Japanese to the inland West.

Equally clear, Eleanor Roosevelt paid more attention than her husband did to the shifts taking place among families, racial and ethnic groups, and other communities as well. If the president's wife sometimes served as his eyes and ears in gathering valuable information and passing it on, she also often functioned as his conscience, noting injustices and prodding her husband to do something for needy Americans.

Not surprisingly, Eleanor Roosevelt was much concerned about the needs of women leaving their homes and going to work during wartime. She particularly fretted about the mounting challenges of child care, with husbands off fighting and mothers working in war-related industries. Worried that children might be neglected, Eleanor urged her husband to do something for children needing care. Following her advice, the president, with congressional support, signed the Lanham Act, which established several child-care centers, including one in Texas. Regrettably, these centers dealt with only about one hundred thousand children when two million or more were in need of care.

Seeing such shortcomings, Eleanor spoke to Henry Kaiser and his son, Edgar, leading wartime builders, about the pressing need for day care. After Eleanor visited the Kaiser shipyard in Portland, Oregon, in which 60 percent of the workers were women, she appealed to the Kaisers to do something specific about child care. They heeded her urging. At the Swan Island Center, one of the Kaisers' two shipyards in the Portland area, a beautiful, commodious, state-of-the-art day-care center was erected. It remained open six days a week, fifty-two weeks a year, and twenty-four hours a day, with three eight-hour shifts of workers. Women could also purchase freshly cooked meals to take home to feed their families. First-rate teachers and staff were hired to provide the best in instruction and guidance. And *all* children were accepted—Indians, Mexicans, blacks, and Asians, along with white children. As historian Doris Kearns Goodwin has written, the child-care center "was a head-start program a quarter of a century ahead of its time."

A fast-paced trip President Roosevelt took in September 1942 introduced him to a West pulsating with wartime production. After stops in the East, the presidential train visited the Twin Cities and then traveled through the agricultural and mining spaces of North Dakota and Montana. In Washington State, the president traveled to the sprawling army base at Fort Lewis and the Bremerton navy yard and then on to the huge Boeing plant in Renton, near Seattle. Boeing had been instrumental in producing B-17 bombers—in fact, had produced more planes per square foot of space than any other plant in the United States. And half of its workers were women, the Rosie the Riveters of the workforce.

Roosevelt went next to Portland to view the Kaiser shipyard. While there, the president's daughter, Anna Boettiger, christened the USS *Teal,* the 576th ship the Kaiser plant had produced in the past eighteen months. The next stop was California, where Roosevelt visited the Douglas aircraft plant in Long Beach. The Douglas facility produced bombers, cargo planes, and large transport ships. When workers in the plant recognized the president in his car, they clapped and cheered him.

The next stop was Texas, where Eleanor Roosevelt joined the president. There they visited the Consolidated plant, which, in an extraordinary assembly line, manufactured B-24 Liberator planes. Eleanor celebrated the outstanding achievement of women workers, which one supervisor verified in pointing out that production shot up when women were hired for the fast-moving assembly line. Writing from Fort Worth, Eleanor told a friend, "FDR seemed happy with his trip and much amazed at the increase in women workers. At last he is interested in nursery schools, family restaurants, etc." Obviously the trip west in 1942 gave Franklin Roosevelt an opportunity to view, firsthand, the war machine he was helping to build and operate, particularly as it roared into action along the Pacific and southwestern edges of the West. The trip, obviously much to Eleanor's delight, also opened his eyes to some of the family needs deriving from the war effort. Revealingly, the president made no visits to the Japanese relocation camps (but Eleanor did); the crowded housing areas of workers; or the fields where hard-pressed Mexican agricultural workers labored.

Roosevelt's direct impact on western politics may be less noticeable than his shaping of western economic and social life, but the influences are evident. When Herbert Hoover lost, and Franklin Roosevelt won, the West in 1932, a trend had begun. In four successive elections from 1932 to 1944, Roosevelt won at least 54 percent of the electorate, climbing as high as 61 percent in 1936. In the elections of 1932 and 1936, Roosevelt took all the states on the Mississippi and to the west. In 1940, Republican Wendell Wilkie won the farm states of North Dakota, South Dakota, Nebraska, Kansas, and Iowa, as well as Colorado; in 1944, Republican Thomas A. Dewy took the same western states and Wyoming. Although Roosevelt's farm policy failed to win over western agriculturist voters, he gained increasing numbers of political supporters on the West Coast. Undoubtedly, the federal contracts and the hundreds of thousands of jobs that the Roosevelt administration sent to the West helped to draw in voters to the Democratic Party. Revealingly, Roosevelt did even better in the Democratic South than in the West, and his strongest western states were those with southern tinges, namely, Texas, Missouri, and Arkansas.

Interestingly, all of Roosevelt's vice presidents were westerners. Texan John Garner helped the president with congressional connections. (Garner had served in Congress from 1903 to 1933.) In 1940 Roosevelt wanted to replace Garner with his liberal secretary of agriculture, Henry A. Wallace, an Iowan, as his vice president. Employing deft strategy and wile, Roosevelt beat down conservative and southern Democratic opposition to win the nomination of Wallace as his running mate. In 1944, the anti-Wallace pressures were too great, so FDR allowed that westerner William O. Douglas or Missourian Harry Truman would be acceptable. Southern Democrats liked Truman, and he became the third of Roosevelt's western running mates.

Not all western political leaders, however, were satisfied with Roosevelt's leadership or major policies. As we have seen, a few independent-minded western governors opposed New Deal stipulations calling for matching funds from the states for government subsidies (matching funds often necessitating tax hikes). Other western politicos like old-time Progressives who supported Roosevelt's domestic policies opposed what they considered his excessive internationalism. In 1943, the Senate voted overwhelmingly—eighty-five to five—to support Roosevelt's plan for postwar reconstruction (a plan sponsored by Texas senator Tom Connally), but western isolationists such as Hiram Johnson of California and Burton K. Wheeler of Montana voted against the measure. These longtime western senators were now themselves isolated as a small but outspoken minority voicing opposition to Roosevelt's internationalism.

At first glance, Roosevelt's impact on western cultural life seemed to diminish under the onslaught of wartime economic transformations. The Roosevelt New Deal policies, especially those evident in the WPA programs, lost much of their influence. On second glance, however, the president's contributions to western cultural development continued. The WPA kept funding writers, artists, and other cultural contributors, even if at a lessened level. In addition, the ubiquitous WPA state guidebooks remained strong influences on westerners, as well as on tourists visiting the West and using the guides for introductions to the region. The important cultural impact of these guidebooks in the mid- to late 1930s persisted through World War II and beyond, an oft-overlooked example of FDR's ongoing impact on the West.

In still another way, through his decisions about the movie industry and Hollywood, Roosevelt shaped western, as well as national, cultural affairs. Even before World War II, the president became concerned that the United States had to develop a propaganda machine to combat the heartless totalitarianism spreading across Europe. After 1941, Hollywood became a major arm in answering Hitler and the Nazis. When FDR established the Office of War Information (OWI) in June 1942, he included a section dealing with movies, and thus impacted Hollywood, the West's omnipresent dream factory. The president and his advisors wanted to turn movies into a popular propaganda machine, touting democracy, helping women and minorities, and creating a brave new world of opportunity. As the war deepened, the OWI urged moviemakers to release films that promoted Americanism, criticized leftist and totalitarian regimes, and promised victory and a new Eden after war's end. In addition, Hollywood produced training films for the U.S. military. Generally, the moving-picture industry, following presidential and OWI suggestions, supported the U.S. war effort.

Another area that revealed Roosevelt's shaping hand in the American West was in science. The expansion of the West as a science center followed the pattern of economic and military development: scatter the scientific laboratories and research sites across the West to protect them from possible enemy attack and to spread the federal financial resources being sent west. In 1940 as world war threatened, President Roosevelt established the National Defense Research Committee. A year later came the creation of the Office of Scientific Research and Development (OSRD), under the apt leadership of scientist Vannevar Bush and the support of the president. Immediately, the OSRD began funneling large research grants to such institutions as the Jet Propulsion Laboratory at the California Institute of Technology; the Radiation Laboratory at the University of California, Berkeley; and science centers at the University of Texas and Rice University in the Southwest. Perhaps as much as $100 million flowed into these scientific laboratories.

Other large grants went to scientists working on atomic projects. Millions of dollars came to Hanford, Washington; Los Alamos, New Mexico; and smaller research sites in Idaho and Nevada for nuclear research and the preparation of an atomic bomb. The Trinity test of an atomic bomb in the New Mexico desert on July 16, 1945, symbolized that the West, the Roosevelt administration, and the whole world had entered the nuclear age. It was indeed "the day the sun rose twice." Gerald Nash concludes in *The American West Transformed* that Roosevelt's encouragement of science, alongside economic and military preparation, "in four short years . . . accomplished more than forty years in peacetime."

ROOSEVELT'S WESTERN LEGACY

Important questions need to be considered at this point. How did Roosevelt view the West? In any specific way? And did his attitude about the region shape his actions and policies during the New Deal and World War II? Generally speaking, Roosevelt did not express extensive, well-organized, and explicit opinions about the West, but enough hints are apparent in his statements and actions that one can draw a few tentative conclusions.

When Roosevelt crisscrossed the West, his speeches often referred to the region as the future, a place to test the usefulness of his policies and to put them to work. In Boise, in September 1937, he pointed out that it was the duty of the president "to think about the future." As he had driven through the Idaho countryside earlier that day, he had thought about ways to protect land, water, and human resources. He spoke then of the mythological character Antaeus, who was reenergized every time his feet touched the ground. Roosevelt felt that same way when traveling in the West. The next year, in Amarillo, Texas, he praised West Texans for their wise uses of land and water. He wished that other Americans could see what was happening there, how they were conserving water, restoring grazing lands, and planting trees. Perhaps the clearest picture of Roosevelt's keen delight in the West was his desire, in CCC planning, to send as many eastern youths as he could to the West, where their energies, outlook, and earning power would be enhanced. For President Franklin Roosevelt, the American West was a special, invigorating place for his mind and heart.

When President Roosevelt died on April 12, 1945, in Warm Springs, Georgia, from a cerebral hemorrhage, journalists, historians, and biographers began to evaluate his legacy as the longest-serving U.S. president. Nearly every writer pointed to the landmark legislation and large impact of the New Deal. Roosevelt's administration had put people to work through relief and public works programs, shored up faith in the American economy, and passed such pathbreaking bills as the Social Security Act. Commentators likewise mentioned that under Roosevelt the central government was now assuming a new, enlarged role in the life of its citizens. Taking a longer look, still other writers emphasized how much Roosevelt prepared Americans for World War II, despite the isolationist hangover of World War I. Finally, there were those difficult-to-define strengths and contributions: Roosevelt's abilities to move from his eastern, elite backgrounds to the needs and dilemmas of millions of middle-class and poorer Americans, and his steadfast determination to act, to experiment, and to try, try again. Most evaluations are positive about Roosevelt's presidency, placing him among the great American presidents.

The leadership Roosevelt exhibited for the entire United States was, by and large, felt in the American West. His contributions included jobs, relief for out-of-work westerners, and financial support for huge public works programs. Briefly put, FDR's administration from 1933 to 1945 so changed the relationship between the American West and the federal government that the region could never return to the status quo before the New Deal. For better or worse, the expanded central government under Roosevelt became the powerful financial overseer of the United States, forming Uncle Sam's West. If hard times came, westerners could expect that relief, recovery, or reform legislation would help them with jobs and loans—and, later, Social Security benefits. Conversely, tax rates went up, and in flusher times westerners could expect to send off more taxes and, generally, face additional governmental guidelines for farmers, ranchers, laborers, and businesses. With Roosevelt's blessing, the federal government had moved into the West, and for the next three-quarters of a century, there would be more shaping of the West. If Thomas Jefferson were yet alive, he would have been startled by, and certainly alienated from, the sprawling bureaucracy that Franklin Roosevelt created in his twelve years in the White House.

Differences existed, however, between Roosevelt's relationships with the West and those with other American regions. When he came into the White House in

1933, the West languished in a colonial relationship with the East and Washington, D.C. When the end of Roosevelt's presidency and of World War II came in 1945, the West had been transformed from a colonial outback to what some would later call a pacesetting region. The more than eight million newcomers to the region, the more than ten million stationed in the West during the war, and economic transfusions that came from New Deal and wartime funding had turned the West into another place. Agriculturists now relied more heavily on the central government, the Dust Bowl problems had been addressed, the West was now primarily an urban region on its way to becoming the most urban of all regions in the country, and it had switched from dominance by the Republican Party to dominance by the Democrats. The millions of newcomers had also transformed the social makeup of the region, where the majority of the nation's Native Americans, Hispanics, Asians, and increasing numbers of African Americans resided. Families had been transformed, too, with men and some women off to war and many wives, sisters, and daughters working in the war plants along the Pacific and southwestern edges of the West. California was booming, well on its way to becoming, within a generation, the country's most populous and powerful state. Military installations, atomic sites, and scientific laboratories dotted the western landscape.

In short, Franklin D. Roosevelt was the instigator and agent of the West's clear transformation from 1933 to 1945. He turned the region into Uncle Sam's West.

FOR FURTHER READING

Arrington, Leonard J. "The New Deal in the West: A Preliminary Statistical Inquiry." *Pacific Historical Review* 38 (August 1969): 311–16.

———. "The Sagebrush Resurrection: New Deal Expenditures in the Western States, 1933–1939." *Pacific Historical Review* 52 (February 1983): 1–16.

Brands, H. W. *Traitor to His Class: The Privileged Life and Radical Presidency of Franklin Delano Roosevelt*. New York: Doubleday, 2008.

Brinkley, Alan. *The End of Reform: New Deal Liberalism in Recession and War*. New York: Alfred A. Knopf, 1995.

Burns, James McGregor. *Roosevelt: The Lion and the Fox*. New York: Harcourt Brace, 1956.

———. *Roosevelt: The Soldier of Freedom*. New York: Harcourt Brace Jovanovich, 1970.

Cook, Blanche Wiesen. *Eleanor Roosevelt*. 3 vols. New York: Penguin Books, 1992, 1999, 2016.

Daniels, Roger. *Franklin D. Roosevelt*. 2 vols. Urbana: University of Illinois Press, 2015–16.

Davis, Kenneth S. *FDR: Into the Storm, 1937–1940*. New York: Random House, 1993.

Freidel, Frank. *Franklin D. Roosevelt*. 4 vols. Boston: Little, Brown, 1952–73.

———. *Franklin D Roosevelt: A Rendezvous with Destiny*. Boston: Little, Brown, 1990.

Goodwin, Doris Kearns. *No Ordinary Time: Franklin and Eleanor Roosevelt: The Home Front in World War II*. New York: Simon & Schuster, 1994.

Hamby, Alonzo. *Man of Destiny: FDR and the Making of the American Century*. New York: Basic Books, 2015.

Hendrickson, Kenneth E., Jr. *The Life and Presidency of Franklin Delano Roosevelt: An Annotated Bibliography*. 3 vols. Lanham, MD: Scarecrow Press, 2005.

Jeffries, John. *A Third Term for FDR*. Lawrence: University Press of Kansas, 2017.

Kennedy, David M. *Freedom from Fear: The American People in Depression and War, 1929–1945*. New York: Oxford University Press, 1999.

Lash, Joseph P. *Eleanor and Franklin: The Story of Their Relationship*. New York: Norton, 1971.

Leuchtenburg, William E. *Franklin D. Roosevelt and the New Deal, 1932–1940*. New York: Harper & Row, 1963.

Malone, Michael P., and Richard W. Etulain. *The American West: A Modern History, 1900 to the Present*. 2nd ed. Lincoln: University of Nebraska Press, 2007.

Nash, Gerald D. *The American West Transformed: The Impact of the Second World War*. Bloomington: Indiana University Press, 1985.

———. *World War II and the West: Reshaping the Economy*. Lincoln: University of Nebraska Press, 1990.

Pomeroy, Earl. *The American Far West in the Twentieth Century*. New Haven: Yale University Press, 2008.

Roosevelt, Eleanor. *This Is My Story*. Volume 1 of ER's autobiography. New York: Harper and Brothers, 1937.

———. *This I Remember*. Volume 2 of ER's autobiography. New York: Harper and Brothers, 1949.

Roosevelt, Franklin D. *FDR: His Personal Letters*. Edited by Elliott Roosevelt. 4 vols. New York: Duell, Sloan, and Pearce, 1947–50.

———. *The Public Papers and Addresses of Franklin D. Roosevelt*. Edited by Samuel I. Rosenman. New York: Random House, 1938–50.

Schlesinger, Arthur M., Jr. *The Coming of the New Deal*. Volume 2 of *The Age of Roosevelt*. Boston: Houghton Mifflin, 1958.

———. *The Politics of Upheaval*. Volume 3 of *The Age of Roosevelt*. Boston: Houghton Mifflin, 1960.

Ward, Geoffrey C. *A First-Class Temperament: The Emergence of Franklin Roosevelt*. New York: Harper and Row, 1989.

White, Richard. *"It's Your Misfortune and None of My Own": A History of the American West*. Norman: University of Oklahoma Press, 1991.

Dwight D. Eisenhower, 1953–1961
LC-USZ62-117123

Chapter 7

DWIGHT D. EISENHOWER
SEARCHING FOR A CENTRIST WEST

The upsetting message came to President Dwight D. Eisenhower from west of the Mississippi in September 1957. Governor Orval E. Faubus of Arkansas was not going to follow the Supreme Court's decision in *Brown v. Board of Education* (1954), ruling that public schools must desegregate. Not only was Faubus refusing to comply with the Court's edict, but he had sent members of the Arkansas National Guard to keep nine black students from attending Little Rock High School. Even after Eisenhower asked Faubus to come to Newport, Rhode Island, for a conference and they had conversed, the governor chose to defy the Court's order.

Eisenhower faced a major dilemma there in the West. The details of his eventual decision to act reveal much about the president's leadership and political philosophy. His steps also demonstrate how his actions in this dramatic incident epitomize his handling of other events that gripped the American West.

Eisenhower delayed, even after seeking the advice of cabinet members and others, before ordering American national troops into Little Rock. These regular army troops would protect the black students who, with a good deal of trepidation, made their way to school despite the threatening taunts hurled at them by segregationists swarming around the high school.

The president explained his actions in the explosive incident in a radio address from the Oval Office of the White House. He assiduously revised and reworked the speech to ensure that it was not an attack on Faubus or those Arkansas residents who agreed with their governor. But Eisenhower also made his position clear. He would brook no stiff-arming of the Court's order. The president explained his action: "Proper and sensible observance of the law then demanded the respectful obedience which the nation has the right to expect from all the people." The law had not been followed in Little Rock, so the executive branch had to move.

Some observers at the time misread Eisenhower's actions, and in doing so, helped push early interpretations of the president off track. Eisenhower was no advocate of a strong central government, such as Franklin Roosevelt engineered in his New Deal policies. Eisenhower, instead, sided with conservatives, decidedly so. He preferred that decisions be made primarily at the state or local level. The government, rather than a dictator of policy for U.S. citizens, should be a partner or advocate for people's rights. Still, if a regional, state, or local entity or leader failed to follow the law, was unable to pass legislation, or fund a much-needed project to enhance or protect the lives of U.S. citizens, Washington, D.C., should do so. Eisenhower sent troops to Arkansas because Governor Faubus was disobeying the Supreme Court's instructions and thereby undercutting the rights and privileges of Americans—in this case, black students out in Little Rock.

Advocates of segregation missed the meaning of Eisenhower's actions when they castigated him as Hitler-like in sending federal troops to Arkansas. Others criticized the president for delaying too long and thought of him as an inadequate leader, a "do-nothing" president in a crisis situation. Both lines of interpretation misidentified Eisenhower. He hesitated because, as a cautious conservative, he wanted state and local leaders to work out the conflicts. He moved, not because he wanted to strike the colors of the central government, but because Governor Faubus and his racist supporters were refusing to obey the law. Eisenhower might not be an FDR-style president, but neither was he an uninvolved onlooker, avoiding hard decisions. Instead, he adopted a middle-of-the-road, centrist position, part advocate of federal strength, part supporter of local control. This approach epitomized his style in dealing with the American West during his eight years in the White House.

PREPRESIDENTIAL YEARS

Dwight David Eisenhower, born October 14, 1890, in Denison, Texas, grew up in Abilene, Kansas. Eisenhower's father, David, was a diligent disciplinarian who worked hard at farming and then took jobs at a creamery and managing a gas company when farming failed to adequately support his family of six sons. Ida Stoner Eisenhower, Ike's mother, was devoutly religious and mild-mannered and was an industrious homemaker. Also a pacifist, later in life she became a Jehovah's Witness. The Eisenhower family never moved to middle- or upper-class status in Abilene; on some occasions, poverty crouched at their door. But the parents modeled discipline, energy, temperateness, and steady lives for their sons. In high school, Eisenhower excelled in athletics but was only an average student, save for his interest in history and mathematics. After graduating in 1908, Ike worked two years at menial jobs and then gained entrance to West Point.

More than a half-century later, in his informal autobiography, *At Ease: Stories I Tell to Friends* (1967), Eisenhower recalled his early years growing up in Abilene. Of note, even though he provided extensive descriptions of family life, boyhood antics, and schooling, he says little or nothing about Abilene as a western setting. He touches on "cowtown" and Wild Bill Hickok episodes, but even his chapter about Abilene, entitled "The 'Gem' of the Plains," lacks thoughtful consideration of the city's role in western history. Even as a schoolboy, Eisenhower was more fascinated with military tales of ancient history and the American Civil War, including Gettysburg, than the close-at-hand American West surrounding him. Though he did not become an inveterate reader of western history, he was to become fascinated with Westerns, the formula fiction of Zane Grey, Ernest Haycox, and Louis L'Amour that captured American readers throughout the twentieth century. More than a few photographs depict Eisenhower with a stack of Westerns on his bedside table.

At West Point, Eisenhower enjoyed the military traditions at the academy and placed, generally, in the top half of his class. His athletic career was notable until a seriously injured knee ended his participation in football, a disappointment he rued for the rest of his life. Graduating in the middle of his class in 1915, he was commissioned a second lieutenant. One year later, he married Marie (Mamie) Geneva Doud, the daughter of a well-to-do businessman. They were the parents of son John, born in 1922, the year after the Eisenhowers had lost their first son, Ikey, who died at three from scarlet fever.

In the 1920s and 1930s, Eisenhower received several increasingly important assignments as he rapidly traveled up the military ladder. He moved to Washington, D.C., where he became a military planner and impressed his supervisors with his diligent work and ability to sort out diverse opinions and deal with conflicting personalities. Even General Douglas MacArthur, a notably difficult man to please and for whom Eisenhower worked in the Philippines, praised his work. In a letter of thanks, MacArthur told Eisenhower, "I write you this special commendation so that you may fully realize that your outstanding talents and your ability to perform these highly important missions are fully appreciated." So rapid was Eisenhower's rise that during World War II, he was named supreme commander of Operation Overlord against the Nazis in 1944. One year later, at the end of the war, he returned stateside as a popular, much-touted military hero.

Eisenhower's burgeoning reputation as a superb leader brought him to the attention of both academics and politicians. After replacing General George C. Marshall as army chief of staff in 1945, he served in that capacity until 1948, when he resigned to become president of Columbia University. Later in the year, both the Republicans and the Democrats made overtures to Eisenhower to run as their presidential nominee. It was even rumored that President Harry S. Truman, worried about the possible negative outcome of the 1948 election for the Democrats, had invited Eisenhower to serve in a joint presidency, with Truman as vice president. Eisenhower rejected the idea but accepted Truman's appointment (1950) as supreme commander of the North Atlantic Treaty Organization (NATO) and served in 1951–52. He resigned from that position to run for the presidency.

Not long after Eisenhower dismissed Truman's unusual idea for a joint presidency in 1948, the Republicans, especially the more progressive leaders of the party, came calling. Chief among them were former New York governor Thomas E. Dewey, who had twice run for the presidency and lost in 1944 and 1948; Dewey's right-hand man, Herbert Brownell; and Senator Henry Cabot Lodge of Massachusetts. They were eastern Republicans with strong global viewpoints—and all opposed Robert A. Taft ("Mr. Republican"), the conservative senator from Ohio. The Atlantic seaboard Republicans—predecessors of the Nelson Rockefeller liberal wing of the party—thought Eisenhower *the* candidate they wanted in 1952. A cautious, moderate internationalist in his perspectives, and in many ways nonpartisan, Eisenhower seemed to epitomize what many progressive Republicans wanted in a party leader.

But Eisenhower frustrated these supporters. He seemed, by turns, uninterested, coy, and then receptive to their overtures. They wanted him to announce his candidacy and ignite a vigorous, multifaceted campaign. He hesitated. Then, in early 1952, Eisenhower allowed his name to be placed in the New Hampshire primary, even though he did not campaign in the state. Surprisingly, he outpolled Taft, considered the frontrunner, 46,661 to 35,838. Although Eisenhower proved, at first, a clumsy campaigner, his reputation as a military hero, his warm smile, and his optimistic personality pushed him ahead of the dour Taft. Choosing to enter the fray and systematically campaign, Eisenhower gained quick momentum in other primaries and won a closely contested Republican nomination from Taft after a vigorous floor fight over which delegations to seat. Listening to advisors and following his own inclinations, Eisenhower chose as his running mate Richard Nixon, California senator, conservative and touted as anti-Communist. They were the first all-western ticket since Herbert Hoover and Charles Curtis had run together in 1928.

In his campaigning for the Republican nomination between spring and summer 1952, Eisenhower gradually revealed some of his opinions on major domestic issues. First of all, he believed in limited power for the central government; the New Deal policies of Roosevelt and Truman, he said, had gone too far in allowing Washington,

D.C., to dictate too much. Second, he favored economic strategies emanating from local and private sources rather than from government funding. Third, he held that states' rights must be protected from infringement by the federal government. As an example, Eisenhower favored Texas over the central government in the competition to control offshore oil rights. Fourth, he wanted balanced budgets; he scored the previous Democratic budgets since the early 1930s that were baptized in red ink. Fifth, not surprisingly for a man of his military background, Eisenhower wanted a strong national defense, heightened security for a nation in deadly Cold War competition with Communists. Revealingly, Eisenhower did not say much about civil rights, which would become such a hot issue in his presidency.

Eisenhower's campaign against the Democratic nominee, Adlai E. Stevenson, sometimes clarified his political positions and revealed the leader he would be. After the Eisenhower-Nixon ticket emerged as victors in the Republican national convention in early July, Eisenhower set up headquarters in Denver. Having first taken time to vacation and plan his actions, Eisenhower set out on a barnstorming campaign at the beginning of September. He had told his followers in Texas he would "lead this crusade"—and he did, with verve and surprising energy. In his fast-moving electioneering, he visited every state but Mississippi; he traveled more than fifty thousand miles, stopped in 232 cities and towns, and gave innumerable speeches. Powered by the ever-popular slogan "I Like Ike," Eisenhower proved that his age—he was now sixty-one and would turn sixty-two in October—would be no drawback to his campaigning or subsequent leadership.

While campaigning in the West, Eisenhower promised he would support legislation helpful to those residing west of the Mississippi. Beginning his Republican campaign in Abilene, he mentioned the necessity of Republicans winning back "the cattle states" from the Democrats. He wanted to do the same in California, where the Democrats had been victorious for nearly twenty years. He told other westerners he would support their dam projects, a promise dear to many western hearts. Eisenhower did much more than Truman had in 1948 to make the West prime campaigning territory.

Eisenhower put distance between himself, the Democrats, and President Truman. When the president invited Eisenhower to White House briefings, to Truman's astonishment, Ike turned down the invitation. He wanted to "remain free to analyze publicly the policies and acts of the present administration," Eisenhower wrote Truman. Among the Republicans, however, Eisenhower mended fences with Taft and tried to skirt the divisive outbursts of Wisconsin senator Joseph McCarthy and his henchmen.

The largest challenge for Ike during the campaign may have been the revelation that his vice-presidential partner, Richard Nixon, had what critics described as a secret slush fund. Upon hearing the report, Eisenhower called for a full examination and urged Nixon to go on national television, explain the fund, and then resign from the ticket—or at least offer to resign. On September 23, Nixon gave his famous "Checkers" speech, playing on listeners' emotions and picturing himself and his wife, Pat, as upright, plain, and dedicated Americans. He did not offer to resign, much to Eisenhower's chagrin. But when Nixon's stubborn defense seemed to win sympathy, Eisenhower changed his mind, and the two Republicans went hesitantly ahead with the campaign. The reconciliation demonstrated that Eisenhower could work out compromises to the benefit of his fellow Republicans—and perhaps for the country as a whole.

Eisenhower's most important campaign speech came on October 24 in Detroit, when he promised his audience, "I shall go to Korea." It was a sustaining vow that appealed to a Cold War–fretting America. A man like Ike, with his burnished reputation as a military leader and hero, would be just the person to settle the fractious war in Korea, now in its third year.

As the November election approached, prognosticators predicted Eisenhower would win easily. Their predictions proved true. Ike carried thirty-nine of the forty-eight states and defeated his Democratic opponent, Adlai Stevenson, in popular votes, 33.9 to 27.3 million, and in electoral votes, 442 to 89. In addition, the Republicans grabbed twenty-two seats in the House to gain a majority, which they would not have again until 1994. In the Senate, the Republicans also gained a two-seat majority—until Oregon senator Wayne Morse defected to the independents, reducing the Republican majority to one. Eisenhower's victory was an electoral revolution. After twenty years of Democratic control, the Republicans had won back the White House. The Eisenhower era had officially begun.

Within a few weeks of his election, Eisenhower had selected his cabinet. One wag referred to them as "Eight Millionaires and a Plumber." Lucius Clay, longtime military associate and advisor of Eisenhower, and Herbert Brownell, another close political advisor, had helped the president pull together this cabinet. They knew the American political landscape better than he did, and he trusted their judgment. John Foster Dulles, an experienced diplomat, became the secretary of state. Dogmatic, self-assured, and loquacious, Dulles was nonetheless more than competent. He was never close to Eisenhower, but the president recognized his knowledge of world affairs. Most of the choices illustrated Clay's and Brownell's ties with midwestern and eastern businessmen and leaders. For secretary of defense,

Charles E. Wilson, president of General Motors, was selected. Ike wanted an elite businessman in charge of defense. Wilson seemed to fill the bill in that he was, at the time, the country's highest-paid executive (receiving a salary of more than $500,000, including benefits), but he and the president never made a close connection. That kind of close connection emerged between Eisenhower and Secretary of the Treasury George M. Humphrey. Also a major business leader, Humphrey was jovial and gregarious, drawing him to the president. Well before the others, Herbert Brownell had become Ike's choice for attorney general. Secretary of commerce was Sinclair Weeks, a New England banker, so conservative that Ike worried about his tightfistedness. Arthur Summerfield, a Michigan car dealer, became postmaster general.

Three cabinet members came from the West. The most important of these was Ezra Taft Benson, secretary of agriculture. Before Benson's selection, Ike and his advisors had considered two Kansas politicians for the post but decided they wanted someone from farther west. Plus, Benson was a favorite of Senator Robert Taft. Unfortunately, Benson proved less malleable in his leadership than Ike had hoped; he alienated thousands of farmers when he lowered the government supports that agriculturists had enjoyed since New Deal times. Still, Eisenhower was drawn to Benson. As retired General Lucius Clay put it, "Benson was one of the twelve apostles of the Mormon Church, and I think President Eisenhower rather liked that." For secretary of the interior, the president wanted a westerner and decided on Arthur Langlie, governor of Washington. But Langlie, having just been reelected for a four-year term, declined the nomination. So Eisenhower chose Douglas McKay of Oregon, a former governor and car dealer. It proved not to be a first-class choice. The selection of Oveta Culp Hobby for secretary of health, education, and welfare worked out better. A well-to-do woman whose family published the *Houston Post* and who had been active in the WACs (Women's Army Corps), Hobby was an extraordinarily hardworking person. Indeed, so diligent was Hobby that she worked herself into exhaustion and resigned in 1955. Over time, the cabinet blended well. One observer explained why: "General Eisenhower was remarkably gifted in bringing people from a variety of backgrounds together and forging them into a successful team."

Eisenhower sandwiched a quick trip to Korea around the cabinet choices. It was a gesture of utmost symbolic importance, launching him, even before he had entered the White House, as one who would "wage peace." Indeed, in the first years of his administration, Eisenhower paid more attention to diplomatic controversies around the world than to domestic challenges.

EISENHOWER IN THE WHITE HOUSE

The successful negotiations in Korea, which led to an armistice in 1953, epitomized Eisenhower's drive to bring peace. Other global tensions pushed at the president. He had to find ways to "peacefully coexist" with the Russians and other Communist countries. Such conflicts kept Americans on edge. Conflicts in Southeast Asia, the Middle East, and Asia, especially with China, kept Eisenhower and his diplomatic corps busy throughout the 1950s. And lurking over all these was the threat of nuclear war. Diplomatic, military, and defense planning kept that horrendous danger at the forefront of their thinking and actions.

These diplomatic decisions had an impact on westerners, as they did on all Americans. But a handful or more of Eisenhower's domestic policies and specific actions had even more direct effect on westerners. These included the president's changing stance on civil rights. His pathbreaking decision to build a network of nationwide freeways also greatly influenced the West. Nor should one overlook his important personal relationships with westerners like Vice President Richard Nixon, Chief Justice Earl Warren, and several other leading persons from the West. These policies, plans, and people greatly influenced Eisenhower's connections with states from the trans-Mississippi West.

Eisenhower's convictions about able leadership and his conclusions about the delegation of responsibility frame and illustrate his presidential dealings with the American West. Based on his long, successful experiences in the military, Eisenhower believed that the best leaders were middle-of-the-road leaders who made good use of a chain of command, up and down. Leaders must trust their lieutenants, give them freedom to formulate and administer policies in their bailiwicks, and then support their decisions and actions. Extremes were to be avoided, compromises and mediating positions embraced. These predispositions played out in all Eisenhower's dealings with westerners.

Conflicts over civil rights loomed large in the two Eisenhower administrations. Those imbroglios played themselves out across the country, including the West. Eisenhower was an uncertain captain on this tortuous journey. Clearly, he was not a civil rights leader, promoting a more balanced playing field for African Americans, for example. Lyndon B. Johnson proved to be that president a decade later, in the mid-1960s. Conversely, Eisenhower was no dyed-in-the-wool segregationist. Here was another illustration of Ike's middle-of-the-road positions as ideologue and as activist. That mediating position upset liberals and conservatives alike, the typical reaction to centrist thinking and acting.

Eisenhower stood where many Americans did on civil rights during the 1950s. His murky, ambivalent attitudes about segregation and integration illustrated what large numbers of other white Americans thought. Eisenhower was clearly not a racist; he had worked with African Americans, he made no antiblack statements, and he did not speak for the division of races. Still, he had grown up in Kansas where segregation was practiced in schools and public facilities. As a military leader, Eisenhower called for enforcement of orders to end segregation, orders that Truman announced but did not implement. Still, the thirty-sixth president did not push for legislation to end segregation.

How intriguing that conflicts over civil rights, especially in the area of segregation of schools, would be one of—if not *the* major—domestic issue of Eisenhower's administration. When the Earl Warren Court announced its *unanimous* decision to end school segregation in *Oliver Brown et al. v. Board of Education of Topeka, Kansas,* on May 17, 1954, it placed a major dilemma before President Eisenhower. This decision on a case from his home state discomfited him, even though, somewhat indirectly, he had a major hand in bringing about the landmark decision. He had named several judges to lower courts who were clearly in favor of integration. Even more important was a notably significant decision—at a higher level.

Eisenhower's actions dealing with the Supreme Court were a tipping point. In September 1953, when Chief Justice Fred Vinson died unexpectedly, Eisenhower, after a few weeks of back-and-forth executive maneuvering with Earl Warren, then governor of California, nominated him for chief justice. Eisenhower had met Warren during the 1952 campaign, liked him, and evidently later promised Warren a nomination after the "first vacancy" on the Court occurred. Eisenhower may have meant an associate justice position, but Warren took a literalist approach and pushed the president for nomination. Eisenhower disliked the pressure, but, influenced by the advice of Attorney General Brownell, sent in Warren's nomination for chief justice.

Warren's role as chief justice in a slightly left-leaning Court became a major shaping force in Eisenhower's administration, even if the president was uncomfortable with that trend. Although evidence is lacking that Eisenhower ever uttered the widely traveled postpresidential statement that naming Warren to the Court was his worst decision, the president did not react positively to the *Brown v. Board of Education* ruling. His actions suggest he was uneasy about what he considered a too-dramatic change, and he worried about strong reactions to the Court's judgment, especially in the South. Still, he would eventually enforce the momentous decision.

Brown v. Board of Education clearly redirected policies toward integration, and Eisenhower exhibited his dissatisfaction over this precipitous change in tradition.

The segregation system had been in effect, legally, for nearly sixty years following *Plessey v. Ferguson* (1896) allowing "separate but equal" transportation facilities, a decision that was gradually adopted for schools and other public facilities. Eisenhower had grown up in the customs of segregation and hesitated to break from them. Civil rights advocates in the mid-1950s, and historians and biographers since, roundly criticized the president for what they consider his foot-dragging on segregation-integration issues.

The fallout from the *Brown* case spread well beyond the South and schools there. Over time, including the *Brown II* order in 1955 calling for integration of schools with "all deliberate speed" (a phrase that originated with Eisenhower), increasing pressure was placed on school systems to integrate all students because separate, segregated schools had been inherently unequal. The tensions over segregation in the West were particularly strong in Texas, Oklahoma, and other western areas proximate to the South. Once the pathbreaking decisions about school integration issued from the Supreme Court in 1954–55, activists in the South, West, and North began to ponder how those decisions might be applied to other aspects of segregation. Some westerners began thinking about separate but unequal schools for Native Americans and Hispanics. And what about other public institutions, neighborhoods, and sociocultural activities? Although these ideas began to percolate in the 1950s, it was not until the 1960s, in the presidential administrations of John F. Kennedy and Lyndon B. Johnson, that civil rights ideas and actions gained center stage.

Searching for a middle-of-the-road position, Eisenhower chose to view the *Brown* decision as a judicial order from the Supreme Court. He did not see the decision as a moral imperative lighting the way for swift, decisive presidential action. Instead, he dismissed "foolish extremists on both sides of the [segregation-integration] question," extremists he wanted to avoid. Still, the "Court has spoken," he told the nation a few days after the May 1954 decision and added in his familiar fractured syntax, "I am sworn to uphold their—the constitutional processes in this country, and I am trying. I will obey." Meanwhile, he had to address another issue in his own party that he considered more pressing.

Even before Eisenhower entered the White House, Wisconsin senator Joseph McCarthy had exploded on the scene. After McCarthy claimed that he had a lengthy list of known Communists in the U.S. government, he became the most-talked-about congressman. Eisenhower had early, negative reactions to the blowhard senator, but he kept those reactions to himself—even after he became the Republican standard-bearer from 1952 onward.

Eisenhower came to the White House desiring to reinstate balance and unity in the American political world. First of all, convinced that the twenty-year Democratic Party domination from 1933 to 1953 had led the country away from its political center, he wanted to cast loose from New Deal moorings and move back to the political midpoint. His winning the presidency for the Republicans was the first step in rebalancing American politics. Second, he had to find and employ a way to unify badly divided elements of his own party. In the first years of his presidency, Eisenhower tried to avoid the negative attacks of Senator McCarthy. In doing so, he would shy away from direct criticism of McCarthy and avoid issues that upset the equanimity the president embraced.

Meanwhile, McCarthy called on several westerners for support. These included Herman Welker of Idaho, Pat McCarran of Nevada, William S. Knowland of California, George Malone of Nevada, Karl Mundt of South Dakota, Henry Dworshak of Idaho, Bourke Hickenlooper of Iowa, Barry Goldwater of Arizona, Andrew Schoeppel of Kansas, and Edward C. Johnson of Colorado. Not all of these men backed McCarthy on every issue, but they stuck close to him in his attacks on people and institutions he considered communistic.

During Eisenhower's early presidential years, he was often harshly criticized for not putting McCarthy in his place. Actually, he did much more to head off McCarthy than contemporaries knew. Political scientist Fred I. Greenstein, in his provocative study, *The Hidden-Hand Presidency: Eisenhower as Leader* (1982), showed, for the first time, how adroit Eisenhower was in dealing, largely off-scene, with the disruptive McCarthy. Avoiding publicly attacking McCarthy, carefully stating his disagreements with extreme conservatives (without using names), privately pointing out McCarthy's undermining actions to advisors and leading Republicans, Eisenhower allowed the senator to pave the way for his own political execution when he took on the army in his vitriolic attacks. Eisenhower wanted criticism of McCarthy to come from other sources rather than from the executive branch. It did. First gradually, and then dramatically, McCarthy's senatorial colleagues moved against him, censuring him in December 1954 by a vote of sixty-seven to twenty-two. Eisenhower had achieved what he wanted—silencing McCarthy—without politically pummeling the senator. Not all of Eisenhower's advisors and fellow Republicans praised his actions, however; more than a few thought he had been too lax and distant in dealing with McCarthy. As Professor Greenstein makes clear, however, he did much more from what seemed to be a sideline position than his critics realized. Most important for the discussion here, getting McCarthy offstage in 1954 helped to reunify the Republican Party, a major goal of Eisenhower's, prepare for his reelection in 1956, and make way for legislation that would impact the West and the entire country.

One issue during Eisenhower's first administration did not work out well. This issue, important to the West but rarely discussed in Eisenhower biographies, was the policy of termination. In the years following the Roosevelt-Truman presidencies, the Indian reforms of Indian Commissioner John Collier fell into disfavor. Conservative commissioners of Indian affairs wanted to reverse policies of the 1930s and early 1940s, ending central government support for Indian-centric efforts and pushing Native Americans toward full assimilation into American society. At first, Indian commissioners William Zimmerman Jr., Dillon Myer (who had earlier headed up Japanese relocation), and Glenn L. Emmons spoke of "freeing," or "emancipating," Indians, but eventually the word "termination" became the most widely used word for Indian policies in the Eisenhower era.

True to form, the president allowed his staff, the commissioners of Indian affairs, and Secretary of the Interior Douglas McKay to work out the specifics of termination. They sold their ideas to Congress, and Eisenhower signed the legislation. Although other Indian tribes, including the Menominees as well as several other Native groups, were terminated, the most significant action for a western tribe was the termination in August 1954 of the Klamaths of southern Oregon. Motives for termination of the Klamath tribe were inextricably mixed. Supporters of termination pushed their familiar idea that wardship and government support should be ended, allowing individual tribal members to own a piece of land or to benefit financially from the sale of their reservation. A few onlookers also coveted the rich, abundant forests the Klamaths owned and supported termination as a way to open those forests for logging. When termination was put before members of the Klamath tribe, three out of four voted for ending tribal identity and receiving a forty-four thousand dollar per-capita share of the sale of tribal lands. Others chose to keep individual shares of the remaining land.

Termination failed. The Klamaths and other tribes were ill-prepared to suddenly leave their reservations and enter American society. Most Indians were inexperienced, too, in handling the funds they received and soon spent or invested the money unwisely or were taken advantage of by unscrupulous advisors. So negative were the outcomes, generally, of termination that subsequent administrations from John F. Kennedy forward abandoned termination and returned to embrace self-determination policies that John Collier had fathered in the 1930s.

Although Eisenhower rarely commented on policies dealing with Indians or other nonwhite groups, he did support termination during his presidency.

Probably two impulses best explain Eisenhower's actions. The more important of the two was Eisenhower's predilection for the status quo. In this regard, he concluded that New Deal policies had gone too far in superimposing government control of Native Americans; instead, Indians should be moved, not toward self-determination and separation, but toward assimilation. Second, Eisenhower backed the policies of his advisors. Not only did Secretary of the Interior McKay push for termination, but so too had recent Indian commissioners and western politicians such as Senator Arthur Watkins of Utah and Representative E. Y. Berry of South Dakota. If these westerners and others, supporters of Eisenhower and the Republicans, advocated termination, Eisenhower leaned in that direction. Regrettably, termination proved to be a disaster for most Native Americans and an ill-advised action in the Eisenhower administration.

Nearly sixty years after Eisenhower's presidency, a leading Republican presidential candidate asserted that "good-guy" Eisenhower had deported 1.5 million illegal immigrants from Mexico during his years in the White House. Some of the accusations of that partisan politician were true: Eisenhower did support "Operation Wetback," which stipulated the deportation of illegal immigrants, the largest numbers of which were residing in Texas and California. The president was convinced that immigrants from Mexico, without legal contracts under the earlier Bracero program, ought to be returned to their homeland. But, contrary to later criticisms, Eisenhower did not advocate slamming the door on Mexican immigrants. Nor did his administration return 1.5 million illegal immigrants— perhaps 250,000 at most, according to historian Kelly Lytle Hernandez. Eisenhower favored the Bracero program's contract system and wanted to keep the Mexican workers' contracts legal and well organized. His stance here gives yet more evidence of Eisenhower's mediated positions on matters that shaped the West.

Overall, Eisenhower's political popularity remained high during his first four years. He had kept his Republican backers and won over independents and even some Democrats. It was clear to nearly everyone that he would be the Republican candidate in 1956. There were health concerns, however. He had suffered a serious heart attack in September 1955, from which he had recovered; but he also was beset with digestive problems (later labeled ileitis) and needed surgery. Not until a doctor cleared him did Eisenhower decide to seek renomination.

The larger political question centered on who would be his running mate. The answer was not clear in the months before summer 1956. Richard Nixon had not been, in all ways, the administrative partner Ike had hoped for. As vice president, Nixon was the most important westerner the president had to deal with, but that relationship was not going very well. One biographer (Stephen Ambrose) suggests that Eisenhower offered Nixon a cabinet position so that the president could choose a new running mate. Whatever Eisenhower truly thought was not even clear when the Republicans gathered in San Francisco for their national convention. When no dump-Nixon movement crystalized, the president allowed his renomination.

As expected, the Eisenhower-Nixon ticket blew by the Democratic Adlai Stevenson-Estes Kefauver team. Eisenhower did even better in 1956 than he had in 1952, polling 35.6 million votes to Stevenson's 26 million, or a 2.5 percent gain over 1952. Interestingly, although Ike still held the West, losing only in Missouri and Arkansas in 1956, he actually lost a percentages of voters in fifteen western states while gaining in six states. On the other hand, Eisenhower became the first Republican nominee to twice win Texas, Oklahoma, New Mexico, Idaho, and Arizona in presidential contests.

INTO THE SECOND ADMINISTRATION

When the Supreme Court announced its decision in the *Brown* case in 1954, Eisenhower had worried that the South would erupt in disagreement. As we have seen, the first major explosion came three years later, unexpectedly, in Little Rock. In Eisenhower's memoir, *Waging Peace, 1956–61,* published about a decade after the events at Little Rock, he depicts the confrontation almost entirely as the necessity of a president's having to send troops to Arkansas to make Governor Faubus obey the law. True enough, but other ingredients complicated the chief executive's actions.

Events in the summer and early fall of 1957 illustrated Eisenhower's persistent reluctance to push hard for integration. On July 18, 1957, the *New York Times* quoted the president as having stated in a recent press conference: "I can't imagine any set of circumstances that would ever induce me to send federal troops . . . into any area to enforce the orders of a federal court. . . . I would never believe that it would be a wise thing to do." Yet the president did that just a bit more than two months later. Why? Because, quite simply, he was forced to do so—much as he was pressured, by surrounding circumstances, to give nominal support for the *Brown* case in the months following the May 1954 decision.

Eisenhower, although no racist or anti-integrationist, was a cautious conservative. When Orval Faubus took on the federal government with his obstructionist, racist actions in September 1957, Eisenhower was compelled to act. If he did not act, Faubus and his segregationist cronies would win the battle by disallowing black students to attend Little Rock High School. When the president ordered troops from the 101st Airborne Division (minus their black members) to Little Rock, he revealed his belief in the executive powers of the presidency and in the court system, as well as the rule of law; yet he lent no strong support for the full integration of American society. His lukewarm backing of integration had delayed its implementation for several years. In that delay, and in his middle-of-the-road approach on reform, he likely reflected the widespread viewpoints of most white westerners in the mid- to late 1950s.

Although attention to race relations in the 1950s in the American West may have focused on black-white contacts, relationships between whites and other groups reveal divided western attitudes not much different from Eisenhower's own. Residue from the Japanese relocation controversy continued to generate tensions between whites and Asians well into the 1950s. Conflicts among braceros, growers, and school officials marked school decisions in more than a few places in the West. Western states, as well as the federal government, were reluctant to sponsor legislation that would aid Mexican immigrants with any of their financial or schooling challenges. Although the federal government passed legislation in the 1950s to aid Indian students, it did not solicit Indian opinions about such matters—not until the late 1960s. Following the guidelines of termination policies and assimilation pressures, western states were not inclined to push for Indian self-determination. Western attitudes toward racial matters, although not as hard and fast as attitudes in the Deep South toward African Americans, did not reflect a notably more progressive stance than that of other Americans, or of President Eisenhower.

As Eisenhower was chaining up for his reelection campaign in 1956, he had signed a legislative act that, eventually, embodied his largest, long-range effect on the American West. The legislation had a long previous history; its ramifications would involve subsequent administrations into the next generation—and more.

Eisenhower had been greatly interested in highways since World War I. In 1919, still in his late twenties and an army captain, he took part in a coast-to-coast trip that revealed the terrible condition of the country's highways. In his autobiographical memoir, *At Ease,* Eisenhower devoted more than ten pages to explaining that cross-continental experience and the impact the journey had on him. In Eisenhower's words, he and "every [other] officer on the convoy had recommended in his report that efforts should be made to get our people interested in producing better roads." The long days and troubling travels across a wide West, where many of the roads (sometimes little more than trails) were treacherous, remained strong in Eisenhower's memory. Adding to this early adventure were

Eisenhower's later experiences in Germany, where he saw the importance of wide highways to Hitler's military regime. Eisenhower resolved "to put an emphasis on road building" when he had an opportunity.

In the first days of his presidency, Eisenhower had spoken for the need of a vastly improved national highway system. But Congress, arguing about sources of funding, federal-state leadership, and the physical layout of the freeways, did not pass the measure until June 1956, which the president promptly signed. The National Highway Program, or Interstate Highway Program, two of the names by which the effort was known, was in every way gargantuan. It would cover, ultimately, 46,876 miles and include 55,512 bridges and 14,756 interchanges. After much congressional wrangling and a major compromise by Eisenhower on the mode of funding, it was decided that the web of freeways would be financed by a four-cent-per-gallon gasoline tax. The federal government would underwrite 90 percent of the construction costs, which ran to more than $100 billion, and provide generous support for later maintenance.

The president provided no entirely clear reasons for his support of the astounding project. His major motivation, he frequently reiterated, was for heightened security. A country in a heated Cold War needed to move its forces and materiel quickly and to many separated sites, as Germany had done in World War II. So military needs were high on Eisenhower's agenda. Less often mentioned was the need to find jobs for unemployed Americans. The country's economy was faltering in the mid-1950s, and the sprawling freeway system would be an invaluable infusion of government funds for something of a make-work project. Thousands of workers found jobs in constructing the huge network of freeways stretching across the country.

Race relations and highway building aside, it was foreign affairs that dominated most of Eisenhower's attention in his second administration. Diplomatic challenges emerged around the globe. The largest, ongoing tension was the continuing Cold War with the Soviet Union. Inconclusive meetings between the president and Russian leader Nikita Khrushchev; the Russian launch of an unmanned satellite, *Sputnik,* in October 1957; and the Russian attack on an American reconnaissance plane within Soviet borders in May 1960—all kept relations between the United States and Russia tense and uncertain. In the Middle East, conflicts continued about the future of the Suez Canal, and blustery rhetoric concerning the offshore China islands of Matsu and Quemoy rattled diplomatic nerves. Turmoil in Vietnam was also becoming evident. The president worried about the rise of Communism in the region but did not come to the aid of France as it was losing control there. Obviously, Eisenhower spent most of his time and energy on these world problems rather than on domestic issues, as he indicated in his later statements in *Waging Peace,* his own history of his administration.

Still, Eisenhower found time to be involved in a handful of other actions that clearly influenced the West, or parts of the region. During Truman's administration it had been decided that the central government would build a huge dam in Hell's Canyon on the Idaho-Oregon border. Eisenhower wanted private companies to build the high dam—or three smaller dams. He told Secretary of the Interior Douglas McKay, who had previously been a federal-power advocate, to push for private companies to build the dam(s), which McKay dutifully did. When Secretary of Agriculture Ezra Taft Benson moved to reduce government subsidies for farmers established under the New Deal and continued under Truman, but which Benson considered wrong and inefficient, Ike backed him on the reductions, even though they elicited negative reactions among western farmers. Toward the end of his presidency, Eisenhower also advocated statehood for Alaska and Hawaii. Although he had reservations about Alaska's unwieldy size and its Democratic tendencies, he signed the bills for statehood, and the two entered the Union in 1959.

Two other Eisenhower actions in the closing days of his presidency affected the West. In his farewell address on January 17, 1961, Eisenhower urged Americans to rein in a mushrooming military-industrial complex. Excessively large armies and an expanding arms industry, when in one another's embrace, he cautioned, would lead the country astray, likely into huge budgets and perhaps into war. When Eisenhower issued this end-of-his-presidency warning, he was speaking to the entire country but especially to the West, where sprawling bases and other military establishments represented the complex that worried the retiring president.

As the election of 1960 approached, reporters wanted to know whom Ike wished to become the Republican candidate for the party's standard-bearer. The president spoke warmly of cabinet member Robert Anderson and also encouraged Oveta Culp Hobby to run, but he accepted the nomination of Nixon at the Republican convention. After the Republican gathering, Ike did not play a major role in Nixon's campaign against the Democratic candidate, John F. Kennedy. There is good evidence that Nixon wanted to win on his own, not riding on Eisenhower's coattails. Not until the final days before the vote did Eisenhower engage in much campaigning for his vice president. Since the outcome was the closest presidential election of the twentieth century—only a 112,881-vote difference out of a total of 68 million ballots—campaigning by the ever-popular Ike on Nixon's behalf might have turned the tide. Clearly, Eisenhower did little to build a friendship with Nixon, the westerner nearest him from 1952 to 1961.

POST-PRESIDENTIAL YEARS

In the years immediately following his leaving the White House, Eisenhower did not fare well in journalistic and historical accounts of his administration. Adopting Truman's earlier castigation of a "do-nothing Congress," reporters and historians depicted Eisenhower as a "do-nothing president." In popular polls, he was pegged as a mediocre chief executive.

In the 1970s and 1980s, however, as more evidence turned up of Eisenhower's "hidden-hand" leadership, he rose rapidly in the estimation of journalists, historians, and biographers. Behind the scenes, diligent researchers found, he had worked to lessen the negative influences of McCarthy, he had used the power of the central government to launch the giant St. Lawrence Seaway and the sprawling national freeway system, and, most important to Eisenhower himself, he had kept the peace. Rather than a "do-nothing" president, Eisenhower, driven by his desire for consensus, agreement, and compromise, had stayed the middle course he had promised. By the 1990s, more than a few interpreters were reevaluating Eisenhower as an above-average, if not near-great, president.

EISENHOWER'S WESTERN LEGACY

The impact of the interstate highway system on the American West was—and is—incalculable. True, the nationwide network of four-lane highways greatly influenced all states, but nowhere was the shaping influence greater than in the West. American historians and Eisenhower biographers often overlook this influence because they misread the demography of the modern American West. The West is the most urban region of the United States; this is especially so in the Far West and in the Southwest from California to Texas, as well as in several interior western states. That is, westerners, more than Americans in other regions, reside primarily in cities and towns. Perhaps scholars are misled by the frontier myths concerning a wide-open West, free from urban concentrations. But more than half a century ago, Texas historian Walter Prescott Webb, in his essay "The American West: Perpetual Mirage," rightly described the West as a land of "urban oases." Space still defined much of the West, but a large majority of westerners lived in those widely separated urban places. From the 1950s onward, the new national freeway system provided the much-needed connections among the West's widely separated cities. One would not be guilty of overstatement in asserting that, like the impact of the New Deal and World War II, the expansive freeway system transformed the American West.

Not all the transformations in the West were positive. With wide new highways leading out from central cities, western residents and newcomers moved to expanding suburbs. Those new neighborhoods surrounding core cities sometimes encouraged quickly constructed, unimaginative tract homes, thereby contributing to the unsightly "sprawl" that characterized western cities such as Los Angeles, Phoenix, Las Vegas, and dozens more. In addition, the ubiquitous freeways added to the tendency of westerners to pave over large sections of their cities and suburbs. Westerners, more addicted to automobiles than other Americans, were cementing their landscapes. No western city demonstrated this unfortunate tendency more than did Los Angeles, where the city had 250 miles of freeway within its limits by 1960.

The burgeoning freeway system, its government funding, and its clear impact should give pause to those wishing to define Dwight D. Eisenhower solely as cautiously conservative in his use of power and in budgetary matters. Here was a president supporting the largest public works program in American history. He was doing it with the power of the national government, and he was asking the federal government to fund most of the costs. The highway project was not undertaken as part of Roosevelt's New Deal; it was a major enactment under Eisenhower's leadership. Had Eisenhower been transformed from a small-government Jeffersonian into a reborn Roosevelt? Any conclusions about Eisenhower, his leadership, and his impact on the West must take into account his unusual actions in leading the charge for a widespread, cross-continental highway system.

In several other areas affecting the West, however, Eisenhower seemed uninterested. Programs that focused on the interests and needs of women and minority groups or the poor did not capture his full attention. He did push for naming one woman to his cabinet, Texan Oveta Culp Hobby, but when she resigned from overwork, he did not replace her with another woman. Although he did name twenty-eight women to offices that needed Senate confirmation—nearly ten more than Truman had—these numbers were miniscule. Nor was he much interested in speaking out for the Equal Rights Amendment. In 1957, when a reporter asked the president about the ERA, he responded: "Well, it's hard for a mere man to believe that a woman doesn't have equal rights. But, actually, this is the first time that this has come to my specific attention now, since, oh, I think a year or so." Not surprisingly, the offhand comment disturbed women's rights activists. Nor did Eisenhower's wife, Mamie, call for action. Her backstage role was similar to that chosen by Bess Truman and Pat Nixon, distinct from the activism of Rosalynn Carter and Hillary Clinton, and furthest from the energetic leadership of the most active First Lady of all, Eleanor Roosevelt.

Eisenhower's dealings with diverse racial groups in the West illustrated his cautious, guarded policies. Race relations was not a topic emphasized in his own writings; this was also true concerning civil rights. When a civil rights bill was introduced in the Senate in 1956, Eisenhower did not push strongly for it—though neither did he oppose it—thinking that such legislation should come from states and that the central government should not impose civil rights legislation on the American people. For the president, changes ought to come only when Americans were willing to embrace them. Eisenhower did not want to admit, of course, that the termination of Indian tribes, as quickly became apparent, had failed to help—in fact, had hindered—Native Americans. Indians remained the poorest, sickest, and most isolated Americans. Eisenhower did continue some farm programs that benefited Hispanic farmworkers, though critics claimed the programs were woefully inadequate. Conversely, according to James T. Patterson, in *Grand Expectations*, conservative senator Barry Goldwater of Arizona carped at Eisenhower for not cutting even more government spending. He asserted that the president was operating a "Dime Store New Deal." Obviously, Eisenhower was conservative on spending and rarely found funds for specific programs aiding racial groups, but he was not a reactionary, trying to return the United States to pre–New Deal days. Throughout his presidency, Eisenhower made clear that he did not agree with FDR's huge expansion of the central government in its multitude of federal programs. Strong government programs aiding needy racial groups were yet to come.

Eisenhower's influences on the West were both conservative and pathbreaking. In his desire to balance budgets, he had reduced government spending that negatively impacted famers and workers and their families in the West. Yet in those cuts he did not go nearly as far as conservatives like Senators Barry Goldwater of Arizona and William Knowland of California wanted. His reluctant acceptance of the Supreme Court's *Brown* decision in 1954 and his dispatch of troops to Little Rock in 1957 were not so much evidence of reform or activism as they were of the president's willingness to back the laws of the land. Those decisions undoubtedly partially opened the door for school desegregation and for more integration, generally, of American society.

The case for a pathbreaking Eisenhower lies in his championing the new interstate freeway system in 1955 and afterward. The construction of the superhighways crisscrossing the region from North to South and East to West remains a tipping point in western history. And Eisenhower was the chief architect and trail boss of the sprawling highway complex. On balance, however, Dwight D. Eisenhower reflected the cautious, conservative, and centrist attitudes of most Americans in the 1950s. Public opinion polls and election results showed that Americans and westerners "liked Ike." In his blend of conservativism and activism, he was a mediating influence on the American West.

FOR FURTHER READING

Alexander, Charles. *Holding the Line: The Eisenhower Era, 1952–1961.* Bloomington: Indiana University Press, 1975.

Ambrose, Stephen E. *Eisenhower, the President.* New York: Simon & Schuster, 1984.

Beschloss, Michael R. *Eisenhower: A Centennial Life.* New York: HarperCollins, 1990.

Branyan, Robert L., and Lawrence H. Larsen. *The Eisenhower Administration, 1953–1961: A Documentary History.* 2 vols. New York: Random House, 1971.

Burk, Robert F. *Dwight D. Eisenhower: Hero and Politician.* Boston: Twayne, 1986.

Divine, Robert A. *Eisenhower and the Cold War.* New York: Oxford University Press, 1981.

Eisenhower, Dwight D. *At Ease: Stories I Tell to Friends.* Garden City, NY: Doubleday, 1967.

———. *Mandate for Change: The White House Years, 1953–56.* New York: Doubleday, 1963.

———. *The Papers of Dwight David Eisenhower.* 21 vols. Edited by Alfred D. Chandler Jr. et al. Baltimore: Johns Hopkins University Press, 1970–2001.

———. *Waging Peace: The White House Years, 1956–1961.* New York: Doubleday, 1965.

Gellman, Irwin F. *The President and the Apprentice: Eisenhower and Nixon, 1952–1961.* New Haven: Yale University Press, 2015.

Greene, John Robert. *I Like Ike: The Presidential Election of 1952.* Lawrence: University Press of Kansas, 2017.

Greenstein, Fred I. *The Hidden-Hand Presidency: Eisenhower as Leader.* New York: Basic Books, 1982

Hughes, Emmet John. *The Ordeal of Power: A Political Memoir of the Eisenhower Years.* New York: Atheneum, 1963.

Johnson, Paul. *Eisenhower: A Life.* New York: Viking, 2014.

Korda, Michael. *Ike: An American Hero.* New York: HarperCollins, 2007.

Newton, Jim. *Eisenhower: The White House Years.* New York: Doubleday, 2011.

Pach, Chester J., and Elmo Richardson. *The Presidency of Dwight D. Eisenhower.* Rev ed. Lawrence: University Press of Kansas, 1991.

Patterson, James T. *Grand Expectations: The United States, 1945–1974.* New York: Oxford University Press, 1996.

Pickett, William B. *Dwight David Eisenhower and American Power.* Wheeling, IL: Harlan Davidson, 1995.

Smith, Jean Edward. *Eisenhower in War and Peace.* New York: Random House, 2012.

Wicker, Tom. *Dwight D. Eisenhower.* New York: Henry Holt, 2002.

LYNDON B. JOHNSON, 1963–1969

LC-USZ62-21755

Chapter 8

LYNDON BAINES JOHNSON
FORMING A NEW AMERICAN WEST

On August 6, 1965, President Lyndon B. Johnson signed into law the Voting Rights Act. This landmark legislation and the Civil Rights Act of the previous year proved to be centerpieces of Johnson's Great Society program. The Voting Rights Act, along with several other major bills, remains chief evidence of Johnson's achievements as a leader, particularly in the areas of civil rights and social and economic justice reforms. All had discernible impact on the American West.

Two weeks earlier, in late July 1965, after intensive meetings with cabinet members and diplomatic and military advisors, Johnson announced he would send a huge new contingent of American troops to Vietnam. He had decided to escalate a complex, continuing war in Southeast Asia. That momentous decision and the unwinnable war that followed during the remainder of Johnson's presidency became his political albatross. Critics and biographers, then and later, condemned Johnson for foolishly committing so many American lives to a ruinous war.

Which was the real Lyndon B. Johnson, and how is he to be remembered? As the formulator of the Great Society and the War on Poverty, or as the misguided leader who deserves to be castigated for the disastrous Vietnam War? And what shaping influence did these decisions have on the American West?

Truth to tell, the ambiguity of Johnson's legacies is but a later stage of an endless series of conflicting tensions that defined his entire life. From his boyhood, during his prepresidential career, and on through his presidency, Johnson felt the buffets of crosscurrent influences and pressures. Those stresses pushed him in several, often conflicting directions. In his youth, the competition was between his influential parents; in his early political career, the conflict derived from liberal and conservative pulls; and as president, he would feel the tug between demands for guns and those for butter. These dualities produced a complex man in Lyndon Johnson. The persistent pressures also helped shape his lifelong links to, and influences on, the American West. Even in his connections with the West, Johnson had to sort out whether he owed more to southern or western influences, both of which were so alive and ideology-shaping in his Texas.

A LIFE SHAPED IN THE WEST

Born on August 27, 1908, in the Hill Country of south-central Texas near the Pedernales River, Lyndon Baines Johnson came to love and to link himself to his home country. No western president so identified with his natal home as warmly and noticeably as did Johnson. In his youth, the clashing influences that would be felt his entire life were embodied in the conflicting dreams of his parents. His father, Sam Ealy Johnson, by turns teacher, farmer, and politician, was a rambunctious, profane man. His mother, Rebekah Baines Johnson, a graduate of Baylor University, was well educated and ambitious. Rather than pursue politics, which Sam Johnson pushed his son toward, Rebekah wanted her firstborn to go to college and become a cultured gentleman. These opposite pulls from his refined mother and his gutsy, sometimes boorish father shaped much of Johnson's early life.

Johnson's formal education influenced his later life much less than did his early experiences as an aspiring politician. After high school, where he showed distinction as a debater, Johnson knocked about before finally attending, and eventually graduating from, Southwest Texas State Teachers College in San Marcos. Following short teaching stints in racially mixed high schools in rural and urban Texas, Johnson left teaching in 1931 to work on the staff of Representative Richard Kleberg in Washington, D.C. Three years later, he married Claudia Alta (Lady Bird) Taylor, a graduate of the University of Texas. They became the parents of two daughters, Lynda (1944–) and Luci (1947–).

Johnson quickly made a name for himself in Washington, D.C., with members of Congress and their staffs. He met and impressed President Franklin Roosevelt and was named director of the National Youth Administration in Texas, where, as the youngest state director, he gained a reputation as a nonstop, energetic worker—in Texas and in Washington, D.C. Building on that mushrooming recognition, Johnson won election to the U.S. House in 1937 and reelection six times. He bonded closely with Roosevelt's New Deal and enjoyed the president's warm support. After one unsuccessful attempt at a U.S. Senate seat in 1941, Johnson won in another run for the Senate in 1948. It was a controversial campaign in which, some said, Johnson stole a victory.

In the Senate, as he had in the House, Johnson quickly lept to the front. Named majority whip of the Senate in 1951, he became the Democratic majority leader in

1955. That year a serious heart attack slowed him for a few months, but he soon returned to lead the charge that passed a civil rights bill in 1957. This compromise legislation, on which President Eisenhower was lukewarm, demonstrated Johnson's skills as a political manipulator and compromiser; it also demonstrated his commitment to civil rights.

Johnson had begun considering a run for the presidency in the early 1950s. In 1956, when his hope that a deadlock among leading Democratic candidates would throw him the nomination did not come to pass, he set his sights on 1960. But he started too late that year, quickly fell behind John F. Kennedy in the vote grabbing, and eventually lost the Democratic nomination to the Massachusetts senator. Then, surprisingly and to the disgust of many of Kennedy's leading supporters, Kennedy turned to Johnson as his vice-presidential running mate. Probably Kennedy chose Johnson to ensure Democratic victory in the South, and perhaps in the West. The Kennedy-Johnson ticket won a razor-thin victory over Richard Nixon and his running mate, Henry Cabot Lodge. Johnson's presence on the Democratic ballot obviously helped in the South, but Nixon captured most of the West.

Johnson's nearly three years as vice president were a series of ups and downs. President Kennedy assigned him to committees dealing with the emerging space program (an important connection that greatly expanded during Johnson's own administration), the Peace Corps, and the Equal Employment Opportunity Commission. He also served as the president's envoy in European and Southeast Asian diplomatic discussions and took part in other conversations around foreign affairs. Johnson got along well with Kennedy but less so with the president's younger brother Bobby, the attorney general, and other Democratic liberals from the Northeast. Generally, Johnson was restless in his role as vice president.

Then tragedy struck. On a campaign trip through Texas in November 1963, Kennedy was assassinated by Lee Harvey Oswald. Within moments, Kennedy was dead, and Johnson was catapulted into the presidency. The position he had hungered and thirsted for during the previous decade was now his. It had arrived with the gunshot of a national tragedy.

A NEW RESIDENT IN THE WHITE HOUSE

Johnson inherited aging, limited, and rather shaky links between the White House and the American West. They were primarily connections that Franklin Roosevelt, during the 1930s and the World War II years, had forged between the federal government and the region. Harry Truman, for the most part, had continued

Roosevelt's strong ties with the states beyond the Mississippi. Then, except for his pathbreaking and sprawling freeway program that linked subregions of the West and the West with the rest of the country, Dwight Eisenhower did little to foster close, explicit ties between his natal region and the White House. Although John F. Kennedy's New Frontier slogan hinted at fresh couplings between his administration and the West, the program was more global and futuristic than focused on specific programs impacting the West. In several ways, Kennedy wanted Vice President Johnson to establish new bonds with the West and the South, which Johnson did vigorously before Kennedy's death in 1963.

This meant that what Johnson inherited were connections largely twenty to thirty years old, and those links had rarely kept up with a dynamic West that was exploding in population and with fresh energy. Johnson was up to the new challenges. He would go on to do more than any president since FDR, and any chief executive since, to strengthen and expand presidential ties with the West. In his general policies, exemplified in his Great Society and War on Poverty programs, as well as in other specific legislation, Johnson continued many of Roosevelt's pioneering programs that shaped the West and went on to engineer important new ones. In his slightly more than five years as the country's chief executive, Johnson connected with, and molded, the West in notable fashion. Some of those presidential influences almost did not come to pass, but unexpected tragic consequences paved the way.

In the opening weeks of 1964, while he tried to deal with the emotional grief and political upheavals that followed Kennedy's assassination, Johnson began to formulate his own plans for the future. In the coming months, it became clear that his policies were to be an amalgamation of Kennedy's ideas, Johnson's own thoughts, and suggestions from his advisors. Most of the plans put into action during 1964 impacted the American West in general, while a few lesser-known policies directly influenced the region.

A few days into his presidency, Johnson made clear that he had ambitious plans. He told one advisor that "we can do it all." He would work closely with Congress, building on his friendships and strong ties on the Hill. About six weeks into his presidency, in his State of the Union speech, Johnson told the nation that his "administration today, here and now, declares unconditional war on poverty in America." This assertion was a bow to some of his predecessor's ideas, but even more a link back to FDR. In the words of historian James T. Patterson, Johnson "wanted to be the President who finished what FDR had started."

Commentators then—and now—misread what became known as Johnson's War on Poverty. The president did not help these commentators with his rather vague statements on the nature of "poverty." He did not mean a new "welfare" program; he would not throw billions of dollars at existing poverty. Instead, his plans were focused on heading off poverty rather than on bailing out poor people with long-range government support. Johnson's War on Poverty would target needy citizens with training and education to get welfare recipients on the road to recovery—and to keep them off later welfare rolls.

Johnson's support for an attack on poverty predated his presidency. When Walter Heller, chairman of Kennedy's Council of Economic Advisors, intimated what Kennedy had been thinking about in dealing with poverty, Johnson declared: "I'm interested . . . I'm sympathetic. Go ahead. Give it highest priority. Push ahead full tilt." Before the end of 1963, Johnson had committed $1 billion of federal funds to launch the poverty program.

Early in 1964, in a hectic six weeks, Johnson and his brain trust hastily threw together plans for his poverty policies. He named Sargent Shriver, previously Kennedy's director of the Peace Corps and the late president's brother-in-law, as the new poverty chief. The programs were national in scope but would also greatly impact the West. For instance, Job Corps programs would educate and train people, especially young men and women, for employment. Community action programs would encourage communities to sponsor their own agendas to help the needy. These and other programs would help not only the young but also blacks, Mexican Americans, migrant workers, and small-margin farmers as well.

When the War on Poverty bill came to Congress, Republicans and conservative Democrats strongly opposed it, denouncing the measure as another example of socialistic legislation. Johnson, diligently working his carefully constructed links with Congress, used the Democratic majority to push through the bill. In the House, he relied heavily on Carl Albert from Oklahoma. In addition to the Job Corps and community action sections, the bill also included VISTA (Volunteers in Service to America), Head Start and Upward Bound programs for preschool children and older students, Neighborhood Youth Corps, and the OEO (Office of Economic Opportunity). The title of the bill was the Economic Opportunity Act.

Sargent Shriver discovered that trying to head up the poverty programs was like riding an unbroken bronc at Johnson's Texas ranch. Without clear directions and goals, the unruly steed he was atop bucked and crow-hopped over wide, uncertain terrain. Gradually, however, Shriver and his lieutenants, drawing on New Deal precedents from the National Youth Administration and Civilian Conservation Corps, practiced a technique by discovery, putting things to work as they planned for today and tomorrow.

The Tongue Point Job Corps camp, a few miles inland from coastal Astoria, Oregon, at a former navy base, illustrated some of the early challenges in a Job Corps location. Founded in 1964–65, and at first catering to inner-city African American young men and later to African American young women, the Tongue Point camp did not become coed for a decade. When racial and cultural frictions arose between the Job Corps enrollees and nearby residents, recruitment shifted to include more camp residents from the Pacific Northwest. Instruction was offered in the trades, much as an apprenticeship program or technical school might provide. The site could accommodate up to five hundred youths, and most graduates found better-than-minimum-wage employment, especially after a local community college began to partner with Tongue Point to strengthen and vary their offerings. In New Mexico, in Job Corps sites in Albuquerque and near Roswell, more residents from proximate areas were recruited, including many Native American and Hispanic youths. In addition to the usual trades and skills training of Job Corps sites, participants in New Mexico were taught conservation and firefighting skills in programs partnering with the U.S. Forest Service.

Even before the Economic Opportunity Act passed Congress and Johnson signed it into law in August 1964, the president was at work on other wide-reaching bills. None was more important and far-reaching than the Civil Rights Act of 1964. Several motivations lay behind Johnson's work on civil rights in early 1964. He was very conscious, in the first place, that he had to build on the legacies of John F. Kennedy, if he were to capture the martyred president's supporters. During 1963, Kennedy had begun to push much more forcefully for civil rights legislation. The obstructionist tactics of Alabama's governor George Wallace, the civil rights demonstrations in the South, Martin Luther King's "I Have a Dream" speech in August 1963, and recent polls indicating a strong upsurge in desired civil rights legislation—all had pushed Kennedy toward embracing civil rights legislation. Now Johnson wanted to build on the draft of a civil rights bill Kennedy had submitted to Congress in 1963.

Johnson had other clear motivations. He wanted to back issues that would gain Democratic support for the fall 1964 elections. Ever the keen politician, Johnson sensed that the public was increasingly dismayed—if not outright angry—at southern and western recalcitrance toward civil rights issues. He realized he needed to move. "I felt the need for change," he wrote later, "in the spring of 1963 when events in Birmingham, Alabama, showed the world the glaring contrast between the restraint of the black demonstrators and the brutality of the white policemen."

Most important, Johnson was sincere in his desire for civil rights reform. Ever since his days teaching poor Mexican American and African American students in rural and urban Texas, he had empathized with the plight of the disadvantaged. When he heard that blacks, especially women, could not use public restrooms and had to locate a convenient bush or tree behind which to relieve themselves, his upset mounted. The president realized that the pending civil rights bill would alienate southerners and some westerners, including his good friend Senator Richard Russell of Georgia, but he would brook no compromises. At a press conference he told his audience, "so far as this administration is concerned . . . its position is firm." No watering down.

Johnson thought the civil rights bill would face tough sledding in Congress, so he went to work on his Democratic supporters and reached out to Republicans. Senator Hubert Humphrey of Minnesota led the charge in the Senate, and, after several sessions of vigorous arm-twisting, Illinois's Everett Dirksen, Republican minority leader in the Senate, helped end southern filibustering and pushed for passage of the bill. Humphrey and Dirksen were the key figures in getting the bill through Congress, but they had the help of such westerners as Thomas Kuchel of California, Mike Mansfield of Montana, and even crusty old Carl Hayden of Arizona. On the other hand, Barry Goldwater, also of Arizona, was a strong opponent of the bill. With skillful marshalling of his forces, Johnson got the act through Congress and signed it on July 2, 1964.

The act included several important ingredients, all impacting the West. It prohibited racial discrimination in privately operated businesses such as hotels, restaurants, theaters, and gas stations. In addition, it gave the attorney general the power to end segregation in schools, hotels, hospitals, libraries, and other public venues. And if federally funded entities were guilty of racial segregation, they would lose their federal monies. Discriminations on the basis of race, religion, color, and natural origin—and later on sexual identity—were verboten.

All these stipulations were not carried out at once, of course, and the Voting Rights Act of the next year was needed to give blacks and others the voting rights promised to them. The provisions of the 1964 act would have the largest impact on African Americans living in sections of the West close to the South—Texas, Missouri, and Arkansas—but also throughout the Southwest, from Texas to California, for Mexican Americans. Racial injustices across large swaths of the West indicated how much such legislation was needed. In 1964, in the Houston school district only 3 percent of the African American students were in desegregated schools. At the other end of the West, in liberal Berkeley, California, de facto segregation reigned, with Berkeley High School integrated, but more than 90 percent of the black elementary students attended neighborhood schools, which were, following racial residential patterns, divided by race. The Civil Rights Act of 1964 was an important beginning; it showed that Johnson would move quickly on this important subject. Seen from the West, the act addressed inequities and racism that had existed in the region for decades.

In other, lesser-known but nonetheless significant moves, Johnson also influenced the West before the end of 1964. In May 1964, in a commencement address at the University of Michigan, Johnson put forth his Great Society plan. As part of the speech, which spoke of needed reform in the areas of poverty, education, and civil rights, he also mentioned the necessity of Americans resurrecting an "America the beautiful."

Even before Johnson entered the White House, he had pushed for conservation of lands, water, and natural resources. And his commitment to environmental reform reached an early peak when he signed the Wilderness Act of 1964, which established the National Wilderness Preservation System. Support for protecting and expanding wilderness areas had been building steadily for nearly a decade. Persons such as Howard Zahniser of the Wilderness Society, David Brower of the Sierra Club, and noted western author Wallace Stegner had spoken widely concerning the concept of wilderness. Stegner's "Wilderness Letter" of 1960, identifying wilderness as the "Geography of Hope," had captured the attention of growing numbers of environmentalists. Zahniser drafted much of the 1964 bill, which went through more than sixty drafts before Congress passed the final version.

The Wilderness Act set aside 9.1 million acres for wilderness sites and established a system by which other areas could come under wilderness protection. Nearly all of the new wilderness areas were situated in the West, with two million acres each in California and Wyoming and about half that amount in each of the states of Montana, New Mexico, and Minnesota. None were within the North Dakota-to-Texas range of states, and only about thirty-five thousand acres were situated outside the West. No roads, vehicles, or permanent buildings would be allowed in these areas; only hiking, camping, and fishing were permitted. As Johnson signed the bill, he told onlookers: "If future generations are to remember us with gratitude rather than contempt, we must leave them with something more than the miracle of technology. We must leave them a glimpse of the world as it was in the beginning, not just after we got through with it." Johnson would follow up this initial environmental legislation with other important measures later on.

When Johnson announced his Great Society slogan in spring 1964, he made space for Native Americans in the War on Poverty. As Native American scholar

Donald Fixico notes in his book, *Indian Resilience and Rebuilding*, Johnson made a place for "Indian civil rights ... [and] in the eyes of indigenous population, Indian rights were more important than civil rights." When Johnson became president, he supported what the Kennedy administration had done to end termination policies and to encourage Indian self-determination. In a conference in Washington, D.C., focused on American Indians, Johnson's secretary of the interior Stewart Udall told the gathering of Indian leaders that the War on Poverty would provide special aids for Native Americans. Udall and other government leaders at the conference were convinced that the gathering displayed a "new determination to help our Indian people help themselves to achieve the very highest that they can achieve."

Johnson's War on Poverty czar Sargent Shriver also made clear that programs under the Economic Opportunity Act (EOA) would not overlook Indian needs. He testified before a Senate hearing in June 1964, telling the senators "we expect broad participation [in the EOA] by Indians and tribal communities all across the nation. . . . Every aspect of this bill can be brought to focus on Indian poverty." Before long, tribal peoples were establishing community action groups, welcoming Head Start funds, and participating in Job Corps, Neighborhood Youth Corps, and VISTA programs. Through his cabinet members and other executive lieutenants, Johnson made sure that Indians participated in the War on Poverty and other Great Society programs. Alongside the rising Red Power movement in the mid-1960s, Johnson continued to be active in support of Native Americans. While launching these important reforms, the president kept his eye on the fall 1964 election.

1964 AND A NEW ADMINISTRATION

The presidential campaign of 1964 carried both immediate and long-range significance. It demonstrated that Johnson, only one year in the White House, proved to be a larger vote-getter than Kennedy was in 1960. The election also propelled Johnson forward with something of a mandate for his domestic plans—the Vietnam War having not yet pushed him off track—during the next four years. In 1964, for the first time in American political history, the Democrats and the Republicans both nominated a western candidate. Although Johnson trounced Republican Barry Goldwater, the election was something of a last hurrah for a candidate strongly and closely linked to the liberal New Deal tradition. The conservative ideas of Goldwater—and later Richard Nixon and Ronald Reagan—coming out of the West, proved to be the trend of the future. Four years later, Nixon's win over Hubert Humphrey and, four years after that, in 1972, his landslide victory over liberal Democrat George McGovern signaled the end of the New Deal liberalism in the White House. The trend in the next two generations of western politics was away from Roosevelt and toward Republican conservatism. Thus, in 1964, the campaigns of Johnson and Goldwater illustrated western political trends, on the one side coming to an end, and on the other just coming on the scene.

Entering the White House in November 1963, Johnson had to begin thinking quickly about campaigning for the presidency a year later. At first he was reluctant, wondering if American voters wanted him, after the Democrats had chosen Kennedy over him in 1960. But his wife, Lady Bird, as well as other intimate advisors, urged Johnson to run, speaking of his need to remain courageous and of the country's needs in tenuous times. But Johnson held back until nearly the last moment before the Democratic National Convention convened in Atlantic City in early August 1964. The previous month, the Republicans, meeting in San Francisco, had nominated Senator Goldwater as their standard-bearer.

The Democrats were happy to hear they would be competing against Goldwater. In their view, he had moved so far to the right that no treasonous Democrats, moderate independents, or Rockefeller Republicans would support him. As Johnson wrote in his presidential memoirs, *The Vantage Point* (1971), "Goldwater moved out of . . . [the] middle and left it to us."

Goldwater's statements during his campaign for the Republican nomination, and later against Johnson for the presidency, captured many headlines. In his acceptance speech in San Francisco, Goldwater told his fellow Republicans "that extremism in defense of liberty is no vice and . . . that moderation in pursuit of justice is no virtue." He also denounced income taxes as an infringement on individual rights, spoke of the possible necessity of sending American troops into foreign lands, and expressed opposition to the federal government's intervening in states to overthrow local social customs. Later in his campaign, his supporters often repeated the slogan, "In your heart, you know he's right." Goldwater's cynical critics grabbed the phrase and translated it into "In your gut, you know he's nuts."

After the nominating conventions, polls showed Johnson far ahead of Goldwater. It might even be a landslide victory. But Johnson campaigned as if he must eke out a close victory. Long, full days of politicking followed other speech- and meeting-filled days. The pollsters were right, however. Johnson smashed Goldwater, winning by sixteen million votes over the Republican candidate, forty-three million votes to twenty-seven million. Equally one-sided was Johnson's win in the electoral vote, 486 to 52. Johnson even surpassed the margin of victory of his hero, FDR, in the election of 1936. In his huge win, Johnson captured every western state, save Goldwater's Arizona. Of major importance, Johnson's landslide carried over into the congressional elections, where the Democrats would now enjoy a 295–140 margin in the House and 68–32 in the Senate. The Democratic president and Congress were ready for action.

After his landslide victory over Goldwater, Johnson was poised to turn full attention to his Great Society and its numerous programs. In the meantime, an ugly serpent was crawling into the president's Eden—the rising conflict in Vietnam. During the previous administration, President Kennedy had waffled on what to do in Southeast Asia. When Communist guerrillas (the Viet Cong) began to rise up in South Vietnam, Kennedy greatly expanded the number of U.S. "advisors" from one thousand to sixteen thousand. He did not send ground troops, however. In fact, some thought Kennedy planned to withdraw from the area if he were reelected in 1964. Before his death, Kennedy had stated, "It is their war. They are the ones who have to win it or lose it . . . the people of Vietnam against the Communists." The hands-off policy was only partially true. The Kennedy administration had meddled in South Vietnam politics, helping to encourage a coup that led to the assassination of the South Vietnamese leader but bringing to power an unsuccessful replacement.

In the first months of his administration, Johnson was uncertain about a Vietnam policy, wavering between keeping out of the rising conflict and sending in the marines, as the hawkish Senator Goldwater had urged. The trend of events did not look good, with the Viet Cong and North Vietnamese seeming to gain the upper hand. Then, in early August, a hazy report indicated that the North Vietnamese had attacked the U.S. destroyer *Maddox* in the Tonkin Gulf region. Perhaps another attack came two or three days later. The reports were not clear. Nor did Johnson tell the public that South Vietnam, with U.S. verbal support, had raided North Vietnamese coastal sites before the firing on the *Maddox*. On the evening of August 4, Johnson told the nation that the attack (attacks) was (were) unprovoked. Three days later, Congress passed the Tonkin Gulf resolution that, one Johnson advisor asserted, was "a blank-check authorization for further action." Only two members of the entire Congress—Democratic senators Wayne Morse of Oregon and Ernest Gruening of Alaska—voted against the resolution.

In early 1965, Johnson was no longer indecisive. The United States launched Operation Rolling Thunder, with air raids over North Vietnam; in March marines were on the ground. For the next three years, Johnson and his political and military advisors escalated the war and predicted eventual victory. By the end of 1965, 180,000 U.S. troops were in Vietnam; 400,000 at the end of 1966; 470,000 late in

1967; and 550,000 in 1968. Not only did the war become a quagmire of uncertain goals, rising opposition, and political division; Vietnam sidetracked and clearly stalled much of Johnson's Great Society and poverty programs. The president soon found he could not have both guns *and* butter; the mounting costs of guns stole away the needed funds and support for butter. Tragically, for the remainder of his presidency, Johnson, bogged down in the morass of an expanding and unsuccessful war, found huge difficulties in keeping his domestic war on track.

Still, there were major achievements ahead, ones that would impact the American West. None was more important to the nation and large groups of rising Americans than the Voting Rights Act of 1965. Seeing that blacks were still not experiencing all the rights he wanted for them, Johnson pushed ahead to ensure that their basic voting rights were being protected. In January 1965, the president told acting attorney general Nicholas Katzenbach to prepare the "goddamndest, toughest voting rights bill you can devise." Johnson hesitated, however, in telling Martin Luther King that he (Johnson) could not "get a voting rights bill through in this next session of Congress." When Johnson delayed, King took his case for a voting rights bill to the streets. Buoyed by polls that revealed 95 percent of Americans agreed that a voting rights bill should be passed, King decided that a march to Selma, Alabama, a citadel of obstructionist segregationists, would serve as a pressure point on the president. Only 2 percent of the blacks in the Selma area were registered voters, even though they made up 58 percent of the population. Violent, bloody marches followed, with city police and state troopers belting the marchers with billy clubs and whips. Two marches to Selma proved unsuccessful, the third finally achieved the marchers' goal of entering the town.

That was enough for national television audiences and President Johnson. A prizewinning movie, *Selma,* released fifty years later, pictured Johnson as very dilatory in moving ahead with the voting rights legislation. Not so. True, he began doubting that he could get the desired legislation through Congress, but after the tragic incidents in Selma, the president moved forward quickly and diligently. A week after events in Selma, Johnson spoke to Congress, calling for a new voting rights act. It would close the loopholes in the Civil Rights Act of 1964 and provide federal guidelines for voter registration if state and local boards discriminated on the basis of race or color. No more literacy tests, no more decisions by southern judges sympathetic to segregation. Any changes in voting practices had to be "pre-cleared" with the Justice Department or the federal district court in the District of Columbia. If any district or region had less than 50 percent of its voting-age residents taking part in the election of 1964 or registered to vote, its voting procedures had to be revised, and new ones without illegal restrictions or discriminatory measures implemented. Although southern and right-wing opposition denounced the voting rights bill as something out of Hitler's regime, the legislation easily passed the Senate and House, and Johnson signed it on August 6, 1965.

JOHNSON LOOKS WEST

Historians have, as they should, emphasized the scene-changing impact of the Voting Rights Act on the South. It transformed large sections of the South's political landscape, with the Democrats, especially those supporting voting rights, losing much of their supremacy and conservative Republicans who opposed the act gaining new ascendency. More white southerners registered, probably to keep political power in their hands, but the largest change came in the mounting numbers of blacks voting for the first time.

Unfortunately, when scholars emphasize the impact of the Voting Rights Act of 1965 on the South, they miss its impact on the West. The fallout on the region west of the Mississippi deserves more attention. In the first place, as African American scholar Quintard Taylor points out in his book, *In Search of the Racial Frontier: African Americans in the American West, 1528–1990*, the West's "multiracial population moved civil rights beyond 'black and white.'" Two examples illuminate Taylor's apt observation. In San Antonio, for instance, the large Chicano population added a sociocultural ingredient missing, for the most part, in the Deep South. Simultaneously, the Asian American presence in Seattle, broadened a racial mix at variance from that in the South. Although neither the Chicanos in San Antonio nor the Asians in Seattle were strongly supportive of African Americans, they too felt the stings of discrimination and benefitted from Johnson's civil rights and voting rights measures in 1964–65.

The political journey of Barbara Jordan, African American legislator in Texas and later in the U.S. House, also illustrates the impact of Johnson reforms. Jordan had tried twice, previous to 1966, to win a seat in the Texas legislature, but not until the Voting Rights Act changed black registration numbers in the Houston area was she able to gain a seat in the Texas senate. She was the first African American woman to serve in the Texas senate and, later, the first black woman from Texas to take a seat in the U.S. Congress. In 1972, she gave the keynote address at the Democratic National Convention. Jordan's rise in Texas, where the largest block of African Americans in a western state resided, epitomized what Johnson's voting rights legislation could do in changing the face of western politics.

Experiences for African Americans in California during the Johnson years were dramatically different from those in Texas. The second largest black population in the West lived in California. African Americans, mainly from the South, had flooded into California during World War II to take advantage of new wartime jobs. By the 1960s, the dream of a rosy future had turned into a nightmare of dissatisfaction.

On August 11, five days after President Johnson had signed the Voting Rights Act, the horrendous Watts riot broke out. When a white policeman attempted to arrest an intoxicated young black man, a violent battle erupted. For nearly a week, shootings, lootings, and numerous other violent conflicts convulsed the Watts area. More than thirty persons, primarily African Americans, were killed, and damages in excess of $40 million resulted from the rioting. President Johnson, dismayed and puzzled about the violent outbreak, established a commission to study the reasons behind it. That group, as well as others examining the outbreak, concluded that racism, ruffians, poverty, and overt discrimination were at the root of the violent days. Johnson's civil rights and voting rights legislation addressed some of the issues facing blacks, but residential, occupational, and income problems were unaddressed dilemmas that quickly added fuel to the civil conflicts raging in Watts in August 1965.

Other near-contemporary happenings in California did not grab Johnson's attention. In October 1966, two young black men, Huey Newton and Bobby Seale, organized the Black Panthers in Oakland. Alienated from the civil rights programs of Lyndon Johnson and Martin Luther King, which they thought much too tepid and tied to white liberals, Newton and Seale called for radical measures to quickly turn around black lives in the depressed inner-city areas. They would make war, literally, on police and other officials who tried to blunt their controversial actions. Newton helped explain his actions by expressing his anger toward California public schools, which, he said, had tried "to [rob] me of my worth . . . and nearly killed my urge to inquire."

Conversely, the Black Panthers also tried to improve black lives with positive efforts in the ghettos. They provided free meals to children, set up health clinics, and operated alternative school programs. Generally, however, although the group attracted widespread media publicity, they were unable to gather many followers. Their misogynist treatment of black women as primarily sex objects and their castigation of more-moderate middle-class blacks largely estranged these two groups. By the end of Johnson's administration, the Panthers were dwindling in numbers and influence. Their quick rise and equally sudden decline had not caught the notice of the president.

Nor did Johnson pay much heed to another, much larger and more successful group in California—César Chávez and the United Farm Workers. In the 1960s and 1970s, the short, quiet, but committed and indefatigable Chávez became the most-well-known Chicano in California—and in the entire country. Speaking especially for U.S. migrant farmworkers (and not so much for undocumented laborers coming from Mexico), Chávez was an organizer par excellence. He and his leading lieutenant, the vivacious and assertive Chicana, Dolores Huerta, led Chicanos on several marches, boycotts, and fasts to gain higher wages, the right to organize as a union, and other fringe benefits. In 1965, Chávez and his organization began a risky venture. They took on a behemoth—the California grape industry—in a five-year boycott. In 1970, they could claim victory when the growers accepted negotiations and gave in on wages and organizing rights. Later, when the more conservative Ronald Reagan won the governor's chair in California, Chávez and his followers found things much more difficult.

In different parts of the West, other Chicano leaders were rising up. In Texas, José Angel Gutiérrez launched a Chicano political party. In Colorado, Rodolfo "Corky" Gonzales attacked the inequities he saw in urban barrios. In New Mexico, Reies López Tijerina organized a movement to recapture lands that Mexicans and Mexican Americans had lost to Anglos after the Mexican-American War. None of these Chicano leaders won the explicit support of President Johnson; nor did he mention them in his presidential memoirs. Robert Kennedy, however, flew to California and joined Chávez on the last day of the fast.

That so much energetic action and discontent emanated out of California should not be surprising. Since the 1920s, the state had been awash in persistent changes flooding into the state. More than a million people had immigrated to the state in the 1920s; they continued to come as Arkies and John Steinbeck's Okies in the Depression; and tidal waves of newcomers arrived in the 1940s and thereafter to work in aircraft, shipping, and other military-related industries. By the early 1960s, California had surpassed New York as the most populous state. These continuing waves of immigrants from other states, from Mexico, and later from Asia meant that many—if not most—Californians had not put down their roots before another huge crest of immigrants pummeled them. California was ripe for discontent—and lots of it.

The yeasty sociocultural movements of "the sixties" found fertile ground in California during Lyndon Johnson's presidency. Anxiety, unhappiness, and anger blossomed and spread like noxious weeds. Rarely were the discontents well organized, clearly intentional, or long-lasting; but, for the most part, they dealt with issues, ideas, and attitudes that were fanning out across the country. Some of the most important uprisings first came on the scene in California and then went blowing in the wind across the country.

Emboldened by the "reform spirit" that was sweeping through the nation and rising up in Black Power, Brown Power, and Red Power movements among blacks, Chicanos, and Native Americans, students also began to organize. Upset about their lack of "rights" on university campuses, the distance between political promises and poverty-stricken realities, sickened especially by the carnage in Vietnam, and fearing the draft, students rallied against university officials, police, and politicians. The SDS (Students for a Democratic Society) and other New Left organizations represented a smaller, more radical contingent of student activists. The great majority seemed satisfied to engage in teach-ins, marches, and peaceful protests.

In the West, the University of California, Berkeley, campus became *the* symbol of student activism. Late in 1964, the Free Speech Movement gained center stage at Berkeley when student leader Mario Savio climbed atop a car to shout his views to a throng of students. "There is a time when the operation of the machine becomes so odious," he asserted, that "you've got to put your bodies upon the gears and upon the wheels, upon the levers, upon all the apparatus and you've got to make it stop. And you've got to indicate to the people who run it, to the people who own it, that unless you're free, the machine will be prevented from working at all." Savio and his fiery coconspirator Bettina Aptheker, the daughter of a well-known Marxist American historian, mocked their opponents: Johnson's government, university officials, and perhaps their parents and older Americans as well. Similar student revolts convulsed campuses at the University of California, Santa Barbara; San Francisco State; Stanford; and others across the West. As the war in Vietnam escalated from 1965 to 1968, so too did student activism in the West—and throughout the country.

Johnson's Vietnam policies also ran into growing opposition among western political leaders. Early on, only Senators Morse and Gruening had voted against the Tonkin Gulf Resolution, but other congressional dissenters began to surface. In September 1965, Senator J. William Fulbright of Arkansas expressed strong reservations about Johnson's handling of the escalating war in Vietnam. Johnson was upset by Fulbright's becoming a "dove" (antiwar) rather than remaining with the "hawks" (prowar). As public opinion polls revealed the American public's growing dissatisfaction with Johnson's Vietnam War policies, other western congressmen became "peaceniks." In November 1966, Missouri senator Stuart

Symington, previously a hawk, was now "thinking of getting off the train soon," that is, dropping his support of Johnson. In early 1967, Johnson's ratings had fallen below 50 percent positive in polls, and the Missouri governor informed Johnson he would lose by one hundred thousand votes if he were now to run in that state, despite his landslide victory there in 1964. Mark Hatfield, "Oregon's dove," had been a lone voice against Johnson's Vietnam actions at previous governors' conferences; now in the U.S. Senate, he was speaking out against war measures. South Dakota senator George McGovern added his voice to the criticism of the war. In addition, Senator Mike Mansfield of Montana, who had previously backed Johnson, was now expressing his reservations. When Idaho's influential senator, Frank Church, also roundly criticized Johnson's actions in Vietnam, the president asked him where he got his information. From journalist/writer Walter Lippman, Church replied. Johnson quickly fired back that when Church wanted to build another dam in Idaho (Johnson had pushed for funding Church's dam-building legislation in 1957), he could go to Lippman for the funding. The drumbeat in the West and other regions against Johnson's ill-adventures in Vietnam continued to rise in 1967 and into 1968, leading to Johnson's difficult decision not to run for reelection in 1968.

Johnson's Great Society and poverty-attacking measures ran into increasing political and budgetary difficulties as the criticism of Vietnam mounted. No longer were guns and butter possible; now, as one wag put it, there could be only guns and margarine. Still, despite the conflicts and opposition, Johnson was able to push through some of his desired legislation in Congress. He also used executive orders to put other measures in place.

Several of these bills added to Johnson's self-generated reputation as a "conservation president." Most of the legislation was national in scope but had strong shaping influences on the West. Sickened by the smog he had seen in the Los Angeles area and the urban blight in Texas cities, as well as in other urban areas of the country, Johnson shoved through the Water Quality Act (1965), the Endangered Species Act (1966), and a handful of other acts attacking water and air pollution and protecting endangered species. Johnson wrote later that he had tried to "restore the balance" in nature with this legislation. Even better known were the much-publicized efforts of Lady Bird Johnson in her "Keep America Beautiful" campaign. Lady Bird's efforts helped to clean up the country's highways by reducing the signage clutter along so many roads and freeways. Although not a policy maker, Mrs. Johnson had inspired the president, Congress, and the American public to pay more attention to the pollution and the rural and urban decay that lurked across America's landscapes.

Even though Johnson did not connect forcefully with most other racial/ethnic groups besides African Americans, he did advocate for Native Americans. Red Power advocates and AIM (American Indian Movement), the latter of which was organized in Minnesota in 1968, were too radical for Johnson, but he found ways to push through legislation that aided tribal groups and individual Indians. In 1966, Congress passed, and Johnson signed, the National Historic Preservation Act, which permitted Native Americans to retain or gain control of "their historic artefacts [*sic*]." In addition, the Office of Economic Opportunity, part of Johnson's War on Poverty package, established its own "Indian desk," which assisted Indian communities in building new housing. It also developed Work Incentive projects for reservations in Idaho, New Mexico, Arizona, Montana, and Oklahoma. Most important, in 1968, Johnson called for a new Indian policy that encouraged Indian self-determination in partnership with ongoing financial support from the federal government. This wise, beneficial marriage of self-determination and government aid continues into the present century.

In the heightened activism of the 1960s, women's issues came increasingly to the fore. Equal rights, equal employment, equal pay, and self-determined reproductive rights stirred emotions and grabbed headlines. They did not capture much of President Johnson's attention, however. He made no ongoing, important contacts with women leaders, including leaders of the newly formed NOW (National Organization for Women), which organized in 1966 with Betty Friedan as its first president. Nor did Johnson's wife Lady Bird, or his two daughters, Lynda and Luci, advocate for women's issues. Yet Johnson did, as western women's historian Glenda Riley pointed out in 2007 in *Inventing the American Woman*, appoint "more women to office than any president before or since, with the exception of President William J. Clinton." Johnson also issued Executive Order 11246 in 1965, which, after further amendments, stated that no government contractor could discriminate in regard to race, color, religion, sex, or national origin.

THE FINAL DAYS

The year 1968, Lyndon Baines Johnson's last full year in office, was twelve months of disappointment and decline. On January 30, in a Tet offensive, Viet Cong rebels blasted their way into the American embassy in Saigon, demonstrating how tenuous was the American occupation of South Vietnam. The attack also proved wrong the repeated American promises of impending victories in Southeast Asia. In the next few weeks, the military shortcomings in Vietnam, the rising antiwar protests, increasing media criticism, stalwart congressional opposition, and falling popularity in polls pushed Johnson to make a gut-wrenching decision. He surprisingly announced at the end of March that he would "not accept renomination." Four days later, a sniper assassinated Martin Luther King. Riots raged across the country after King's violent death. Mounting discontent and protest reached another violent peak with the assassination of Robert Kennedy in early June, just after he had won the Democratic primary in California. The increasing political and social chaos exploded at the Democratic National Convention in late August in Chicago. Hubert Humphrey, Johnson's vice president, won the nomination, but limped out of the city, politically wounded by the violence and turmoil of Chicago. Then, in the fall, the resurrected westerner, Richard Nixon, after several political disappointments, bounced back to defeat Humphrey and the Democrats. During the 1968 campaign, Nixon had launched sharp attacks on Johnson's presidency, especially his handling of the Vietnam War.

Johnson left the White House in January 1969, like a beaten dog after a disastrous fight. Returning to his Texas ranch, he was, by turns, disappointed, angry, and depressed. At first, he defended himself against his most vicious critics, but then he turned away. So down was Johnson, according to historian Doris Kearns Goodwin, that he found it difficult to write his presidential memoirs, *The Vantage Point: Perspectives of the Presidency, 1963–1969*, published in 1971. That finished, he turned to a more enjoyable task, diligently—almost obsessively—operating his ranch and taking care of his cattle. Increasingly, he stayed out of the limelight and distanced himself from the American political scene. Failing health led to his death, from another heart attack, on January 22, 1973.

The rush to judgment of Johnson's presidency in the years immediately after his death led to conclusions wobbling between criticism of his missteps in Vietnam and praise for his achievements in Great Society and poverty-addressing domestic measures. Over time, historians and biographers, while keeping in mind the Vietnam tragedy, have turned increasingly to lauding Johnson's memorable role as a reformer.

JOHNSON'S WESTERN LEGACY

Most of Johnson's significant reform policies obviously impacted Americans living west of the Mississippi, even as they shaped the lives of persons residing in other regions. The Civil Rights Act of 1964 and the Voting Rights Act of 1965 greatly influenced the rights of African Americans. Biographer Charles Peters does not exaggerate in asserting that Johnson did "more for African Americans and the cause of civil rights than any president since Abraham Lincoln." Clearly, that impact was strong in the West, where increasing numbers of African Americans were living, but the civil rights legislation also notably altered the lives of Native Americans and Mexican Americans, the great preponderance of whom were in the West.

In similar ways, the War on Poverty programs spilled out over the West. The Job Corps, VISTA, Upward Bound, Head Start, and Community Action programs were national in focus but also markedly affected students and families in the American West. Johnson's Wilderness Act of 1964 particularly focused on the West. The president also pushed through specific legislation to aid Indians and to encourage their self-determination.

In other areas, Johnson's impact on the West was more negative. In making unwise—even if sometimes understandable—decisions about the conflict in Vietnam, he decidedly undermined his own Great Society and War on Poverty efforts. One wonders how much more he might have been able to do with the War on Poverty had the Southeast Asia war not sideswiped his budgets.

The tragedy of Lyndon Baines Johnson is that he allowed the Vietnam War to steal away his attention, presidential energies, and government financing from his valuable reforms in the West and the rest of the United States. His triumph is that, despite the tragedy, he accomplished much in addressing the country's needs and helped so many Americans—in the West, and throughout the rest of the nation.

FOR FURTHER READING

Andrew, John A., III. *Lyndon Johnson and the Great Society.* Chicago: Ivan R. Dee, 1998.

Beschloss, Michael R. *Taking Charge: The Johnson White House Tapes, 1963–1964.* New York: Simon & Schuster, 1997.

Bornet, Vaughn Davis. *The Presidency of Lyndon B. Johnson.* Lawrence: University Press of Kansas, 1984.

Bullion, John. *Lyndon B. Johnson and the Transformation of American Politics.* New York: Pearson, 2007.

Caro, Robert A. *The Passage of Power: The Years of Lyndon Johnson.* Vol. 4. New York: Knopf, 2012.

Caroli, Betty Boyd. *Lady Bird and Lyndon: The Hidden Story of a Marriage That Made a President.* New York: Simon & Schuster, 2015.

Conkin, Paul K. *Big Daddy from the Pedernales: Lyndon Baines Johnson*. Boston: Twayne, 1986.

Dallek, Robert. *Flawed Giant: Lyndon Johnson and His Times, 1961–1973*. New York: Oxford University Press, 1985.

———. *Lyndon B. Johnson: Portrait of a President*. New York: Penguin Books, 2004.

Darman, Jonathan. *Landslide: LBJ and Ronald Reagan at the Dawn of a New America*. New York: Random House, 2014.

Farber, David. *The Age of Great Dreams: America in the 1960s*. New York: Hill and Wang, 1994.

Fernlund, Kevin J. *Lyndon B. Johnson and Modern America*. Norman: University of Oklahoma Press, 2009.

Hodgson, Godfrey. *JFK and LBJ: The Last Two Great Presidents*. New Haven: Yale University Press, 2015.

Isserman, Maurice, and Michael Kazin. *America Divided: The Civil War of the 1960s*. New York: Oxford University Press, 2000.

Johnson, Lady Bird. *A White House Diary*. New York: Holt, Rinehart and Winston, 1970.

Johnson, Lyndon Baines. *The Vantage Point: Perspectives of the Presidency, 1963–1969*. New York: Holt, Rinehart and Winston, 1971.

Kearns [Goodwin], Doris. *Lyndon Johnson and the American Dream*. New York: St. Martin's Press, 1976.

Leuchtenburg, William E. *The White House Looks South: Franklin D. Roosevelt, Harry S. Truman, Lyndon B. Johnson*. Baton Rouge: Louisiana State University Press, 2005.

Miller, Merle. *Lyndon: An Oral Biography*. New York: Ballantine Books, 1980.

Patterson, James T. *Grand Expectations: The United States, 1945–1974*. New York: Oxford University Press, 1996.

Peters, Charles. *Lyndon B. Johnson*. New York: Times Books, 2010.

Public Papers of the Presidents of the United States: Lyndon B. Johnson, 1963–69. 10 vols. Washington, DC: U.S. Government Printing Office, 1965–70.

Wilson, Robert H., et al. *LBJ's Neglected Legacy: How Lyndon Johnson Reshaped Domestic Policy and Government*. Austin: University of Texas Press, 2015.

Woods, Randall B. *LBJ: Architect of American Ambition*. Baton Rouge: Louisiana State University Press, 2005.

Zelizer, Julian E. *The Fierce Urgency of Now: Lyndon Johnson, Congress, and the Battle for the Great Society*. New York: Penguin Books, 2015.

JAMES E. "JIMMY" CARTER JR., 1977–1981

LC-USZ62-13039

Chapter 9

JAMES E. "JIMMY" CARTER JR.
DEALING WITH A DISTANT WEST

One month after Jimmy Carter entered the White House in 1977, he made a momentous decision that began his strained relationship with the American West and with Congress. Convinced that nearly twenty water and dam projects, several of which were located in the West, were largely congressional pork-barrel schemes, he moved to eliminate presidential support and funding for them. The outcry from Congress was immediate and shrill. The new president had stepped on the toes of many westerners in Congress.

This presidential decision, though not without considerable merit, was particularly unwise if Carter wanted smooth relations with Congress and the West. Some western members of the U.S. House and Senate, in whose districts the dam and water projects were located, barked back at the new president. Rather than meet with the western legislators and work out a compromise before his announcement, Carter had unilaterally done what he considered "right." Those who came to view Carter as high-handed and a hopeless moralist point to this decision in February 1977 as prime evidence for their conclusions. Journalist Marc Reisner, in *Cadillac Desert: The American West and Its Disappearing Water*, viewing the act in light of Carter's entire presidency, was even more critical: the action illustrated Carter's "typical capacity for mind-boggling political naivete." Carter, even while understanding some of the complexities and fallout from his decision, was still convinced many years later that he had made the correct decision. However one viewed the controversy, it signified that Carter, one of our presidents most interested in "doing the right thing," had gotten off on the wrong foot with Congress and the American West.

BEFORE THE WHITE HOUSE

Jimmy Carter's roots in his native South were as deep as any U.S. president's in a home region. Those strong ties proved a mixed blessing for Carter in the White

House: tradition, stability, and southern experiences provided durable foundations; but they also limited Carter's understandings of other regions and their political and cultural traditions. Even though stationed for a few months in the West while in the service, Carter knew little about the region. Nor during his four years in the White House did he remedy this lack of knowledge. Unfortunately, on several occasions Carter's distance from westerners undermined his efforts to win over the West as his presidency unfolded.

Carter's ties were strongest to the rural, agricultural South. Born on October 10, 1924, in Plains, Georgia, Carter grew up, was educated in public schools, and entered his adult years while living in Plains. His father, James Earl Carter, who exerted more influence on Jimmy than any other person, came from a farming, business, and landowning background. His mother, Bessie Lillian Gordy, trained as a nurse, was notably forward-looking on race relations, a perspective her oldest son came to share. After graduation from high school in 1941 and a short stint at a regional college, Jimmy was appointed to the U.S. Naval Academy, where he graduated in 1946 and shortly thereafter married Rosalynn Smith, a Plains girl he had known since childhood. That match gave Carter an extraordinarily supportive marriage and an increasingly valuable political helpmate. In 1952, Carter was accepted into a nuclear submarine program and stayed in the Navy for another year.

The death of James Earl Carter in 1953 changed Jimmy's life. Jimmy and Rosalynn, much to her disappointment, returned to Plains to take charge of the Carter holdings. After stabilizing the family business, Jimmy turned to politics. In 1962, in a tightly contested vote, he was elected to the Georgia state legislature. Eight years later, he was elected the state's governor. After only two years in the governor's chair, Carter made the unexpected decision to run for the U.S. presidency. The long-range plan worked well, with Carter defeating Gerald Ford in 1976 in a close election.

Carter's victory in 1976 may have been his most surprising achievement. In the national political shadows in 1972, having served only two years as Georgia's governor, and not listed among the most likely Democratic presidential possibilities, Carter nonetheless announced his candidacy in late 1972 and launched what proved to be a superbly organized, enthusiastic, and indefatigable campaign for the Democratic nomination. Ironically, the very successful ingredients of the plan for winning the presidency in 1976 proved to be an inadequate strategy once in the presidency.

The run for the White House revealed Carter's manifold strengths. Ambitious (perhaps driven, some thought), supremely self-confident, extraordinarily well organized, and tireless, Jimmy Carter, his family, and a small group of loyal friends and advisors began, in December 1972, to plan for a presidential contest nearly four years in the future. In several ways, the campaign started from zero: Carter was virtually unknown nationally, southerners suffered from a clear regional bias against them, Carter supporters lacked the necessary finances, and Carter wanted for national Democratic connections. Still, his almost magical campaigning strategy, accompanied by one or two strokes of luck, overcame the major drawbacks he faced at the outset of the campaign.

Carter made several key decisions between 1972 and 1976 that worked well. He decided to cooperate most closely with a team of advisors, largely from Georgia, who had helped him in his gubernatorial contests. He would rely heavily on his family, particularly his wife, Rosalynn, his sons and their wives, and his mother and his sisters to fan out across the country to meet people, get his name before hundreds of thousands, and make important political, financial, and intellectual connections. This small cadre of energetic volunteers, the core of Carter loyalists, worked endlessly to boost Carter's recognition and to link him with officials who would support his campaign.

None worked harder than did Carter himself. Stretching out his hand, flashing his wide smile, he greeted newcomers with the same words: "Hello, my name is Jimmy Carter. I'm running for president." He kept his comments at formal and informal gatherings rather general, sometimes labeling his perspective as "benevolent conservatism." Playing on post-Watergate anxieties and distaste, he clarified his background: "I am not from Washington, I do not hold public office, and I am not a lawyer."

Following the suggestion of one of his advisors, Georgian Hamilton Jordan, Carter decided to enter all state primaries. "Our strategy was simple," Carter remembered; "make a total effort all over the country." It was a herculean task that other candidates avoided. Blanketing Iowa and New Hampshire with visits by his family. his advisors and himself, Carter did surprisingly well in states not usually supportive of southern politicians. Next, the win in Florida's primary in March 1976 over Alabama governor George Wallace and Senator Henry "Scoop" Jackson of Washington pushed Carter to the forefront of centrist candidates. When he won again in Pennsylvania, he became the frontrunner and stayed there, despite later primary losses in New Jersey and California to westerners Senator Frank Church of Idaho and Governor Jerry Brown of California. More than anything, Carter's nonstop campaigning and his superb, tireless support team led him to victories over westerners like Jackson, Church, and Brown. Building on his impressive primary wins, Carter gained the nomination on the first ballot of the Democratic National Convention in July. His sudden leap to the front seemed to be a political miracle to many observers.

Carter's Republican opponent in the fall vote, Gerald Ford, had survived a close, bruising battle with California governor Ronald Reagan for the nomination. At first, Carter surged ahead of Ford, largely because of the continuing fallout from Watergate, Ford's pardoning of Nixon, and anti-Republican sentiments in general. But he gradually lost much of his large lead. An unfortunate interview in *Playboy* quoted him as stating that he had "committed adultery in [his] heart many times." No one expected such an unlikely comment from a highly touted evangelical. Carter faltered, too, in the first debate with Ford in the fall. When it looked as if Carter's edge would disappear, Ford slipped badly in the second debate when he declared that there was "no Soviet domination of Eastern Europe and there never will be under a Ford administration." Ford critics had a field day with that blooper, harpooning the president as an innocent abroad, a flawed leader unaware of clear Russian domination. Ford's campaign stumbled, and Carter won a very close election, forty-one million votes to Ford's thirty-nine million, and 297 to 240 electoral votes. Revealingly, in the states west of the Mississippi, Carter won Texas, Minnesota, Missouri, Arkansas, and Hawaii, but did very poorly in Alaska, Idaho, Nebraska, Utah, and Wyoming. Carter would have to woo the West if he wanted the region to back his policies. It was a major lesson that Carter never did learn.

CHALLENGES FOR A NEW PRESIDENT

In January 1977, Carter faced several problems that had emerged in the previous half-dozen years or so. Large numbers of American voters were in a sour mood. Discontent reigned. Controversy over the unsatisfactory ending of the Vietnam War, disgruntled hangover from the tumultuous 1960s and early 1970s, and the stink of Watergate were still in the air. Many Americans continued to wonder if they could trust their leaders after the demise of Vice President Spiro Agnew in 1973 and the disgraceful fall of President Richard Nixon in the Watergate scandal of 1974. In addition, President Gerald Ford's controversial pardoning of Nixon left a deep distrust of their leaders with many Americans.

From 1974 to 1977, Ford had tried to serve as a healer. He thought his pardoning of Nixon in September 1974 would put the Watergate debacle in the past, and the country could move on to better times. But the initial reactions were more negative than positive, with the Republicans losing badly two months later in midterm elections. Ford's popularity had plummeted to 37 percent by January 1975. Critics accused Ford of flip-flopping, of changing his mind on taxes, energy policies, and spending—clear evidence of weak leadership, they said. The inexperienced Ford also had difficulty in foreign affairs. He seemed unable to deal with the hangover from the Vietnam War, particularly in not heading off the Communists' takeover of South Vietnam in 1974. Critics, especially hardnose Senator Henry "Scoop" Jackson of Washington, also thoroughly opposed Ford's efforts at détente with the Russians.

These conflicts in domestic and foreign affairs weighed heavily on Ford in the final days of his administration. And they continued to face Carter as he entered the White House in January 1977.

Westerners, of course, were among the Americans experiencing the challenges that had plagued President Ford and now awaited the new president, Jimmy Carter. Still other region-specific issues were lurking in the West. They, too, had vexed Ford, and would soon Carter.

Westerners were particularly on edge about their water supplies and access to them. They had been for several decades. Although competition for water sources had erupted all over the West as agriculture expanded and urban areas boomed in the twentieth century, none was more contentious than the conflicts over the Colorado River system and central California water. Supreme Court decisions had allocated water resources—fairly, the justices thought—among Arizona, Indian nations, and the largest and thirstiest petitioner, Southern California, but the contest for water continued into the 1960s and 1970s. As Southern Californians by turns begged for and demanded more water, their supporters launched a California Water Project to bring down precious water from the northern part of the state. These competitions were front and center in early 1977.

No less a hot political potato were the clashes over energy supplies and needs. In 1973, when the OPEC (Organization of the Petroleum Exporting Countries) consortium embargoed invaluable shipments of oil to the United States because of its pro-Israel stance and, at the same time, American petroleum production dipped, the country was in trouble. The problem carried forward from the Ford administration to Carter. The western oil states of California, Texas, and Oklahoma were strongly impacted. Other oil shale, coal, and uranium states especially felt the energy crunch. Colorado, North Dakota, South Dakota, Montana, Utah, New Mexico, Arizona, and Wyoming, with about 50 percent of the country's coal and uranium, nearly all of its shale oil, and large deposits of oil and natural gas loomed as new areas of decision making about energy development and use at the outset of the Carter presidency.

Bust-and-boom cycles facing farmers were a third challenge for Carter. Difficult times for agriculturists came in the early 1970s, but an extraordinarily large grain sale to Russia in 1972 encouraged farmers about looming demands and markets. Earl Butz, President Nixon's energetic secretary of agriculture, encouraged farmers to plant, fertilize, irrigate, and harvest as never before. But what if the sale to Russia and other needy countries was a demand of the moment, undependable and risky? That question confronted Carter in 1977.

Other western challenges also stood in front of the president. What should he do about federal land policies? Would he expand wilderness areas, sell off public lands? These questions and others surfaced with new rhetorical intensity when they morphed into the so-called Sagebrush Rebellion toward the end of Carter's presidency.

Carter inherited the contentious issue pitting the federal government against state and local governments over land policies. The arguments had begun in the nineteenth century, and the passage of the Taylor Grazing Act (1934) was but one, more recent example of the ongoing controversy. Farmers, ranchers, developers, and advocates of local control wanted the remaining government lands open for state or private control or ownership; conservationists, wilderness advocates, and federal government agencies wanted continuing federal wardship.

Late in Carter's presidency, the conflict escalated to new heights and spilled over into the Reagan presidency. The war heated up in Utah when newly elected Orrin Hatch of Utah introduced a bill in the Senate in 1979 calling for more state control of federally owned lands. President Carter did not support the legislation, and neither did his secretary of the interior Cecil Andrus, but as many as fifteen members of Congress (almost all from the West) cosponsored the bill. The controversy reared up even more in Nevada, where roughly 85 percent of the state's lands were federally owned. In the election of 1980, Republican candidate Ronald Reagan supported Hatch's ideas, calling himself a "rebel" in league with the Sagebrush Rebellion. Carter's position on this controversy coincided with his strong push to conserve wilderness areas throughout the West.

Alongside these environmental debates was the question of Indian rights and self-determination. Out of the activism of the 1960s, a new Red Power movement had quickly gained strength. Then, in early 1973, nearly two hundred armed Indian activists took over the small town of Wounded Knee on the Pine Ridge Reservation in western South Dakota. After a seventy-day occupation and standoff, compromises prevailed, but not until two Indians were killed and a federal marshal severely wounded. Events such as Wounded Knee and the earlier establishment of AIM (American Indian Movement) signaled that Native Americans wanted to be in control of their lives and to see improved conditions on reservations. Those wishes—even demands—were circulating in early 1977.

The judicial branch of the federal government was more involved than the executive branch with Indian affairs during the Carter administration. The Supreme

Court upheld the sovereignty of tribal law over the Constitution in legal matters and guaranteed fishing and treaty rights in other cases—all dealing with the American West. Carter's White House did not sponsor any major new legislation focusing on Native Americans, but he did support Indian self-determination. He also expanded Indian leverage in naming, to a new position, an assistant secretary of the interior for Indian affairs. Carter's first appointment was Forrest J. Gerard, an enrolled member of the Blackfeet tribe. Moreover, the president signed into law the American Indian Religious Freedom Act, with Carter declaring the right of all Indians, Eskimos, Aleuts, and Native Hawaiians "to believe, express, and exercise their traditional religions."

Another shift was also underway in the American West that caught some political observers by surprise. Gradually, beginning with conservative Republican Barry Goldwater's unsuccessful run against the incumbent president, Lyndon Baines Johnson, in 1964, western politics began swinging right in many sectors of the region's political landscape. The election of conservative westerner Richard Nixon in 1968, and his reelection in 1972, provided strong additional evidence of a mounting conservative and Republican force in the West. Not many political observers noticed or commented on this trend at the time. In the first years of his administration, neither Carter nor his advisors acknowledged this political course. Behind the scene, however, the right wing of the Republicans was taking control of the party in several parts of the American West. The startling and unexpectedly large victory of Ronald Reagan over Carter in 1980 proved irrefutable evidence of the victorious swing to the right.

CARTER AT WORK

Jimmy Carter's fateful decision to deny financial support for dams and water projects in February 1977 revealed much about his thinking and his presidential actions. Carter's attempt to block the projects stemmed from his conservative economic position, his desire to balance budgets, and his attempts to end projects he considered environmentally unsound. Unlike liberal Democrats like Senator Edward Kennedy and House Speaker Tip O'Neill, Carter favored holding in check any programs or projects extraordinarily expensive and budget-breaking. As the governor of Georgia, he had been a budget-watcher; among other economies, he had denied support for costly reclamation projects. Now he wanted to follow the same kind of watchful, balanced spending on the national level. Not only were the dam and water projects budget-busters, but most were also, Carter was convinced, environmentally unsound.

Carter was neither blind nor insensitive to what the political fallout might be following his controversial stance on the water projects. As he recorded in his White

House diary, "I know this is going to create a political furor, but it's something that I am committed to accomplish. These projects ultimately would cost at least $5.1 billion, and the country would be better off if none of them were built. It's going to be a pretty touchy legislative fight to get these projects removed permanently."

Even though Carter saw the looming political conflicts, he failed to understand, at the time, how large those contests would be and how much they would strain his relations with Congress. The discontent of westerners not only did not go away, it heightened over the years. As Carter wrote in his *Keeping the Faith: Memoirs of a President* (1982), "None of the leaders in either House [of Congress] supported me." Seeing that enough votes were available to override his threatened veto of a public works bill, Carter relented and signed the bill in early August 1977. A few years later, he considered his compromising a major mistake because the bill contained too many "wasteful items." Plus, his giving in "was accurately interpreted as a weakness on my part." It "was not the worst mistake" he made, he wrote, but he "regretted it as much as any budget decision I made as president."

The discontent on the water and dam issues roiled on. Two months later, Carter, trying to "put out fires," met "with thirty or forty western senators who had been irate about our water policy." The president tried to explain the need to let up on the water projects in order to help keep the budget balanced. At the same time, he expressed his desire "to learn about specific regional problems," even while urging members of Congress to work with him on a program helpful for the entire country. Carter thought members on the Hill "went away assuaged." The following week, he again gathered with "western state members of Congress" to formulate a "comprehensive national policy on water."

The water-and-dam problem did not disappear: in fact, it continued to vex the president throughout his administration. In the summer of 1978, he expressed his discouragement about the differences that divided the Democratic Congress on dams and other issues. Not until much later did Carter come to understand how potent the water conflict had been in shaping—or misshaping—his presidential-congressional relations. Well into retirement he concluded that a "somewhat less rigid approach to these sensitive issues [including the reclamation projects] could have paid rich dividends." Bert Lance, a close friend of the president's and director of Carter's Office of Management and Budget, put a sharper point on Carter's handling, early on, of the water projects: it was, Lance wrote, "the worst political mistake he made, and its effect lasted the rest of his term and doomed any hopes we ever had of developing a good, effective working relationship with Congress."

Another crucial western issue, a matter equally environmentally important but less tied to budget concerns, proved that Carter could work successfully with

Congress. Early in his administration, he declared that he wanted to set aside Alaska wilderness areas in order to protect their rivers, establish national parks, and hold off despoiling developments. But opposition from oil and gas interests, other developers, and even the Alaska congressional delegation stalled legislation embodying Carter's wishes in the first year of his presidency. When Alaska senators Ted Stevens and Mike Gravel seemed to be dragging their feet on what Carter wanted in the Alaska land legislation, he urged his able secretary of the interior, former Idaho governor Cecil Andrus, "to be very strict" in holding the line.

When delays continued through 1978–79, Carter decided to make the Alaska land bill one of his top agenda items in 1980. With matters seemingly stalled in Congress, he instructed Secretary Andrus, following executive provisions in the Antiquities Act of 1906, to set aside and protect large wilderness areas in the sprawling state. By summer and early fall 1980, Carter and Andrus were pushing hard to get Congress to act on a comprehensive wilderness lands act for Alaska.

Carter succinctly summarized the complexities of the issue. "It provoked intense struggles among the state government, private landowners, Indians, Inuits, hunters, fishermen, timber interests, environmentalists, the oil industry, and their highly paid lobbyists in Washington." The hard work finally paid off; a compromise bill passed in Congress on November 12, a week after Carter's defeat for reelection to the White House.

The contents of what was officially named the Alaska National Interest Lands Conservation Act were nothing short of astounding. As one historian has written, the Alaska lands bill was "the most sweeping proposal of its kind ever approved by Congress." The contents of the bill were pathbreaking: seven national parks, four national forests, sixteen national wildlife refuges, and ten national preserves were established. In all, the act set aside conservation areas larger than California and doubled the size of the country's national parks and wildlife refuge areas.

Still, some provisions of the Alaska Land Bill were upsetting to die-hard environmentalists. Wanting to at least examine sources for possible energy development to win an ongoing battle against the OPEC nations, Carter encouraged oil and gas explorations in nearly all the lands being set aside as wilderness areas. That possibility was anathema to environmental purists. Still, realizing that the Carter-supported legislation set aside 104 million acres, or nearly one-third of Alaska, and understanding the difficulties in getting the bill passed as his political support dwindled, later historians and biographers have labeled Jimmy Carter one of the country's leading environmental presidents. For Carter himself, the legislative victory was "among the most gratifying achievements" of his presidency.

Still another environmental issue of the Carter years would, over time, greatly influence the American West. With his background in nuclear engineering, Carter understood better than most Americans the threats of spent nuclear fuel and waste. He urged Congress to pass legislation addressing these dangers. In addition, the chemical disaster in 1977 in the Love Canal area of Niagara Falls, New York, was another spur for Carter to deal with the dangers of nuclear and other toxic wastes. In February 1980, with an executive order, the president established a committee to put together a nuclear waste policy. The following July, he urged congressional leaders to establish a "Superfund to deal with waste dump areas." Carter continued to push for the Superfund legislation up to and after his defeat for reelection in November.

Success on the compromise Superfund bill came in early December. Congress responded with the Comprehensive Environmental Response, Compensation, and Liability Act, which became known as the Superfund. Carter signed the legislation on December 11, 1980. Although the Superfund bill focused more on chemical misuses and spills, it motivated westerners and other Americans to think more creatively and consistently about nuclear wastes so evident at western sites such as Hanford, Washington; Los Alamos, New Mexico; and Yucca Mountain, Nevada. To the disappointment of some environmentalists, the Superfund bill did not cover oil spills.

Carter dealt with other concerns significant to western environments. In April 1977, he signed a bill to control strip mining. The next year, in February, the president put his name on the Endangered American Wilderness Act, which added 1.3 million acres to protected wilderness areas. Throughout his presidency, Carter exhorted Americans to be more conscious of their and the world's endangered environments. Toward the end of his administration, he summed up his attitudes on the subject: "From the perspective of space our planet has no national boundaries," he wrote. "It is very beautiful, but it is also very fragile. And it is the special responsibility of the human race to preserve it." Even though the most enthusiastic environmentalists thought Carter had not pushed valiantly enough against dam builders and petroleum and mineral exploiters, others saluted him as a superb environmentalist. Reviewing Carter's achievements in dealing with environmental challenges, including several that were immensely important to residents of the West, Senator Gaylord Nelson of Wisconsin, a founder of Earth Day, praised Carter as "the greatest environmental president the country ever had."

Overlapping Carter's environmental policies were his diligent actions addressing energy challenges. Carter's experiences in his prepresidential years, as an officer on a nuclear-powered submarine and a tightfisted governor of Georgia, inclined him toward thoughtful, budget-balancing energy policies. Plus, the entire country, beset by the obstructionist actions of the OPEC nations and by its own growing thirst for energy, demanded that its leadership think about rising energy costs and alternative energy options. Much more than his predecessor, Gerald Ford, or his successor, Ronald Reagan, Jimmy Carter focused on energy plans and decisions. Yet, despite his concentrated attention, easy solutions seemed beyond his grasp.

Carter lost little time in placing his intentions on energy policy before the American people. Two weeks into his presidency, Carter appeared on national television. Dressed in a cardigan sweater and urging his fellow Americans to turn down their thermostats, he promised his listeners a comprehensive energy policy. It would be two-pronged: (1) deal with the Arab oil embargo and erratic policies; and (2) cut consumption and/or increase production in the United States. Carter realized, however, that his goal of establishing a cabinet-level department of energy and launching a comprehensive program might "be . . . his most important domestic challenge." Or, as he noted after leaving the presidency, his attempts at moving the Congress and country toward a sustainable energy program was "like chewing on a rock that lasted the whole four years" of his administration.

In mid-April 1977, Carter brought elements of his energy policies into focus. He told a nationwide audience that his energy program would be the "moral equivalent of war, except that we will be uniting our efforts to build and not to destroy." He would be working with James Schlesinger, whom the president had named to head up his energy program and who later became a cabinet secretary when a department of energy was established the following August. Schlesinger, working in secret, would have ninety days to formulate a comprehensive energy proposal that the president could support and that would boost Americans' confidence in a fast-acting chief executive. Within the allotted three months, Schlesinger and the president came up with what was named the National Energy Plan.

The new plan aimed at several goals, all of which would have general or specific impact on the American West. Higher prices on oil and natural gas would be allowed, in the hope that this decision would help consumers understand the need for less consumption and more production. The federal government would more closely regulate high-energy users, provide incentives for energy conservation, and fund additional research on alternative energy sources. Even more controversial were the Schlesinger/Carter decisions to keep federal control on natural-gas pricing rather than to deregulate the prices, as Carter had promised. Equally complex were the stipulations on oil pricing, which allowed the central government to control pricing but also instituted several price levels for consumption and returned taxes on oil usage to the public. Critics thought Carter was a duplicitous waffler, keeping White House control while still speaking of deregulation. One wag said Carter could never be placed on Mount Rushmore because there was insufficient room for a two-headed president.

Carter understood some of the pushback that would occur when he launched his energy plan. Still, he was convinced circumstances demanded change. About 50 percent of the country's oil supply—nearly nine million barrels daily—came from an accelerating demand and from foreign sources. The president noted that the United States was the only leading nation of the world that did not have an organized, specific energy plan. He would provide that plan, even if it meant political fallout. And it did.

The most vociferous opposition to Carter's energy bill in Congress came from oil- and natural-gas-producing states, several of which were in the West. Oil and gas lobbyists in those states pressured state representatives in the Senate and House to vote for deregulation, allowing prices in a worldwide free market to regulate themselves. The companies failed to realize, even though Carter pointed out their mistaken notions, that no such free market existed; the OPEC nations, by controlling a large share of the world's oil supply, were holding hostage developed countries such as the United States with their control of oil prices.

Other major problems divided the Senate, where powerful committee chairmen Russell Long of Louisiana and Scoop Jackson of Washington clashed and refused to compromise on their own energy plans. Throughout the final months of 1977 and well into 1978, Carter tried to get members of the Senate to support his complicated, but comprehensive energy plan. For varied reasons, other conservatives and liberals from the West, including Paul Laxalt (Nevada), Barry Goldwater (Arizona), and George McGovern (South Dakota), opposed the several, separate energy bills in the Senate.

Carter moved more directly on his energy legislation as 1978 wore on. Convinced that oil and gas interests were twisting congressional arms, Carter urged Democratic leaders (and a few Republicans who would support him) in the House and Senate to coordinate efforts to turn back the lobbyists and pass the energy bills. The differences among legislators on Capitol Hill, particularly in the Senate, stalled combined efforts as much as the delaying tactics of the lobbyists. The House finally passed Carter's energy bill by the closest of margins, 207 to 205, in October 1978. Two days later, the Senate, which had divided the energy legislation into five separate bills, also passed these bills. Senators had wrangled, primarily, over the question of deregulation of natural gas prices. A few days later, Carter signed the energy package. Although the congressional bill, as Carter wrote later, encompassed only "about 60–65 percent of the energy savings we had projected earlier," he considered his energy legislation one of the major achievements of his administration. To Carter's disappointment—even disgust—subsequent presidents, particularly Ronald Reagan, reversed or ended some of Carter's energy policies.

CHALLENGES FOR CARTER

Carter's position as a southern, moderate Democrat had helped land him in the White House, but his divergent viewpoints also brought on major challenges. One of these challenges was linked to Carter's connections to the West. Even though his defense considerations were of less moment than his environmental and energy policies in dealing with the West, they were nonetheless an important consideration. Carter's defense policies owed a good deal to his background as well as to prevailing Cold War attitudes.

Carter had enjoyed his experiences at the Naval Academy and serving onboard a nuclear-powered submarine. Unlike many Democratic leaders, he entered the White House with a very positive attitude toward the military; he wanted to make sure defense budgets were sufficiently large to provide more-than-adequate protection against Cold War opponents. Only when the military budget threatened to throw his entire budget off track and bring on floods of red ink did Carter back away from adding to defense spending.

The tensions between balanced budgets and the push for a B-1 bomber program had special implications for the American West. The military-industrial complex that had mushroomed after its birth in the West in Franklin Roosevelt's World War II policies needed a healthy budget to be kept alive. Cold War pressures to keep ahead of the Russians were just the fuel the war-related industries needed, particularly those scattered up and down the West Coast, but also through the Southwest, and in various military installations sprinkled widely across the West. The plan to build a fleet of B-1 bombers would provide exactly the kind of financial support plane-building companies wanted.

Plans for a B-1 bomber followed a circuitous route. As early as the 1960s, planners, deciding that the B-52 lacked what American leaders wanted in their bombers, called for a new kind of long-range, low-flying strategic bomber. Several designs were produced, and proposals put before aircraft-building companies such as Boeing, General Dynamics, and North American Rockwell. Delays continued, with costs spiraling out of sight. No previous president and no Congress had yet made a final decision. Carter did, in the negative. He had hinted what he would do when, during the election of 1976, he stated forthrightly, "The B-1 bomber is an example of a proposed system which should not be funded and would be wasteful of taxpayers' dollars."

Carter announced at the end of June 1977 that the United States would not build the B-1—because of its costliness and questionable effectiveness. In this difficult decision, the president had the support of his effective secretary of defense Harold Brown, who had been president of the prestigious California Institute of Technology before he joined Carter's cabinet. A majority of Congress seemed also to agree with Carter's rejection of the B-1.

But some influential congressmen dissented. The hawkish Senator Scoop Jackson, who alternatively tormented and buoyed Carter with his erratic statements, spoke for Boeing in opposing Carter's cancellation. Representative Robert Dornan, a Republican from California, voiced other discontents of Cold Warriors bent on a stronger—and more expensive—defense budget. Following Carter's decision, Dornan retorted, "They're breaking out the vodka and caviar in Moscow." Later, Carter expressed his deep chagrin when his successor, Ronald Reagan, reversed Carter's decision on the B-1.

Carter was convinced that other, better offensive and defensive weapons could be put in place. They must not be budget-destroyers, however. One of the weapons that caught Carter's attention was the MX (missile experimental) system. Again, Cold War anxiety pushed presidents and Congresses toward some kind of missile system that could protect the United States and possibly demolish strategic sites in Russia. Changing times, costs, and conflicting opinions about the best system stalled decisions—and actions.

In 1979–80, Carter announced a plan to place a huge MX system in the Basin West, chiefly in western Utah and eastern Nevada. Spread over a sparsely populated area roughly the size of Pennsylvania, the sprawling system would honeycomb these arid lands with an astounding network of underground tunnels. To avoid detection and destruction, nuclear missiles could be transported from tunnel to tunnel via subterranean rail tracks. Not surprisingly, the fantastic system, a kind of underground Star Wars, would cost an estimated budget-bruising $100 billion. Moreover, it would bring in thousands of newcomers into isolated western areas, threatening to overthrow established social patterns and dry up already threatened water supplies.

Carter, the engineer and steadfast opponent of the Russians, strongly supported the MX plan. A surprising group of opponents to Carter's incredible idea quickly surfaced. Westerners had not griped much about earlier nuclear facilities established from the 1940s to the 1960s, but the MX idea spawned immediate reactions. Some critics worried about escalating cancer rates in nuclear areas. Other naysayers spoke out on environmental threats to western lands and the atmosphere. Even the conservative-trending Latter-day Saints (the Mormons) criticized the possible social and environmental disruptions that would likely follow the MX installations. Because of the rising opposition, the missile plan stumbled. Then, in an increasingly familiar pattern in the early 1980s, Ronald Reagan withdrew his support for the MX system and moved in other directions with his Cold War defense measures.

WESTERN FOES AND FRIENDS

Perhaps Carter's closest contacts with the American West came more through people than policies. Some of these personal connections emerged during Carter's gubernatorial period, some in the election of 1976, and still others during his presidency. Some were decidedly negative, others positive and beneficial for both parties.

While governor of Georgia and attending national governors' conventions, Carter met Cecil Andrus, governor of Idaho. That friendship blossomed and led to Carter's asking Andrus to serve as his secretary of the interior. A low-key, dependable administrator, Andrus was a loyal lieutenant and served all four years of Carter's administration. During Carter's challenges on environmental and energy questions, Andrus was a bulwark of support. A symbol of their warm friendship came when the president, Rosalynn, and daughter Amy traveled with the Andruses down the Salmon River (the "River of No Return") for a few days in Idaho.

Carter's spirited contests with leading western politicians in the 1976 presidential campaign shaped his relations with them during the next four years. The most influential of these was Henry "Scoop" Jackson of Washington, who also hungered and thirsted for the White House. As strong-willed and ambitious as Carter, Jackson carried decision-shaping powers as a senior senator. Ironically, Carter's contact with Jackson had begun with obvious friendship: he had nominated Jackson for president at the Democratic Convention in 1972. Things seemed to fall apart after the vigorous, hard-fought campaign of 1976. A hawkish liberal Democrat, Jackson was decidedly pro-Jewish and anti-Soviet, often disagreeing with Carter's diplomatic initiatives. Frustrated with Jackson's lack of support and know-it-all attitude, Carter declared that Jackson thought he "knew everything that was going to happen five or six years before it did happen"—and that Jackson denigrated any ideas different from his own.

Frank Church, the forceful senator from Idaho also competed for the Democratic nomination in 1976. Entering the campaign late, he did well in the western primaries but was not strong enough to head off the Carter steamroller. Competition between the two continued during the next four years. Church, still flexing his aspiring presidential muscles, challenged several of the president's major policies. As chairman of the powerful Senate Foreign Relations Committee, Church was often an opponent or staller of Carter's diplomatic agenda. On one occasion, when Carter met with Democratic congressional leaders and faced the opposition of Church and Jackson, he concluded that they both were "acting like asses."

Not all of Carter's western relationships turned sour after the election of 1976. Texan Lloyd Bentsen proved to be an aid to Carter. So did Congressman Morris Udall, particularly when Carter pushed for the passage of the Alaska Lands bill. The tightest links were forged with a contingent from Minnesota. Hubert Humphrey, former vice president for Lyndon Johnson and unsuccessful Democratic candidate in 1968, and his protégé Senator Walter Mondale were both listed as possible candidates in 1976. After Carter's win, Humphrey and Mondale were bastions of encouragement. After considering Jackson and Church as possible running mates, Carter turned to Mondale. The two proved to be a compatible, very supportive team. Carter also selected another Minnesotan, Robert Bergland, as his secretary of agriculture.

In fact, a surprising number of Carter's cabinet members were native westerners or longtime residents of the region. These included G. William (Bill) Miller (Treasury), Harold Brown (Defense), Cecil Andrus (Interior), Robert Bergland (Agriculture), Philip M. Klutznick (Commerce), Ray Marshall (Labor), Brock Adams (Transportation), Neil Goldschmidt (Transportation), Charles M. Duncan Jr. (Energy), and Shirley Mount Hufstedler (Education). Perhaps even more surprising is how little these western connections seemed to play out in Carter's policies. In fact, save for Miller, Brown, and Andrus, the names of the other cabinet members rarely surface in Carter's voluminous writings. Carter's discussions in his two most important books about his presidency—*Keeping Faith: Memoirs of a President* (1982) and *White House Diary* (2010)—mention these westerners only infrequently. Judging from these two accounts, the American West and many of its political leaders were a distant country for President Carter, off the scene during much of his administration.

Two other westerners, Harold Hughes and Mark Hatfield, connected with Carter, as much on religious as on political grounds. Hughes, former governor and senator from Iowa, had gained notoriety for his work, based on his own experience, in helping recovering alcoholics. He also led in establishing prayer groups for senators. Hughes supported and encouraged Carter's leadership and joined him in evangelical gatherings. The other political-religious contact from the

West was Oregon senator Mark Hatfield. More from the Nelson Rockefeller than the Richard Nixon–Barry Goldwater wing of the Republican Party, Hatfield, in his progressive stances, proved an inspiration to Carter. "Mark Hatfield was a kind of hero of mine," Carter wrote; "I was filled with admiration for him." A superb middle-of-the-road senator and evangelical, Hatfield most resembled Carter's balance of politics and religion, even though they were from opposite parties. Still, as much as Carter admired Hatfield and Hughes, they were something of political loners and did not bring a large following of western supporters to Carter.

Carter made a few other efforts to build political support in the West. These included one-or two-day trips to the West Coast to deliver speeches or participate in fund-raisers for Democrats. In 1978, sensing that he was losing support in the western states, he sent Vice President Mondale to Aspen, Colorado, to meet with western political leaders, hoping to improve relations with them. Surprisingly, when his decision to embargo grain sales to Russia after its invasion of Afghanistan set off angry reactions among midwestern and western farmers, Carter and his lieutenants did little to salve raw feelings. Nor had Carter forged strong, valuable links with such western leaders as Governor Jerry Brown of California. Even when Reagan's popularity began to zoom up in late summer and early fall of 1980, Carter seemed hesitant, even reluctant, to campaign in the plains or mountain states. By the second half of his presidency, Carter's connections with West, never strong, were crumbling.

The election of 1980 revealed how much support Carter had lost in the American West. The first challenge, from Edward Kennedy in the Democratic primaries, bruised Carter and demonstrated how little encouragement he was getting from the liberal wing of his party. The Democratic progressives thought Carter was far too conservative, unwilling to follow the New Deal traditions of a strong central government through funding and direction, addressing the problems of the poor and the needy. But there was no coherent core of political and sociocultural values among all Democrats for Carter to follow. When Reagan won the Republican nomination, he and his party attacked Carter's flawed leadership; his inability to free the hostages Iran had taken in the American embassy in November 1979; and what they considered his arbitrary actions in cancelling American participation in the Moscow Olympics and embargoing American wheat to Russia (both prompted by the Russian invasion in Afghanistan).

Generally, Reagan capitalized on the growing conservative movement, nationally and in the American West. His terms as California's governor symbolized the swing to the right that captured increasing numbers of westerners. Carter and his political lieutenants were slow to realize how formidable an opponent Reagan was. Also, the president got bogged down in the time-consuming negotiations to free the American hostages being held in Iran. When Carter should have been out campaigning in a nearly deadheat contest in September-October, he frequently stayed in the White House, trying to free the American captives. Plus the Carter-Reagan debate in late October went better for Reagan than for Carter, especially when the former movie star and California governor asked the nationwide television audience if things were going better for them now than when Carter had taken office four years earlier. High interest rates, gasoline and oil shortages, and the trouble in Iran suggested to most listeners that Carter had not been up to the demanding challenges. Domestic difficulties outweighed his first-rank diplomatic achievements in negotiating a short-term peace in the Middle East.

Probably the unresolved hostage crisis was the most important ingredient in Reagan's victory in 1980. Pollsters suggested that when undecided voters learned Americans held in Iran would not be freed by election time, they decided to give Reagan a chance because Carter had not done enough to free the hostages. Reagan won 51 percent to Carter's 41 percent—or 43.9 million to 35.5 million votes. The third-party candidate, the liberal John Anderson, won 5.7 million votes, or 6.6 percent. Most of Anderson's votes probably came from Democrats, especially liberals, dissatisfied with Carter's leadership.

Carter's loss of support was clearly evident in the West. In 1976, he had won five states west of the Mississippi, but won only Hawaii and Minnesota (Vice President Fritz Mondale's home state) in 1980. He did very poorly in the western interior and agricultural states, winning less than 30 percent of the votes in Colorado, Idaho, Nebraska, Nevada, North Dakota, Utah, and Wyoming. Generally, Carter seemed never to have understood or to have courted westerners.

CARTER'S WESTERN LEGACY

Many historians have been very critical of Jimmy Carter, considering him at best a mediocre president. Some of this widespread criticism has a sound basis; much of it also reflects his connections—or lack of them—with the American West.

Critics provide often-repeated lists of Carter's major and less-major snafus. The major list includes four limitations: (1) Carter came to the White House with an excessively long and complex agenda of desired policies; (2) Carter failed to reach out to Congress to gain additional support for his agenda; (3) Carter relied far too much on his Georgia-trained and too little on Washington-connected advisors; and (4) Carter was a narrow-minded moralist who lacked the necessary pragmatic political acumen to lead the country. These criticisms pertained to nationwide issues as well as those affecting the West.

Once these shortcomings are acknowledged, other, less-negative perspectives merit elaboration. Carter's dilemma was that of the classic moderate—in politics as well as in religion. Criticism of his political stances came largely from the left and right wings of the American political spectrum. Edward Kennedy, a left-leaning senator speaking for the New Deal heritage of Franklin Roosevelt, criticized Carter for paying too much attention to a balanced budget and too little to liberal social programs. Western politicians were also among the most prominent critics. Conservatives like Barry Goldwater, Paul Laxalt of Nevada, and Orrin Hatch of Utah attacked Carter, not for a balanced budget, which they favored, but for not spending enough on the military, blocking support for reclamation projects they favored, and paying too much attention to foreign affairs.

A major reason for Carter's failure to link up with the American West mimicked similar problems other presidents had encountered in the past and problems that would face future presidents. When an outsider president enters the White House with a coterie of his earlier advisors, he often falls victim to his own previous—and sometimes misguided—agendas. While running for the presidency, Carter defined himself as not a politician and not from Washington, D.C. He also brought a group of close advisors from Georgia who had served him well there. That gang of Carter supporters continued to serve *him* well in Washington, but too often they failed to connect with Congress or with other important bureaucrats in the nation's capital. Similar problems faced John F. Kennedy when he brought his New England and Harvard contacts to Washington, Bill Clinton and his "Bill's friends" from Arkansas, and George W. Bush's Texas advisors. Kennedy and Clinton, once in the White House, were able to forge new relations with other important advisors; Bush less so. Carter was too tied to his political "mafia" from Georgia, whose members, like Carter, knew almost nothing about the West. Except for strong ties to Cecil Andrus and Walter Mondale, Carter failed to enlarge his western contacts. And when relationships with powerful westerners such as Senators Scoop Jackson and Frank Church broke down—and a relationship with Senator Barry Goldwater never took off—Carter lacked the necessary links to shape the West.

Carter's middle-of-the-road position on religion came under similar attack. Liberals, including leaders of the women's group NOW, denounced Carter for not favoring personal choice for women and government-funded abortions. In his evangelism, Carter was far too conservative for many secular or mainline Protestants. Conversely, both right-wing evangelicals who came to the fore under the leadership of Jerry Falwell and the fundamentalist Moral Majority in Carter's own Southern Baptist denomination, and later westerner James Dobson and his Focus on the Family organization berated Carter for not pushing harder to oppose abortion and to support prayer and Bible reading in classrooms. Interestingly, although Carter was touted as an evangelical in the White House, he was unable to bond with any of the major evangelical leaders in the West.

For the harshest of critics, Carter's achievements were nonexistent. First these critics overlooked his accomplishments in foreign affairs. They did not mention his region-changing diplomacy that brought decades-long peace in the Middle East between Israel and Egypt. Nor was there praise for the Panama Treaty that reminded our Latin American neighbors that we could revive the earlier Good Neighbor policy. The time-consuming attempts to sign SALT II with the Russians, as well as the successful work to normalize relations with China, went unmentioned.

Other faultfinders were unwilling to admit Carter's successes in domestic affairs, several of which had strong impact on the West. His work with the Alaska Lands Act was extraordinary. His setting aside of other wilderness areas was also of note. And in the field of energy, Carter taught Americans to be more thoughtful in their use of oil and gas, even as he called their attention to western areas where shale oil, coal mining, oil and gas industries could be developed, as could wind and solar energy. Even when Carter was unable to gain all he wished from Congress and the American public, he led them in thinking about the future of energy and how it could be more wisely developed and used.

Carter's own opinions about his connections with the West are revealing. When the authors of this book asked him what he considered his "most important connections with the American West" during his presidency, he cited the "passage of the Alaska Lands Legislation, (ANILCA)." When a second question was raised—"How would you evaluate how . . . connections with the American West worked out during your four years in the White House?"—he answered that his administration had "doubled [the] size of national parks and tripled wilderness areas & protected 25 rivers." Most historians and biographers would also single out these areas as Carter's major contributions to the West. So have recent pollsters. They rank Carter very high as an environmentally conscious president, behind only Theodore Roosevelt and Richard Nixon in his efforts.

Even while keeping those considerable achievements in mind, Carter's West was a distant region. Once he made the fateful decision in the first days of his administration to cancel the water and dam projects in the West—without first seeking strong congressional or western support—he was off on the wrong track with the American West, his major and long-lasting achievements in environmental and energy matters notwithstanding, Carter was unable to capture the West politically, losing it to his successor Ronald Reagan.

FOR FURTHER READING

Balmer, Randall. *Redeemer: The Life of Jimmy Carter*. New York: Basic Books, 2014.

Bourne, Peter G. *Jimmy Carter: A Comprehensive Biography from Plains to Postpresidency*. New York: Lisa Drew Book/Scribners, 1997.

Brinkley, Douglas. *The Unfinished Presidency: Jimmy Carter's Journey beyond the White House*. New York: Viking, 1998.

Carter, Jimmy. *A Full Life: Reflections at Ninety*. New York: Simon & Schuster, 2015.

———. *Keeping Faith: Memoirs of a President*. New York: Bantam Books, 1982.

———. *White House Diary*. New York: Farrar, Straus and Giroux, 2010.

Carter, Rosalynn. *First Lady from Plains*. Boston: Houghton Mifflin, 1984.

Etulain, Richard W. *Beyond the Missouri: The Story of the American West*. Albuquerque: University of New Mexico Press, 2006.

Etulain, Richard W., and Michael P. Malone. *The American West: A Modern History, 1900 to the Present*. 2d ed. Lincoln: University of Nebraska Press, 2007.

Fink, Gary M., and Hugh Davis Graham, eds. *The Carter Presidency: Policy Choices in the Post-New Deal Era*. Lawrence: University Press of Kansas, 1998. See especially the chapters on Carter and the environment and his energy policies.

Frisch, Scott A., and Sean Q. Kelly. *Jimmy Carter and the Water Wars: Presidential Influence and the Politics of Pork*. Amherst, MA: Cambria Press, 2008.

Hargrove, Erwin C. *Jimmy Carter as President: Leadership and the Politics of the Public Good*. Baton Rouge: Louisiana State University Press, 1988.

Kaufman, Burton I. *The Presidency of James Earl Carter*. Lawrence: University Press of Kansas, 1993.

Mollenhoff, Clark R. *The President Who Failed: Carter Out of Control*. New York: Macmillan, 1980.

Morris, Kenneth E. *Jimmy Carter: American Moralist*. Athens: University of Georgia Press, 1996.

Nash, Gerald D. *A Brief History of the American West since 1945*. Fort Worth, TX: Harcourt College, 2001.

Patterson, James T. *Restless Giant: The United States from Watergate to Bush v. Gore*. New York: Oxford University Press, 2005.

Public Papers of the Presidents of the United States: Jimmy Carter (1977–1981). 9 vols. Washington, DC: Government Printing Office, 1977–1982.

White, Richard. *"It's Your Misfortune and None of My Own": A History of the American West*. Norman: University of Oklahoma Press, 1991.

Zelizer, Julian E. *Jimmy Carter*. New York: Henry Holt, 2010.

RONALD REAGAN, 1981–1989

LC-USZ62-13040

Chapter 10

RONALD REAGAN
RENEWING A CONSERVATIVE WEST

Ronald Reagan stood triumphantly before the just-past-midnight inaugural crowd on January 2, 1967, in Sacramento, California. Two months earlier he had won the governorship of the most populous state in the Union and brought down the two-time incumbent governor, Pat Brown, in a surprising turnabout. Even more remarkable, Reagan had gained his victory without having held political office before. He came on the scene as an avowed conservative who would get California out of the clutches of New Deal liberals and back in the embrace of capitalistic and democratic traditions. That conservative stance would be his political hallmark throughout his career, in the West and across the nation.

Reagan repeated his successful strategy to be reelected in California in 1970 and, later, in his runs for the presidency in 1980 and 1984. Capitalizing on the economic and social unrest of the '60s, Reagan promised to cut expenditures—especially for welfare programs—balance budgets, and crack down on violent disruptions, including those of students on California campuses.

Reagan communicated his goals in an appealing manner, particularly attractive for those dissatisfied with previous officeholders. He portrayed himself as a man who could lead, solve large fiscal problems, and restore peace and harmony. His masterful, "aw-shucks" personality also appealed to Californians, and later to Americans in general.

Reagan's political journey included one especially unusual turn. He was raised in a Franklin Roosevelt–supported and New Deal–loving home and remained a Democrat until the early 1960s. Some think that his alienation from leftist moviemakers and actors and his publicity work for General Electric turned him into a conservative. His "coming out" in a memorable speech in the Goldwater campaign of 1964 brought him forward as a possible gubernatorial candidate for California. Gaining widespread support among conservative and moderate Republicans, Reagan rode on the discontent in his home state and gained a victory of nearly 60 percent of the vote over the twice-elected Pat Brown.

Later, Reagan would use similar methods to win his way to the White House. Playing on the dissatisfactions with Jimmy Carter's administration, Reagan promised to cut expenses, balance the budget, and restore America's patriotic pride. He also vowed to strengthen the military as part of resurrecting the United States as a dominant world power. His skills in speaking and in use of other public media won him accolades as the Great Communicator and the restorer of American power and pride.

ORIGINS OF A POPULAR PRESIDENT

Reagan's background was lower middle class, with definite economic and social challenges in his family. Although Reagan provided sunny, delightful accounts of his early years, biographers, digging deeply into his formative experiences, furnish much less optimistic stories, suggesting that financial and parental tensions shadowed his life through high school.

Reagan was born February 6, 1911, in Tampico, Illinois. He lived in Illinois until he graduated from college. In fact, he was the only American president born and raised in Illinois.

Reagan's father, John "Jack" Reagan, unable to earn much of a living as a shoe salesman, moved his wife, Nelle Wilson Reagan, and their two sons in and out of several small Illinois towns and Chicago before settling in Dixon when Ronald was nine. Jack Reagan, a loyal Democrat, a Catholic, and later a New Deal employee, was also an alcoholic, which added tension to Reagan's boyhood and youth. Conversely, Nelle Reagan was strongly evangelical in her religious faith, a dedicated homemaker, and an encourager of her sons. She particularly urged Ronnie to participate in sports and neighborhood plays.

Reagan was an average student academically but a popular athlete and student leader. He played football and other sports in high school and college, was student body president of his high school and president of his college student council, and took part in several plays. In nearby Eureka College, a Disciples of Christ denominational school, Reagan majored in sports and social life rather than in his sociology and economics courses. Graduating in 1932, he embarked on a career in radio broadcasting.

Reagan hoped to land a radio job in Chicago, maybe even broadcasting the Chicago Cubs games. When that did not happen, he took a job in Davenport and then Des Moines, Iowa. He soon became recognized as a fluent and lively sports announcer. Receiving sparse telegraphic accounts of out-of-town ballgames,

Reagan expertly filled in the details, which, some thought, prepared him well for a career in politics. While on a trip to California, he gained a tryout with Warner Brothers, impressed his interviewers with his voice and manner, and landed a seven-year movie contract at two hundred dollars a week. California would be his home, save for his eight years in the White House, for the rest of his life.

From 1937 to 1965, Reagan acted in a variety of films, with the total exceeding fifty. He became a good, solid, but not superior, actor, landing lead roles in B movies and supporting roles in A films. He gained attention for his supporting role as a dying George Gipp in *Knute Rockne—All American* (1940), in which, as the dying Gipp, he told another character to send the boys into the game to "win just once for the Gipper." Slightly revised, these words would later become a popular catchphrase for Reagan. After spending three years in the army (1942–45), Reagan returned to Hollywood and signed a second seven-year contract with Warner for $3,500 a week. Meanwhile, he met, wooed, and married Jane Wyman in 1940. They had two children, Maureen (1941–2001) and a second, premature daughter who died early; they also adopted a son, Michael (1945–).

Reagan never became a widely touted movie star, but he was well known and liked among his Hollywood colleagues. In 1947–52 and again in 1959–60, he was elected president of the Screen Actors Guild. When his movie career stalled, he became a representative of General Electric and hosted the General Electric Theater on television. When that job ended in 1962, he joined the Death Valley Days series as its host. As Reagan's career declined and Jane Wyman's flourished, the marriage floundered. Wyman sued for divorce in 1949, stating privately that Reagan's increasing political activity was a major cause of the breakup. In 1952, Reagan married Nancy Davis, an aspiring actress. They became the parents of Patti (1952–) and Ronald Prescott (1958–).

Reagan's political journey had, in the meantime, undergone a dramatic shift. His ties to the Democratic Party continued through the 1930s and 1940s—and into the 1950s. Like his father, Reagan much admired President Franklin D. Roosevelt, drawn to FDR's genial ways of leading and his handling of public appearances, including his "fireside chats" on radio. In the 1950s, Reagan defended Hollywood from conservatives who criticized leftist tendencies among owners, directors, and stars. But he gradually feared even more the Communist influences among the movie crowd, became an FBI informer, and aided studios in getting rid of liberals. In 1948, Reagan supported Harry Truman's election, but in 1952, he stood for Republican Dwight Eisenhower. In the early 1960s, Reagan, abandoning the moderate Republicanism of Eisenhower, came out as a Republican; in 1964, he backed conservative Barry Goldwater. By Reagan's own gloss, he had not left the Democrats; "the Democratic Party left me," he said. Although Goldwater lost badly to Lyndon Johnson, Reagan gained strong support for his campaign speech entitled, "A Time for Choosing." It was vintage Reagan, a mix of humor, strong attacks on overblown and centrist governments, and telling quotes from Franklin Roosevelt, Abraham Lincoln, and others. Americans had "a rendezvous with destiny"; we were "the last best hope of man on earth." Soon after Goldwater's defeat and Reagan's attention-catching speech, a small group of influential and conservative Californians gathered to organize a committee touting Reagan for governor in 1966.

CALIFORNIA GOVERNOR

Reagan's campaign and victory in the California governor's contest of 1966 were but prologue for what he would do and say for much of his political career. Reagan and his handlers—and he willingly used many of them in his political career—realized that the sitting governor, Pat Brown, was vulnerable in several areas. The Watts riot in 1965, the Berkeley student protests, and the escalating costs of higher education and sprawling freeway systems—those would become the prime targets for Reagan and his campaign lieutenants. Students must, Reagan asserted, "observe the rules or get out." Governor Brown, he added, had not led well, letting costs and budgets get out of hand. Reagan, repeatedly and winningly, told California voters he could handle these problems and return the government to them by rescuing it from bloated bureaucracies. He contended that solutions were simple but not easy. California's citizens believed Reagan, giving him 3,742,913 votes to Brown's 2,749,174.

Reagan's executive leadership came from lessons learned on the fly. The ingredients of those lessons were what he gradually realized about himself and with which he became comfortable. The foundations of his governorship began with the small group of well-to-do men who had earlier pushed him to run against Governor Brown. Among those at the center of this group were Holmes Tuttle, a millionaire car dealer in Los Angeles; A. C. Rubel, chairman of the Union Oil Company; and lawyers William French Smith, Caspar Weinberger, and Ed Meese. These rich men and adept administrators formed something of a "kitchen cabinet" that advised Reagan in California; some went with him to Washington, D.C., in 1981.

Reagan made clear his conservative political philosophy. That manner of executive leadership in California was doubly important because, while shaping his actions in Sacramento, it foreshadowed what he would do later in the White House. One conviction was central to his thinking. As he told one group, "[T]he truth is that outside of its legitimate function, government does nothing as well or as economically as the private sector of the economy." It followed logically, for Reagan, that he would need to cut costs, rein in spending, and make sure the numbers of state government employees did not get out of hand.

Reagan achieved some of his goals—at least to his satisfaction. For one, he struck most observers as standing up to student radicals, sending in troops when he thought young troublemakers were disrupting classes and campus life. He made traditionalists happy, too, when he denounced hippies: they have "hair like Tarzan, look like Jane, and smell like Cheetah," he told one group. Reagan also implemented cuts in the budget of the Department of Mental Hygiene, which operated California's mental health hospitals. To the surprise of some of his backers, Reagan also organized new departments to address the state's waste and pollution problems, supported the establishment of Redwood National Park, and stopped the building of a dam that would have inundated a scenic valley and forced resident Indians to relocate. Generally, Reagan was middle-of-the-road on environmental issues, all the more intriguing when he previously had denounced governmental meddling in issues he thought individual or private in nature.

Not surprisingly, Reagan could not achieve all of his many campaign promises in California. Most significantly, he fell far short in balancing his budgets. In fact, during Reagan's eight years in Sacramento, the annual budget more than doubled, from $4.6 billion to $10.2 billion. Reagan also vowed to revise legislation supporting abortions, but the bill he signed contained so many loopholes that abortions moved on apace. The governor later rued signing the legislation, considering it one of the worst political blunders of his career. At first Reagan also called for uniform 10 percent cuts in all state departments but then backed away when he realized such actions penalized strong departments along with the weak. Nor did the governor carry out all his belt-tightening threats to public schools and higher education.

Reagan's largest successes, however, were with the general public. They liked him, even if some of his ideas seemed hazy, vague, and unenforceable. Conservatives and moderates were pleased with the way he stood up to student radicals, strikers, and dissenters. As journalist-biographer Lou Cannon adeptly points out in his thorough study *Governor Reagan: His Rise to Power* (2003), "Reagan was ideological and practical in nearly equal measure, and this balanced combination of attributes was crucial to his political accomplishments." Put another way, Reagan spoke as a conservative but also worked as a pragmatic leader, willing to compromise to achieve better-than-average success. Californians were drawn to Reagan both because of his promises to bring about changes (many of which he did not achieve) and because he offered something different in leadership and temperament, qualities central to his popularity as California's governor.

In the last years of his governorship, from about 1973 to 1975, Reagan seemed to drift. He promised not to run for a third term as California's governor (the majority Democrats in the state legislature were giving him headaches), and he was considering whether to run for the presidency. When the Watergate scandal broke in 1973–74 and fellow Californian Richard Nixon resigned under the threat of impeachment, many Republicans and more than a few conservative Democrats, especially in the South, quickly turned to Reagan as the bright new star from the West to lead their next charge for the White House.

In 1976, Reagan launched his candidacy against incumbent Gerald Ford by attacking what he (Reagan) thought were the president's moderate, misguided policies. Reagan and his advisors criticized Ford for naming liberal Republican Nelson Rockefeller as his vice president. (Reagan, some think, had wanted that position for himself in 1974.) They also scored Ford for suggesting partial amnesty for some Vietnam draft resisters. Generally, for Reagan, Ford lacked sufficient conservative credentials to be acceptable. Between the end of his governorship in California and the 1976 presidential race, Reagan went on what he called "the mashed potato circuit," making speeches at $5,000 an appearance, writing for popular journals, and spreading a conservative gospel. A misstep hurt Reagan, however. He promised to cut federal spending by $90 billion. That drastic reduction would have thrown thousands of federal and state employees out of work, severely cut Medicaid, and greatly reduced educational and transportation funding. Reagan critics pointed to those cuts as prime examples of how little he knew about governing the country.

Despite what some considered a gaffe and Reagan's mistake in not working hard to win the New Hampshire primary, he bounced back and was breathing down Ford's neck by late spring. Reagan had lit a fire under conservatives who had earlier supported two westerners, Barry Goldwater and Richard Nixon; now they were Reagan men and women. Reagan and Ford were neck and neck when Republicans met for their national convention. Rallying all the forces available to an incumbent, Ford eked out a close, first-vote nomination, with 1,187 ballots to Reagan's 1,070. But when Ford lost to Jimmy Carter in fall 1976, he was effectively out of the running for 1980. Reagan had become the Republican candidate for 1980 well before the formal campaigning began.

As we have seen in the previous chapter, Carter traveled a bumpy road in the last two years of his presidency. Interest rates skyrocketed, oil and gas prices reached new highs, and, most of all, the public grew increasingly dissatisfied with Carter when fifty-two Americans remained captives in the hands of radical militants in Iran. Once Reagan vanquished Robert Dole of Kansas and John Connally of Texas, among others, and then George H. W. Bush as the Republican candidate, he turned his big guns on Carter. The president had proved to be not up to the job of chief executive, Reagan charged. He had allowed things to get out of hand economically, he did not work well with Congress, he had alienated many members of that body from the West, and his inability to free the hostages in Iran proved his limitations as a leader. All these failures of Carter's, as pointed out by Reagan, influenced westerners as they did all other Americans.

In two ways, Reagan's foes misunderstood him and the shifting political-cultural currents that now moved toward him. Some opponents denounced Reagan as an "amiable dunce" or an "apparent airhead." These off-track denunciations revealed more about the critics than about Reagan. He was an optimist, undoubtedly, and he communicated that sunny disposition in a way that won over voters. Behind the smiles, however, was a person who understood himself and the dreams of many Americans. When critics, including President Carter, could not see how Reagan could govern, they were overlooking the shrewd insights behind the grin.

Besides winning followers through his demeanor, Reagan was buoyed by the political-cultural shifts taking place in the Sunbelt. From Florida to California, increasing numbers of Americans were moving right politically. Blue-collar workers, middle-class suburbanites, and evangelical Christians were becoming more conservative. Nonunion laborers and small businessmen, throughout the South and Southwest, were turning away from New Deal legacies and embracing the political credos of conservatives, from Goldwater to Nixon and on to Reagan. These three men from the West had similar goals: less government (at the federal level), more balanced budgets through less spending on social programs, and more support for the military. One political wag, studying the expansions in the Sunbelt from the 1960s onward, pointed to air conditioning as one reason for the rise of western conservatives like Reagan.

Another ingredient of the right turn in politics deserves mention. When Carter won the presidency in 1976, he enjoyed the support of most evangelicals, who were voting for a fellow evangelical. At the end of his presidency, in the election of 1980, Carter lost the evangelicals to Reagan and other conservatives. For one, the Reverend Jerry Falwell had established the Moral Majority and raised, it is estimated, $100 million for his group, much more than had the Democratic National Committee. Three westerners added much to mushrooming numbers supporting the Moral Majority and similar organizations. Tim LaHaye, of Southern California, captured evangelical readers in his coauthored Left Behind series of novels, and his wife, Beverly LaHaye, organized the conservative Concerned Women for America. James Dobson, of Southern California and Colorado Springs, spread conservative views in his widely influential Focus on the Family radio program. These and other conservative leaders and programs swung away from Carter when he refused to support a constitutional amendment outlawing abortions, seemed hesitant to marshal larger support for the military, and was too liberal, they thought, on other causes. The Religious Right, as these combined groups became known, were Reagan supporters in 1980, abandoning their own kind in the White House.

In the late stages of the 1980 election, Reagan and Carter were even in the polls. Then Reagan began to surge ahead after besting Carter in a television debate. Reagan's jump forward was even more noticeable when it became obvious in the closing days of the campaign that the hostages would not be freed before the election. Reagan won by a landslide, capturing 489 electoral votes (forty-four states) to Carter's 49 (representing six states and the District of Columbia). Reagan's margin of victory—10 percent—was the largest for a challenger since FDR's defeat of Hoover in 1932. Reagan's win was also the most one-sided electoral college victory for a nonincumbent president in the history of U.S. elections. In the twenty-three states on or west of the Mississippi, Reagan did even better than he did in the rest of the United States. He captured more than 60 percent—sometimes more than 70 percent—of the vote in the inland West states of Colorado, Idaho, Nebraska, Nevada, North Dakota, Utah, and Wyoming. Of the states west of the Mississippi, Carter won only Minnesota and Hawaii.

A CONSERVATIVE IN THE WHITE HOUSE

In his presidential campaign of 1980 and in speeches immediately after his victory and in early 1981, Reagan outlined what he intended to do while in the White House. These proclamations, not surprisingly, varied little from what he had stated in the West beginning in 1966. His central ideas were encapsulated in one sentence of his inaugural address in January 1981. "In this present crisis," he told the crowd gathered at the Capitol, "government is not the solution of our problem, government is the problem." The country was in an economic mess, but, Reagan made clear, massive government spending—like Lyndon Johnson's Great Society program—was not the answer. Rather, diminished government outlays, tax cuts, and large reductions in social welfare programs were the mechanisms to get the economy and country moving again. These were key elements of what was labeled supply-side economics. These popular conservative ideas, lacking hard evidential support, had nonetheless captured Reagan well before he moved to Washington. In fact, so shaky was the thinking behind sharply cutting taxes so that spending would increase and thus, in the end, add to government revenues, that George H. W. Bush, Reagan's future vice president, labeled the theory "voodoo economics" when he campaigned against Reagan in 1980.

Just as Reagan brought to the presidency ideas he had tested during his California governorship, so he brought to Washington a corps of people he had worked with in the West. No recent American president did more to get westerners in his cabinet than did Ronald Reagan. He particularly selected cabinet members from California. Most, but not all, turned out to be strong supporters of the president's policies, even though Reagan often paid little attention to their activities.

After Reagan's first secretary of state, Alexander Haig (1981–82) resigned, frustrated by what he considered directionless policy, Californian George P. Shultz (1982–89) had the president's backing as the new secretary of state. Caspar W. Weinberger (1981–87), also of California, served as secretary of defense and engineered the Star Wars defense system. Still another Californian, William French Smith (1981–85), was named attorney general and led the attack on the air traffic controllers in 1981. When Smith resigned, Californian Edwin Meese (1985–88) took over. After John R. Block (1981–86) quit as secretary of agriculture, Californian Richard E. Lyng (1986–89) succeeded him. Elizabeth H. Dole, wife of Kansas senator Robert Dole, became secretary of transportation in 1983 and served for the next four years. In 1982, when James B. Edwards resigned as secretary of energy, Donald P. Hodel served until he became secretary of the interior. John S. Herrington, also from California, replaced Hodel in 1985. Over his eight years as president, Reagan named more than ten westerners to cabinet positions.

All of these cabinet members seemed to get along well with Reagan. Following his nondirective manner of leadership, Reagan did not look over the shoulders of these people but encouraged them to bring to him ideas or legislative matters for his consideration. He also connected with another unofficial cabinet of advisors. This group included James A. Baker III, his chief of staff, with a Texas background and an Ivy League education; David Stockman, director of budget and a general advisor on economic policies; Reagan's longtime friend, Ed Meese, known at first as a counselor before he became a cabinet member; and Michael Deaver, deputy chief of staff, a man with a California background who had been with Reagan since 1967. Overall, these cabinet members and the clutch of close advisors provided opinions that Reagan asked for, thereby illustrating what one writer labels a "delegated presidency." They supported his tax cuts, his downsizing of government control, and his diminished funding of social programs. On a few occasions, they disagreed on details but kept the differences to themselves—or offered the president dissents in the most palatable form.

Two other westerners got along less well in Reagan's cabinet. Terrel H. Bell, from Utah, with extensive administrative experience in educational programs, served from 1981 to 1985 as secretary of education. At first, Bell and the president seemed in accord about shutting down the department because, they thought, of its excessive oversight of public education. That guidance should come from the states. Bell reduced federal aid to elementary and secondary schools and made less funding available to college students. Bell and Reagan seemed on the same track. But, later in his book *The Thirteenth Man: A Reagan Cabinet Memoir* (1988), Bell expressed his disappointment about how little presidential support he received from Reagan in attempts to address some of the educational inadequacies that had surfaced in a government-sponsored report on American education, "A Nation at Risk" (1983). Opponents—Bell denounced them as "right-wing idealogues"—had hijacked the president away from support of funding for handicapped students, implementation of civil rights programs in schools, and other projects Bell favored. After his reelection in 1984, Reagan no longer called for shutting down the education department, but neither did he support it in the manner Bell wanted.

Bell's disappointment was as a molehill compared to the mountainous problems surrounding Secretary of the Interior James G. Watt. Reared in Wyoming and something of a protégé of the distinguished and politically conservative Simpson family of that state, Watt came to Reagan's cabinet with considerable legal experience in the nation's capital, particularly in cases dealing with land and water issues. In 1977, Watt had become the president of the Mountain States Legal Foundation, a legal support group and conservative think tank in Denver. Strongly identifying with the Sagebrush Rebellion that President Carter had opposed and that presidential candidate Reagan espoused (Reagan called himself a Sagebrush Rebel), Watt seemed at first to be Reagan's right-hand man, calling for cutting, trimming, and squeezing federal government control of land, water, and other natural resources. His promise to "mine more, drill more, and cut more timber" was far to the right of most Americans, when public opinion polls in the early 1980s—and Congress—called for retaining present conservation laws, protecting parks, and reining in wilderness leasing. One critic asserted that Watt had "out-Reaganed Reagan."

Watt's largest problem was his ever-active mouth, into which he often placed a foot, or two. Even though Reagan liked Watt, considering him a "soul mate," and agreed with most of his stances on environmental issues, the interior secretary's unbridled tongue finally led to his demise. His fundamentalist religious views and hawkish negativity were continuously getting him into trouble. His denouement came when he defended the diversity of one of his groups by stating that it had "every kind of mixture you can have. I have a black, I have a woman, two Jews and a cripple." That out-of-bounds comment was even too much for Reagan. No cabinet member had engendered more negativity and caused the president more grief than had James Watt. Although asking Watt to step down, which he did in November 1983, Reagan never publicly criticized his controversial friend.

In the early months of his administration, Reagan set out to overturn some of Carter's policies already on the books and others in the planning stage. Unlike Carter's missteps in attempting executive actions early in his administration without working with Congress, Reagan began to woo members of Congress, for instance Speaker of the House Tip O'Neill, even before he launched his presidency. In the days following his inaugural, Reagan scheduled dozens of gatherings with members of Congress, attempting to evangelize them to support his campaign promises. He repeated again his desire to markedly downsize budgets, cut taxes dramatically, and notably reduce the federal government's role in American business. All these changes, later dubbed the Reagan Revolution, were seen as turning back Carter's policies.

Other Carter legislation impacting the West was also overturned. Early in his presidency, Reagan lifted the grain embargo against the Soviet Union, which Carter had used to penalize the Soviets for their invasion of Afghanistan but which Reagan was convinced had hurt American farmers. In fall 1981, Reagan announced his opposition to the MX (Missile Experimental) plan that President Carter had promoted. Reagan's announcement had foreign and domestic policy implications. He did not want to drop the defensive missile program entirely, so he effected a compromise to place the missiles in existing but strengthened silos. Political and religious (Latter-day Saint) leaders of Nevada and Utah, where the missiles were to be based, had opposed the system on economic, environmental, and moral grounds. In a masterstroke of a decision, Reagan cut costs, delayed construction, and calmed negative reactions in the West. However, another Reagan appointee,

Ann Gorsuch (Burford), raised hackles among western environmentalists. As Reagan's director of the Environmental Protection Agency (EPA), she led a James Watt–like program to cut back on government regulation of offshore drilling, oil leases, and coal mining, seemingly intent on allowing a "privatizing" of the resource-rich West. Her agenda aroused so much controversy that she was removed from office. Alongside these West-specific changes, the impact of Reagan's cuts to national programs dealing with public housing, the lessening of Social Security and Medicare benefits, and the elimination of aid for needy students was also felt in the West.

Even as he was stiff-arming more than a few Carter endeavors, Reagan went on the offensive with his own programs. A few days after his presidency commenced, Reagan was on the move. He signed an executive order freezing federal salaries. He placed strong advocates of deregulation on several commissions and went after what he and his advisors considered unnecessary and stifling economic and legal regulations. In February 1981, building on previous budget-cutting ideas, Reagan announced his specific proposals: reduce Carter budgets by more than $40 billion, reverse the deficit spending of Democrats, and, down the road in two or three years, engender government surpluses. Although economic forecasters worried about the supply-side ingredients of these policies, Reagan called on conservative Democrats, including Democratic representative Philip Gramm of Texas (who would later become a Republican), to push his economic package through Congress. Reagan's quick recovery from a near-fatal assassination attempt in late March and the resulting sympathy for the president—much like that following Kennedy's assassination in 1963—helped propel Reagan's economic plan through Congress in late summer.

Even before he gained the White House, Reagan promised to beef up American defense and the military. When Democrats howled about his cuts in social programs, the new president told them he was going to hike defense spending. "I was determined to *increase* military spending," Reagan wrote later in his autobiography, "to reverse the effects of years of neglect of our armed services." Since Carter had also been an advocate of defense spending—but not beyond balanced budgets—Reagan was not accurate in speaking of "neglect." He also made clear, as he told audiences during his first administration, that if he had to decide between balanced budgets and defense spending, he would "come down on the side of national defense." All these changes—the cuts in social programs, the attempts at balanced budgets, and the hikes in defense spending—had implications, as we shall see, for the American West.

OTHER REAGAN POLICIES

After the United States recovered from an economic downturn in 1982, Reagan was a shoo-in for renomination in 1984. The Democrats, after competition among several candidates, including westerners Gary Hart of Colorado, George McGovern of South Dakota, and Alan Cranston of California, settled on Walter Mondale of Minnesota, who had been Carter's vice president. Once Reagan's popularity bounced back after the earlier fiscal challenges, the Democrats faced an uphill battle. A catchy phrase, "It's Morning Again in America," although not explicitly mentioning the president, suggested that a Reagan America had recaptured a sunny, upbeat, and promising future. Although Democrats denounced the slogan and much of Reagan's commentary as superficial—if not hokey—the critics were shooting blanks. Even intimations about Reagan's age—he was now seventy-three—lacked impact, and he scored an even more impressive victory than he had in 1980, snatching 525 electoral votes to Mondale's 13. Reagan also captured forty-nine states, with Mondale (narrowly) winning only his home state and the District of Colombia, which had never voted for a Republican. Reagan's winning margin in the West was even larger than it had been four years earlier.

Women's issues were never central to Reagan, although his statements and actions shaped some policies, in California and the nation, on some of these issues. As a happily married man with his supportive, homemaking wife, Nancy, Reagan, as governor and later as president, spoke often for "traditional families." In addition, Nancy, unlike Eleanor Roosevelt and Rosalynn Carter before her and more like Bess Truman, Mamie Eisenhower, and Pat Nixon, rarely spoke out on, or became involved in, issues related to women. While in Sacramento, Reagan had avoided women's matters for the most part. As governor and president, he was an opponent of the Equal Rights Amendment and dismissed the measures that the National Organization for Women (NOW) tried to promote. The controversies surrounding abortion and freedom of choice forced themselves on Reagan, however. The bill he supported in California was designed to limit abortions to cases of assault and incest or those that threatened the physical or psychological welfare of mothers-to-be. However, determined doctors discovered escape hatches in the legislation, and the rate of abortions went up precipitously in California during Reagan's governorship. Reagan also added to the misery of many poor wives and mothers when he signed a "no-fault" divorce bill, meaning that women who left their husbands had little support. He was also instrumental in the firing of radical activist Angela Davis from the California university system for being a self-identified Communist.

Reagan's conservative advisors kept him from advocating legislation supporting women during his presidency. For the most part, he tried to avoid abortion
issues; they were too fiery to touch. Still, his counselors, even while advocating
hands-off on legislation dealing with women, worried that such actions would
alienate women voters. They did. The discontent of women voters mounted when
Reagan vetoed a Civil Rights Restoration Act, but Congress overrode his veto.
Plus, Reagan's critics accused him of failing to enforce Title IX stipulations calling
for support of women in public school and college athletics equal to that of men.
Overall, throughout his political career, Reagan enjoyed more support from men
than from women.

Still, Reagan surprised many Americans and angered some of his most conservative advisors when he nominated Arizona judge Sandra Day O'Connor for the
Supreme Court in 1981. Right-wing Republicans opposed O'Connor because of her
support of the Equal Rights Amendment and abortions, but when rightest Senator
Barry Goldwater supported his fellow Arizonian for the Court, most conservative
opposition melted away. Reagan also appointed Jeane Kirkpatrick as ambassador
to the United Nations and named Ann Dore McLoughlin as secretary of labor,
Margaret M. Heckler as secretary of health and human services, and Elizabeth
Dole as secretary of transportation. He appointed women to other lesser positions,
but fewer in number than had Johnson and Carter, for example.

Reagan's policies both positively and negatively impacted the West. His increased
defense and military spending greatly benefitted most residents of the West involved
in those programs. Especially was this new prosperity true for middle-class westerners, but less so for poorer residents of the region. Nearly every western state's
financial support for military and defense spending jumped noticeably in the 1980s.
Utah, for example, the state that gave Reagan the widest margin of any state in
the elections of 1980 and 1984, gained $95 million more in federal funding than
it paid in taxes. California led the nation in that regard, receiving $100 billion in
annual federal support. In fact, in the range of western states from North Dakota
to Texas and to the west, and including Alaska and Hawaii, twelve of the twenty
states receiving the most federal dollars were in the West. In the 1980s, six of the
top ten cities with the largest number of Department of Defense employees were
in the West. In addition, in the years from 1983 to 1986, seven out of every ten
contracts for Reagan's Strategic Defense Initiative landed in five western states. Even
though Reagan spoke of cutting government support, those in the military-defense
industries benefitted from hikes in funding. As western historian Richard White
perceptively observes in *"It's Your Misfortune and None of My Own": A History of*

the American West, the "Reagan administration . . . did not represent a decline in federal influence in the West as much as a shift in that influence."

Regrettably for others in the West, the Reagan cuts were near-disastrous, particularly for Native Americans, most of whom resided in the West. In 1981, the federal support for Indian programs was cut by one-third, meaning that Indians suffered the largest per capita cut of all Americans. As the reductions came into play, Indian income plummeted. When the average annual American income in the mid-1980s stood at $9,000, individual members of the Navajo tribe were earning $1,700. Government support for Americans in general stood at $3,681, but that figure was $2,497 for Indians. Western states with large Indian populations, including Oklahoma, Arizona, California, and New Mexico, were hit hard with these reductions. Interior Secretary James Watt, who was likely more conservative—and certainly more outspoken—than Reagan, might have spoken for Reaganites to the Right when he stated in 1983: "If you want an example of the failures of socialism, don't go to Russia. Come to America and go to the Indian reservations." Policy makers in Reagan's administration saw funding for Indians as out of control and over the top, so they cut that support severely in the 1980s.

Conversely, for persons of Mexican and Mexican American heritage, Reagan made a surprisingly positive decision. Indeed, conservatives much later in the Obama administration, trying to block that president's executive actions on immigration, seemed to have forgotten Reagan's support for legislation aiding immigrants, mostly Chicanos. The Immigration and Reform and Control Act of 1986, which Congress passed and Reagan signed into law, granted amnesty to millions of undocumented immigrants, allowing them to apply for jobs, open bank accounts, buy their own homes, and, through a series of steps, become full citizens. Ironically, as one conservative critic noted, with a measure of truth, Reagan's amnesty decision helped pave the way for Obama's later election because many of the immigrants, particularly those of Mexican heritage, voted for the Democratic candidate in 2008 and 2012.

In his second administration, Reagan's domestic programs lost much of their fire. Undoubtedly, his increased involvements in time-consuming foreign affairs stole his attention away from domestic demands. His flagging energies also played a role, and, like the administrations of several other two-time U.S. presidents, Reagan's second term suffered from the lame-duck syndrome. The energetic legislative program tailed off from 1985 to 1989.

In his vow to restore American greatness—its power and patriotism—Reagan promised to deal harshly with terrorists and others he considered evildoers. He attempted to do that in conflicts with Middle Eastern revolutionaries, particularly with Muammar al-Qaddafi, the assertive leader of Libya. Reagan also promised to oppose leftists and Communists as he did in Grenada and Nicaragua. Such efforts sometimes led him down a troubled path, as when his administration illegally sold arms to Iran to gain release of hostages and used profits from the sales to support Contra rebels in Nicaragua. Reagan, at first, claimed innocence regarding the dealings but then admitted that some of his underlings had broken the law in these underhanded maneuvers. Reagan's exact role in the cloak-and-dagger affair has never been fully clarified, although he seems to have understood that selling arms to Iranians might bring release of the hostages.

Most time-consuming were Reagan's down-and-up negotiations with the Soviet Union. Earlier in his presidency, Reagan spewed out hot rhetoric aimed at the Soviets, perhaps to twist the tail of the Russian bear. He sent billions into the arms race and Star Wars program and chastised the Russians for their negativism and imperialism. The election of Mikhail Gorbachev allowed for a new path, however, and a warming of U.S.-Soviet relations. Reagan gradually was less driven to continue the arms race and his space-based missile system. Even though summit meetings between Reagan and Gorbachev failed to achieve diplomatic breakthroughs, relations between the two leaders improved. The Cold War was thawing.

On June 12, 1987, speaking in Berlin at the 750th anniversary of the founding of the city, Reagan challenged Gorbachev to "open this [Brandenburg] gate . . . [and] tear down this wall." Reagan devotees make much of this speech, pointing to it as a tipping point in American history, even though the best evidence reveals that not many West or East Berliners heard the speech and that the press said little about it at that time. Perhaps the crumbling Russian economy, victimized by the ruinous costs of the arms race, had more to do with the East Germans breaking through and tearing down most of the wall shortly after Reagan left the presidency. Clearly, though, even if Reagan's Berlin speech did not in itself bring about *glasnost* (transparency) and *perestroika* (restructuring), it did encourage the resultant epoch-making shifts in U.S.-Russian relations.

Even as Reagan was devoting increasing attention to these global matters, he continued working with western political leaders. Chief of these, of course, was George H. W. Bush, a New Englander and New Yorker, who had moved to Texas in 1947. After unsuccessfully competing for the presidency with Reagan in 1980, Bush became his loyal but rather subdued vice president. More moderate politically than Reagan, Bush nonetheless supported the president's economic policies and traveled worldwide on assignments from the White House. Bush was also sufficiently involved with Reagan's actions that he probably dirtied his hands in the Iran-Contra controversy. In his relations with another westerner, and largely behind the scenes, Reagan listened to the advice of Richard Nixon, a decade and more after Nixon's Watergate embarrassment. Reagan had remained loyal to Nixon well into the Watergate imbroglio, which prepared the way for later good communications between the two presidents, especially in foreign affairs.

Reagan also worked well with several other western politicians. Chief among these was Paul Laxalt, the Basque governor and then senator of Nevada. Although he may have been more conservative than Reagan, Laxalt was a longtime friend. In fact, strong rumors traveled in 1980 that Laxalt would be Reagan's running mate. Not until eastern Republicans of the Rockefeller stripe reminded Reagan and Laxalt that two very conservative candidates from the West—and living less than two hundred miles apart—were not a team likely to capture eastern voters did the idea die. Still, Reagan listened to Laxalt's advice on policies and people and often followed them, as he did on Laxalt's misguided touting of James Watt. On one occasion, Reagan even attended one of Laxalt's notorious barbecues of lamb fries (also known as "Basque Beans"); despite Reagan's love of masculine symbols, the menu of broiled lamb testicles was too much for him.

Reagan maintained curious connections with the leading conservative Republican in Congress, Barry Goldwater of Arizona. Even though Reagan boosted Goldwater in his failed run at the presidency in 1964 and they shared similar positions on Reagan's favorite policies, their meetings were hit-and-miss during Reagan's White House years. Goldwater supported Reagan's nomination of Sandra O'Connor, but railed against the MX missile plan and was "pissed," as he put it, with Reagan's meddling in Nicaragua. He also advised against Reagan's trip to China in 1984. Perhaps the lack of strong, persistent connections with Goldwater showed how much more closely Reagan worked with his "kitchen cabinet" of advisors than he did with members of Congress.

Sometimes Reagan and a leading western politician clashed. Senator Mark Hatfield of Oregon, a progressive Republican seriously considered as Nixon's running mate in 1968, often stubbornly opposed Reagan's militarism. After Reagan failed on one occasion to talk Hatfield into backing one of the president's defense measures, and knowing Hatfield wanted deep cuts rather than additions to defense spending, Reagan confided to his diary, "With some of our friends we don't need enemies." Hatfield represented the Rockefeller wing of the Republican Party in the West, a diminishing group that was, at best, lukewarm in supporting Reagan.

REAGAN'S WESTERN LEGACY

Ronald Reagan closely identified with the American West. He loved the West, or more specifically, his idea of the West. His West was a Hollywood West, more linked to John Wayne and Louis L'Amour than to urban Los Angeles, troubled reservations, or a region strongly tied to federal government subsidies. Like Lyndon Johnson, and more than other recent western presidents, including Richard Nixon and George W. Bush, Reagan felt *his* California West to be a retreat, a symbol of the freedom and openness that he thought an earlier frontier West symbolized. During his eight years in the White House, Reagan spent more than three-hundred days, nearly one-eighth of his presidency, at his California ranch.

Rancho del Cielo (ranch in the sky, or heavenly ranch) was at the center of Reagan's magical, mythic West. Purchased in 1974 for slightly more than a half-million dollars, the property of nearly seven hundred acres thirty miles northwest of Santa Barbara was located in the Santa Ynez Valley. Rebuilding the Spanish-style adobe home, chopping wood, riding horses, building fences, taking care of such duties—here Reagan worked with vigor and enthusiasm. If the ranch wasn't exactly heaven, he told Nancy, it "probably has the same ZIP code."

What happened in the Far West at the Rancho del Cielo symbolized what Reagan thought the West could or should be. A man labored to build his own place, without outside help or oversight. The place ensured freedom and independence, two virtues all persons should cherish. Governments, whether local, regional, or national, should ensure the same for all Americans: hard work, diligence, and the absence of outside interference would bring a healthy and happy future. The West Reagan saw and experienced at Rancho del Cielo symbolized what he wanted to achieve as governor and president.

And it was to this retreat in Southern California that Reagan retired when he left the White House in 1989. He quietly remained at the ranch for the next few years, absent from the hurly-burly of politics. Tragically, as Reagan announced in 1994, he was suffering from Alzheimer's disease. From then until his death in 2004, he remained largely out of sight.

What is one to make of the Reagan legacy, especially as related to the American West? To find the answer, one can look to his major ideas. Whether labeled supply-side economics, Reaganomics, or the Reagan Revolution, the president's ideas and policies made a difference in the American West in the 1980s. Critics who have harpooned Reagan as an airhead, or described his presidency as "sleepwalking" through two administrations, have misfired. He had ridden into California's governorship on a western conservative political movement that began with Barry Goldwater and that grew in the next fifteen years. Reagan entered on that steed, and he brought it under increasing rein during his presidency.

The Reagan moves—both in California and then in Washington, D.C.—were aimed at reducing debts, cutting costs, backing off an overreaching central government, and adding strength to the military-industrial complex that had so worried President Eisenhower when he left the White House. Reagan both succeeded and failed in his goals. He did cut back on the costs of social programs, and he reduced the reach of the federal government in some areas. He certainly built up the military, spending billions and opening thousands of new positions for men and women in the armed forces. But he utterly failed in balancing budgets, and he left the presidency with overruns escalating well beyond what his predecessor had left.

From another, a later perspective, Reagan's stamp is clear on the trends in western politics. In the Reagan landslide in 1980, strong political liberals like Frank Church and George McGovern were tossed out of office. Reagan's ideas about conservative politics would also extend well beyond him in the stances of Republican president and Texan George W. Bush, Republican candidate and Arizona senator John McCain, and Republican president Donald Trump. Reagan provided, more than any other Republican since the New Deal, a track for western politicians to follow. His conservative West is still much in evidence, particularly in the interior of the region, from the plains states to the eastern ends of western coastal states. And for Republicans, in the West and the nation, Ronald Reagan remains *the* symbol of recent Republicanism at its best, much as FDR does for the Democrats.

Indeed, historian H. W. Brands, in the most extensive biography to date of Reagan, advances a provocative thesis, one uniting Franklin Roosevelt the Democrat with Reagan the Republican. "What [Franklin] Roosevelt had been to the first half of the twentieth century," writes Brands, "Reagan was to the second half." If one limits the comparison to powerful leadership, a strong presence in foreign affairs, and popularity with voters, Brands's comparison is on track. But the power of FDR's domestic policies during the New Deal and World War II far outshine Reagan's influence on the nation and the West. Still, Reagan, the westerner, must be numbered among at least the near-great in his impact on all regions of the United States.

FOR FURTHER READING

Brands, H. W. *Reagan: The Life*. New York: Doubleday, 2015.

Brownlee, W. Elliot, and Hugh Davis Graham, eds. *The Reagan Presidency: Pragmatic Conservatism and Legacies*. Lawrence: University Press of Kansas, 2003.

Cannon, Lou. *Governor Reagan: His Rise to Power*. New York: PublicAffairs, 2003.

———. *President Reagan: The Role of a Lifetime*. 1991. Reprint. New York: PublicAffairs, 2000.

———. *Reagan*. New York: Putnam, 1982.

Dallek, Robert. *Ronald Reagan: The Politics of Symbolism*. Cambridge, MA: Harvard University Press, 1984.

Ehrman, John. *The Eighties: America in the Age of Reagan*. New Haven, CT: Yale University Press, 2005.

Jenkins, Philip. *Decade of Nightmares: The End of the Sixties and the Making of Eighties America*. New York: Oxford University Press, 2006.

Johnson, Haynes. *Sleepwalking through History: America in the Reagan Years*. New York: W. W. Norton, 1991.

Morris, Edmund. *Dutch: A Memoir of Ronald Reagan*. New York: Random House, 1999.

Patterson, James T. *Restless Giant: The United States from Watergate to Bush v. Gore*. New York: Oxford University Press, 2005.

Pemberton, William. *Exit with Honor: The Life and Presidency of Ronald Reagan*. Armonk, NY: Routledge, 1997.

Reagan, Nancy, with William Novak. *My Turn: The Memoirs of Nancy Reagan*. New York: Random House, 1989.

Reagan, Ronald. *The Reagan Diaries*. Edited by Douglas Brinkley. New York: HarperCollins, 2007.

———. *Ronald Reagan: An American Life*. New York: Simon & Schuster, 1990.

Reeves, Richard. *President Reagan: The Triumph of Imagination*. New York: Simon & Schuster, 2005.

Rossinow, Doug. *The Reagan Era: A History of the 1980s*. New York: Columbia University Press, 2015.

Schaller, Michael. *Reckoning with Reagan: America and Its President in the 1980s*. New York: Oxford University Press, 1992.

———. *Ronald Reagan*. New York: Oxford University Press, 2011.

Tygiel, Jules. *Ronald Reagan and the Triumph of American Conservatism*. 2nd ed. New York: Pearson, 2004, 2006.

Walsh, Kenneth T. *Ronald Reagan*. New York: Park Lane Press, 1997.

Wilentz, Sean. *The Age of Reagan: A History, 1974–2008*. New York: HarperCollins, 2008.

Wills, Garry. *Reagan's America: Innocents at Home*. Reprint. New York: Doubleday, 2000.

Chapter 11

RECENT PRESIDENTS
AND THE AMERICAN WEST
GEORGE H. W. BUSH to BARACK H. OBAMA

In the quarter-century following the end of Ronald Reagan's presidency, the trans-Mississippi West played an increasingly larger role in American politics. In 1990, the twenty-three states on or west of the Mississippi (save for Louisiana) were holders of 210 electoral votes. By 2016, based on the census of 2010, westerners had 222 of 538 electoral votes in hand.

All four of the presidents after Reagan—George H. W. Bush, William "Bill" Clinton, George W. Bush, and Barack H. Obama—were westerners or had spent at least a dozen years of their life in the West. Clinton and George W. Bush were longtime westerners, Bush senior and Obama less so. More and more presidential candidates, cabinet members, and executive advisors were also coming from the West. But the election of New Yorker Donald Trump in 2016 broke from this tradition.

The national and even international policies of the quartet of post-Reagan presidents obviously shaped the lives of many westerners. Decisions on taxation, immigration, and health care, for example, affected westerners, as did diplomatic negotiations with Russia, China, and Middle Eastern countries. Interestingly, none of these western presidents is known for specifically region-centered policies. Still, their connections with the West provide examples of how our most recent presidents have dealt with the region.

GEORGE H. W. BUSH, 1989–1993

LC-USZ62-98302

GEORGE H. W. BUSH

Like so much of George H. W. Bush's up-and-down presidency, his links with the American West were in and out. Born, raised, and educated in the East, Bush and his wife, Barbara, and their family moved west to Texas in 1948, where they have resided off and on to the present. Failing in a bid for the U.S. Senate from Texas in 1964, Bush won a term in the U.S. House two years later. After being defeated in his reelection bid to that body, he held several appointive positions, including ambassador to the United Nations (1971–73) and director of the CIA (1976–77). Bush then served eight years as Ronald Reagan's vice president (1981–89) and won his own bid for the White House in 1988.

Bush's presidency was defined more by foreign than domestic affairs; he had little time to focus on interests or legislation specifically western. Still, some of Bush's national policy decisions molded the West, while also shaping other regions. His secretary of education, Texan Lauro Cavazos, pushed hard to solve educational challenges such as raising test scores and high school graduation rates, but the failure to gain necessary funding hamstrung the reforms. Much the same occurred in Bush's "war on drugs." On the other hand, his support for the Disabilities Act and the Clean Air Act, both in 1990, were two national policies that impacted the West.

Bush's actions vis-à-vis racial tensions in the West illustrated his yes-and-no tendencies. When the arrest of African American Rodney King for speeding—and the subsequent beating of King by the police—ignited a series of violent riots in Los Angeles in 1991, Bush reacted ambiguously, first pointing to "liberal social programs of the 1960s" as a cause of the horrific upheaval. Then he called for "weed and seed" programs that would weed out violence and crime and seed crime-ridden areas with "helps" (jobs, improved schools, and expanded health care) to quell the discontents in the needy areas. Unfortunately, the president did not push hard for funding the seeding programs.

Bush's policies dealing with Native Americans were as indecisive as those treating African Americans. Bush succeeded in getting Congress to pass the important Native American Grave Protection and Repatriation Act in 1990; he pushed for more funding than Reagan had in supporting Indian self-determination; and he hired more Indians for government jobs. But he did not twist congressional arms to add funding for much-needed new programs to address occupational, training, and health challenges that Indians across the country faced.

Bush gathered several influential westerners around him as cabinet members and advisors. Among these were his secretary of state, James A. Baker, a Texan, as well as Texans Lauro Cavazos in Education and Robert Mosbacher in Commerce. Elizabeth Dole of Kansas served briefly in Labor before leaving to head up the Red Cross. The most influential of the westerners surrounding Bush was Richard Cheney, the no-nonsense secretary of defense from Wyoming. Ramrod-like, Cheney pushed Bush on military affairs. Impressed with Cheney, Bush later successfully recommended him as a running mate for his son George's presidency. Active and opinionated, Cheney may have been the country's most significant nonpresidential leader in the years after 1990.

Historians with an environmental bent remain ambivalent about Bush's policies. Early on, Bush promised to be an environmental president, and he did more in that area than Reagan had. By executive order, he restored or newly protected 1.7 million acres of wetlands and secured much more funding for national parks and wildlife refuges, many of which were in the West. On the other hand, critics pointed to the president's slow response when the *Exxon Valdes* tanker broke up and spilled thousands of gallons of oil into the ocean off Alaska. Revealingly, though the harshest critics condemned Bush for his inaction, their comments were as light jabs compared to the knock-out blows aimed at President Obama after the British Petroleum oil spill in the Gulf of Mexico in spring 2010.

When Bush's popularity fell dramatically in the second half of his administration, he faced serious challenges from two westerners in the election of 1992. The more serious threat came from the ebullient young governor of Arkansas, Bill Clinton; the other competitor was Texan Ross Perot. Bush could not bounce back from his downturn, with Clinton winning the election, gaining 43 percent of the vote, to Bush's 38 and Perot's 19.

One perceptive commentator on Bush's connections with the West observed that, in the White House, the president "invoked his western ties with less frequency. Vacations to Maine were more common than an annual hunting trip to Texas." True enough, and one might also add another commentator's perceptive conclusion: "George Bush's relationship with the American West remained out of clear focus when he left the White House." Conversely, just sixteen years later, his son George W. Bush left the White House to reconnect with and reside in his boyhood Texas.

WILLIAM J. "BILL" CLINTON, 1993–2001

LC-USZ62-107700

WILLIAM J. "BILL" CLINTON

Bill Clinton was a boy wonder. Born and raised in Arkansas in challenging circumstances, the "comeback kid" exhibited extraordinary energy and ambition,
gained a superb education, including a coveted Rhodes Scholarship, and earned a
law degree from Yale. Returning home to his natal Arkansas, Clinton was elected
its governor in 1978 at age thirty-two. Serving for four terms, he bested incumbent
George H. W. Bush in the election of 1992 and entered the White House the next
year.

Building on his extensive administrative experience as Arkansas's governor,
Clinton established himself as a "New" or "Third Way" Democrat, supporting
welfare and social justice programs without plunging the federal government
into the red. After a defeat on a too-early and too-hazy health care plan, Clinton

settled into a series of clashes with leading Republicans like Congressman Newt Gingrich, most of which the president won.

About half of Clinton's cabinet members were westerners who aided him in implementing national policies that helped shape the West. The advisors included Bruce Babbitt, from Arizona, serving ably as secretary of the interior, pushing for environmental policies that impacted the West. Clinton also named two Chicanos to his cabinet: Henry G. Cisneros of Texas, secretary of housing and urban development, and another Texan, Federico Peña, secretary of transportation. Alongside and surrounding the cabinet members was an unofficial group known as FOB (Friends of Bill), several of whom came from Arkansas. The best known of these friends was Vince Foster, a White House consul whose tragic death by suicide was mourned by Bill and Hillary Clinton.

In Congress, Clinton found westerners who led or supported his initiatives. A key member of Clinton's congressional team was House Speaker Tom Foley—until his defeat in 1994. In addition, Tom Daschle, the Senate majority leader from South Dakota, could be counted on for budget support and opposition to Republican attempts at a government shutdown. Moderate Republican Mark Hatfield of Oregon, chair of the Senate Appropriations Committee, also aided the president on several occasions.

Clinton prided himself on his work with minority groups and environmental legislation. He invited Indian representatives to Washington and pushed congressional measures to improve Indian health. He also pledged additional support for Indian education and vowed to add government aid to buttress tribal sovereignty. In addition, wanting to be known as an environmental leader, Clinton pushed legislation to protect wilderness and park areas in California, Colorado's wilderness sites, and monument areas in Utah. He also worked with Bruce Babbitt to name additional historical places along the Lewis and Clark Trail.

Three tragic events in the West, none of the president's making, linked him further with that region. In April 1993 in Waco, Texas, David Koresh and his followers in the Branch Davidians became the target of an FBI invasion. Their defiance of the government led to a fiery destruction of the compound and the death of nearly eighty of Koresh's disciples. Clinton took full responsibility for what seemed to be an unnecessary tragedy. Two years later, in Oklahoma City, Timothy McVeigh, an angry paramilitary dissident, set off a truck bomb that severely damaged the Murrah Federal Building, killing 168 people. Clinton, after investigating the calamity, flew with his wife to meet with victims' families and delivered a heartfelt speech at a memorial service. The third traumatic event in the West was a shooting at Columbine High School in Littleton, Colorado. Again the Clintons traveled to the site, with the president urging listeners to work together to "help America build a safer future because of what they had endured." Clinton used the tragic event to push for stronger gun control, but fierce opposition from the National Rifle Association and gun supporters in Congress derailed the president's efforts.

Clinton's ties with the West had political fallout. In 1992, in defeating Bush senior and Perot, he won the Democratic states of California, Oregon, and Washington, but lost the less-populated mountain and plains states. About half of Clinton's 370 electoral votes came from states west of the Mississippi. Four years later, Clinton again won the vote-rich Pacific coast states but lost the interior states in the Rockies and on the plains to Republican candidate Bob Dole, who was from Kansas.

Clinton was proud of his accomplishments in the West. He trumpeted his environmental legislation, pointed to his work for minority groups, and cherished his victories over fellow westerners—Bush and Perot in 1992 and Bob Dole in 1996. He was part of the western political contingent that led American politics from the 1980s onward.

GEORGE W. BUSH, 2001–2009
LC-DIG-PPBD-00371

GEORGE W. BUSH

Unlike his father and his siblings, George W. Bush reveled in his proud, stand-up-like-a-man western heritage. From his early years in West Texas, through his presidency and beyond, Bush emblemized the bulldog tenacity and assertion associated with western heroes. He learned early on how to govern, how to fasten on a few key issues and hold on. Of the recent presidents, he was the most western, at least symbolically.

After his close, controversial win over Al Gore in the election of 2000, Bush soon found his presidency diverted during the traumatic days and months following the violent attack of September 11, 2001, on the World Trade Center in New York City and the Pentagon in Washington, D.C. Those emotional events and the later Iraq War shaped much of Bush's presidency—similar to the way affairs in the

Middle East had dominated his father's administration. Sidetracked by foreign affairs, Bush paid limited attention to his home region.

Still, in several areas, Bush's national policies impacted the West. Particularly was this the case in legislation dealing with tax cuts, education, and immigration. As Texas governor and as president, he was committed to large tax cuts, thinking, like Ronald Reagan had, that tax cuts would stimulate the economy through expanding domestic spending. Montana conservative Democrat Max Baucus, chairman of the Senate Finance Committee, helped steer the tax reductions through Congress. Unfortunately, those large cuts hurt more than they helped the economy, sending the country into huge deficits by the end of Bush's administration.

Bush entered the White House with educational reform in mind. Gaining the support of liberal Democrat Edward Kennedy, he helped ram the No Child Left Behind program through Congress. Conservative western states, particularly those in the Rockies and on the plains, favored the demanding program much more than did the blue, or Democratic, states of the West.

Bush had always been sympathetic to immigrants, especially Hispanics. As president, he supported legislation to help undocumented Mexican workers find ways to become citizens, but he could not get the measure through Congress.

Environmental issues were not high on Bush's agenda. He did not spend much time or effort on the environment. Advisors spoke of Bush's being a "green" president, but he opposed legislation coming out of Clinton's Congress that called for the reduction of greenhouse gas emissions and refused to support Clinton's ban on road building in western wilderness areas.

No westerner played a more central role in Bush's administration than did Vice President Richard "Dick" Cheney. Born and reared in Nebraska and later in Wyoming, Cheney helped stiffen Bush's stances on tax cuts, opposition to climate change, and approach to the Iraq War.

Toward the end of Bush's second administration (2005–9), observers commented on his Texas-imprinted behavior. He was, one critic opined, an intransigent leader, a man of Alamo-style swagger. Bush convinced himself, however, that he was courageous and stout, like the fighters who held out at the mission in Texas. When Bush's popularity fell dramatically in the final years of his presidency, he happily left the White House to return to the haven of his home country in Texas.

BARACK H. OBAMA, 2009–2017
LC-DIG-PPBD-00358

BARACK H. OBAMA

Barack Obama spent approximately a dozen of his first twenty-one years in the western reaches of the West, in Hawaii and California. Once he left the region for the remainder of his college years, law school at Harvard, and early jobs on the East Coast and Chicago, he rarely spent much time in the West thereafter, save for brief vacations in Hawaii. Nor could one say he was, by and large, a "western" president. Yet a few of his national and regional policies influenced the West and its residents.

Several westerners played significant roles in Obama's attempts to implement his presidential policies. One of the most influential was Senator Harry Reid of Nevada, longtime Senate majority leader. When Obama's complicated health care bill (the Affordable Care Act) came before the Senate in 2009–10, Reid moved to fend off damaging amendments, pushing from the table anything that would water down or complicate a bill already running more than a thousand pages. Representative Nancy Pelosi of California, the Democratic Speaker of the House, although less overtly supportive of Obama, nonetheless worked assiduously to push his health care bill through the House in 2009.

Obama was the first African American—indeed, the first person of color—to occupy the White House, but he was not an outspoken leader for racial or ethnic peoples. Still, he appealed to minority voters, winning more than 70 percent of the Hispanic vote and majorities of Asian and African American voters in 2012. By the time of Obama's electoral victories in 2008 and 2012, minority groups made up more than 25 percent of the American voters. Obama did best, as have other recent Democrats, in the rich harvest of West Coast votes.

When Obama took office in 2009, he assured the country he would be a "green" president. He promised to address the detrimental effects of climate change, encourage new and beneficial modes of energy development, and rein in pollution. When Congress failed to pass his environmental legislation, he turned to the Clean Air Act of 1970 to further regulate air pollution in an attempt to reduce smog, soot, and carbon excesses in the atmosphere. When the Deepwater British Petroleum oil spill fouled huge areas of the Gulf of Mexico and Obama was wrongly criticized for the disastrous event, he became more cautious in regard to offshore drilling. Toward the end of his administration, he did open other, previously protected wilderness areas of Alaska for limited drilling.

What will Obama's legacy be? How will historians and biographers evaluate his influence on the country, and on the West specifically? If the health care legislation continues to benefit millions of Americans and if it becomes increasingly clear that his handling of the recession early in his presidency helped the country, his legacy will be on solid ground. Both of these achievements, of course, were national—and even international—in scope, but they have also greatly influenced the American West. Undoubtedly, the political euphoria that accompanied Obama into the White House in 2009 diminished considerably as his first administration wore on. Still, he survived the lowest points of his presidency and began to climb back as he worked on other policies that influenced both the country as a whole and the American West.

In the closing days of his eight-year administration, Barack Obama made a decision that exhibited both long-range and present-day implications for under-standing presidential connections to the American West. Using his executive authority and provisions of the Antiquities Act of 1906, an act that he used more than any previous president had, Obama set aside important historical sites and expanded on wilderness and national monument areas in Oregon and California.

Obama's actions were of more than contemporary significance. His 2016 decision represented the huge shift that had taken place in presidential actions vis-á-vis the West. If earlier presidents—Thomas Jefferson, Andrew Jackson, James Polk, and Abraham Lincoln—had purchased, taken, or given away huge expanses of what became the American West, later chief executives such as Theodore Roosevelt, Jimmy Carter, and Barack Obama, among others, set aside hundreds of thousands of acres as protected parks, wilderness, and historical monument areas. For more than two centuries, presidential actions have clearly shaped the West. Whether as procurers or protectors, White House leaders have played large roles in the history of the American West. Seeing and understanding these vital links between the country's presidents and the American West enlarges the meanings of national and regional history.

FOR FURTHER READING

George H. W. Bush

Bush, George H. W. *All the Best, George Bush: My Life in Letters and Other Writings.* Rev ed. New York: Scribner, 2013.

Bush, George W. *41: A Portrait of My Father.* New York: Crown, 2014.

Greene, John Robert. *The Presidency of George H. W. Bush.* 2d ed., rev. and exp. Lawrence: University Press of Kansas, 2015.

Meacham, Jon. *Destiny and Power: The American Odyssey of George Herbert Walker Bush.* New York: Random House, 2015.

Mervin, David. *George Bush and the Guardianship Presidency.* New York: Palgrave Macmillan, 1996.

Parmet, Herbert S. *George Bush: The Life of a Lone Star Yankee.* New York: Scribner, 1997.

Sunumu, John H. *The Quiet Man: The Indispensable Presidency of George Bush.* New York: Broadside Books, 2015.

Wicker, Tom. *George Herbert Walker Bush.* New York: Penguin Viking, 2004.

William J. "Bill" Clinton

Branch, Taylor. *The Clinton Tapes: Wrestling History with the President*. New York: Simon & Schuster, 2009.

Clinton, Bill. *My Life*. New York: Alfred A. Knopf, 2004.

Harris, John F. *The Survivor: Bill Clinton in the White House*. New York: Random House, 2005.

Klein, Joe. *The Natural: The Misunderstood Presidency of Bill Clinton*. New York: Doubleday, 2002.

Maney, Patrick J. *Bill Clinton: New Gilded Age President*. Lawrence: University Press of Kansas, 2017.

Maraniss, David. *First in His Class: A Biography of Bill Clinton*. New York: Simon & Schuster, 1995.

Morris, Roger. *Partners in Power: The Clintons and Their America*. New York: Henry Holt, 1996.

Nelson, Michael, et al., eds. *42: Inside the Presidency of Bill Clinton*. Ithaca, NY: Cornell University Press, 2016.

Renshon, Stanley. *High Hopes: The Clinton Presidency and the Politics of Ambition*. New York: New York University Press, 1996.

Smith, Sally Bedell. *For Love of Politics: Bill and Hillary Clinton; The White House Years*. New York: Random House, 2007.

Tomasky, Michael. *Billy Clinton: The 42nd President, 1993–2001*. New York: Macmillan, 2017.

George W. Bush

Bush, George W. *A Charge to Keep.* New York: William Morrow, 1999.

———. *Decision Points*. New York: Crown, 2010.

Draper, Robert. *Dead Certain: The Presidency of George W. Bush*. New York: Free Press, 2007.

Frum, David. *The Right Man: The Surprise Presidency of George W. Bush*. New York: Random House, 2003.

Greenstein, Fred I., ed. *The George W. Bush Presidency: An Early Assessment*. Baltimore: Johns Hopkins University Press, 2003.

Ivins, Molly, and Lou Dubose. *Shrub: The Short but Happy Political Life of George W. Bush*. New York: Vintage, 2000.

Mann, James. *George W. Bush*. New York: Henry Holt, 2015.

Zelizer, Julian E. *The Presidency of George Bush: A First Historical Assessment*. Princeton, NJ: Princeton University Press, 2010.

Barack H. Obama

Alter, Jonathan. *The Center Holds: Obama and His Enemies.* New York: Simon & Schuster, 2013.

Garrow, David. *Rising Star: The Making of Barack Obama.* New York: William Morrow, 2017.

Kloppenberg, James T. *Reading Obama: Dreams, Hope, and the American Political Tradition.* Princeton, NJ: Princeton University Press, 2012.

Maraniss, David. *Barack Obama: The Story.* New York: Simon & Schuster, 2012.

Obama, Barack H. *The Audacity of Hope: Thoughts on Reclaiming the American Dream.* New York: Crown, 2006.

———. *Dreams from My Father: A Story of Race and Inheritance.* New York: Three Rivers Press, 1995, 2004.

Todd, Chuck. *The Stranger: Barack Obama in the White House.* Boston: Little, Brown, 2014.

CONCLUSION

The introduction to this book encouraged readers to notice continuities between the western policies of ten presidents who were especially significant in shaping the American West during the past two centuries. In this conclusion, the authors would like readers to consider some of the changes that have occurred in the American West and in the American presidency during the past two hundred or so years, and the ways newer attitudes and realities may redefine future presidents' views of, and interactions with, western issues.

Especially important changes relate to the land itself and the people. U.S. presidents no longer pursue additions of land to the West. The annexation of Hawaii in 1898 marked the nation's last acquisition of land, and the admission of Alaska and Hawaii, both in 1959, completed the union of fifty states. Along with these actions came the end of government's need to control or eradicate indigenous peoples in the West. Attention has turned instead to establishing policies that will help the West's polyglot population live together in some degree of harmony and protect the weak from the aggressive.

Nor is it any longer necessary for presidents to urge people to move westward. The census of 1910 indicated that 24.8 million Americans resided in the nineteen states on or west of the Mississippi River. A century later, in 2010, those states, with the addition of New Mexico, Arizona, Hawaii, and Alaska, were home to 116.2 million persons. Certainly, this influx of people has resulted in some western areas in troublesome situations, such as overcrowding, poverty, crime, and drug abuse. Especially since the 1960s, presidents and their Congresses have tried to help in the fields of education, health, welfare, and civil rights, but the issues remain.

Despite progress, a number of unfortunate holdovers from earlier eras continue to demand attention. One is the reservation system for Native Americans. Despite government programs and the gambling casinos that financially alleviate some reservations' problems, poverty and disease continue to disadvantage many American Indians. Another negative legacy is discriminatory treatment of people of color, not just Native Americans, but Asian Americans, black Americans, Mexican

Americans, and Hispanics as well. A hopeful sign is that public thinking no longer stamps these groups as automatically inferior and deserving of unequal treatment. And a major advance is that many people of color have formed such action coalitions as the American Indian Movement, or AIM, which lobbies representatives of local, state, and federal governments, including presidents. Because the largest number of American people of color live in the West, their organizations exert pressures that are difficult for anyone making western policy to ignore.

Air travel and transport have added new dimensions in the development of transportation in the West. Because so many roads now cross the sky, western transportation has to focus on airports, on takeoff and landing fields, and, increasingly, on air-traffic control. For example, training of traffic controllers has to mesh with military demands and needs. After all, such conflicts as World War II, Vietnam, and crises in the Middle East have dramatically turned much of the West into staging areas for military personnel, ordnance, and heavy equipment. One listing of U.S. Army installations at the turn of the twenty-first century shows some eighty sites in the West, as opposed to eighty-two in all the rest of the states. Army listings include forts, camps, ammunition plants, chemical depots, proving grounds, training bases and centers, and a missile range and demolition range in New Mexico, all of which give a new meaning to the title, Commander-in-Chief.

In the political realm, the West also has undergone numerous transitions, going from a developing frontier to a major player in American politics. Nowhere is the growing influence of the West on U.S. presidents and national politics more evident than in the expanding number of electoral votes in the West. In 1800, no electoral votes existed west of the Mississippi River, but by 2016, the West had amassed 230 votes out of a total of 538. Because the two largest states, population-wise—Texas and California—as well as other growth areas, are in the West, the region's electoral heft will presumably continue to grow. As a result of the West's increased weight in the electoral college, presidents have to reach out more and more for ballot-box support from western areas and from such groups as black and Hispanic voters.

Another of these growing constituencies is western women, both white and of color. Except for Native American women and indigenous women in Alaska and Hawaii, American women gained the right to vote in 1920 by the authority of the Nineteenth Amendment to the U.S. Constitution. But it was in the West that woman suffrage, as the movement was called, made its first, and definitive, gains. As early as 1869, Wyoming Territory granted the right to vote to approximately one thousand women. The next states, all in the West, to give women the vote were

Colorado (1893), Utah (1895), Idaho (1896), Washington (1910), California (1911), and Oregon, Kansas, and Arizona (1912). The West's attitude toward woman suffrage added to the region's image as liberal and democratic. In fact, western women had long exerted more rights than women in other parts of the country, especially in employment, education, land ownership, ease of divorce, and officeholding. Today, every president recognizes women as important potential supporters and as a source of appointees to national office. Accordingly, the country's chief executives will continue to include planks in their platforms aimed at western women.

The importance of the West in national politics is particularly evident in the election of western presidents, especially after 1948. In the seventeen elections from 1948 to 2012, candidates who were either born west of the Mississippi or who had spent at least a dozen years of their earlier lives in the West won all the presidential contests, save for New Englander John F. Kennedy and southerner Jimmy Carter. In addition, in more than half these elections, the defeated candidates were also from west of the Mississippi. By the twenty-first century, the American West was not only home to most American presidents, but vice presidents, cabinet members, and influential members of Congress also tended to come from the West.

Lastly, although preservation and conservation remain a priority of presidents in dealing with the West, the emphasis has shifted from the establishment of historic and natural sites to the protection and wise use of western resources. Environmental groups and residents in specific areas often oppose management's decisions. An example is the Trans-Alaska Pipeline System, or TAPS, whose operations are often criticized by environmental organizations as well as by Alaska Indians.

In summary, we would argue that sorting out continuities and changes—which we hope readers will do on their own—makes apparent the intricacy of relationships between the West and American presidents. To gain this wide view, the definition of the West here has been inclusive. Despite scholarly controversies over exactly what constitutes the West in any given era, looking at the entire trans-Mississippi region and beyond gives the most comprehensive, and perhaps the most insightful, perspective. This interpretation of the term "West" also shows the diversity of the West—how Texas is not California, the Southwest not the Rocky Mountains, the plains states not the West Coast, and Alaska clearly not Hawaii.

Against this inclusive West we have set sketches of ten presidents. Information has included a brief biography of an individual president, a snapshot of his relations with the West, and an evaluation of his actions on the West, both then and later. The intended outcome is to reveal the tremendous effect presidential policies can have on the West and whether a president's looking West had a favorable outcome, or not, on the region. As far as we know, this method has not been attempted before. We hope that our "cross-continental" approach has helped readers picture a larger West, one linked to, and influenced by, the dominant figure in the Oval Office, the White House, and the nation.

FOR FURTHER READING

U.S. PRESIDENTS

Beschloss, Michael. *Presidential Courage: Brave Leaders and How They Changed America*. New York: Simon & Schuster, 2007.

Brinkley, Alan, and Davis Dyer, eds. *The American Presidency*. Boston: Houghton Mifflin, 2004.

DeGregorio, William A., ed. *The Complete Book of U.S. Presidents*. 8th ed. New York: Barricade Books, 2013.

Freidel, Frank, ed. *Our Country's Presidents*. Washington, DC: National Geographic Society, 1966.

Graham, Otis. *Presidents and the American Environment*. Lawrence: University Press of Kansas, 2015.

Greenstein, Fred I. *The Presidential Difference: Leadership Style from FDR to Clinton*. New York: Free Press, 2000.

Kunhardt, Philip B., Jr., et al., eds. *The American President*. New York: Riverhead Books, 1999.

Leuchtenburg, William. *The American Presidency: From Teddy Roosevelt to Bill Clinton*. New York: Oxford University Press, 2015.

McPherson, James, and David Rubel, eds. *"To the Best of My Ability": The American Presidents*. New York: Dorling Kindersley, 2000.

Neustadt, Richard E. *Presidential Power and the Modern Presidents*. Rev. ed. New York: Free Press, 1991.

Rossiter, Clinton. *The American Presidency*. 2nd ed. New York: Harcourt, Brace and World, 1960.

Skowronek, Stephen. *The Politics Presidents Make: Leadership from John Adams to Bill Clinton*. Cambridge, MA: Harvard University Press, 1997.

Thomas, Norman C., et al., eds. *The Politics of the Presidency*. 3d ed. Washington, DC: Congressional Quarterly, 1993.

THE AMERICAN WEST

Etulain, Richard W. *Beyond the Missouri: The Story of the American West*. Albuquerque: University of New Mexico Press, 2006.

Etulain, Richard W., and Michael P. Malone. *The American West: A Modern History, 1900 to the Present*. 2nd ed. Lincoln: University of Nebraska Press, 2007.

Hine, Robert V., and John Mack Faragher. *The American West: A New Interpretive History*. New Haven: Yale University Press, 2000.

Limerick, Patricia Nelson. *The Legacy of Conquest: The Unbroken Past of the American West.* New York: Norton, 1987.

Lowitt, Richard. *The New Deal and the West.* Bloomington: Indiana University Press, 1984.

Lowitt, Richard, ed. *Politics in the Postwar American West.* Norman: University of Oklahoma Press, 1995.

Nash, Gerald D. *The American West in the Twentieth Century: A Short History of an Urban Oasis.* 1973. Reprint, Albuquerque: University of New Mexico Press, 1977.

Nugent, Walter. *Into the West: The Story of Its People.* New York: Alfred A. Knopf, 1999.

Pomeroy, Earl. *The American Far West in the Twentieth Century.* New Haven: Yale University Press, 2008.

———. *The Pacific Slope: A History of California, Oregon, Washington, Idaho, Utah, and Nevada.* New York: Alfred A. Knopf, 1965.

Prucha, Frances Paul. *The Great Father: The United States Government and the American Indians.* 2 vols. Lincoln: University of Nebraska Press, 1984.

Riley, Glenda. *Building and Breaking Families in the American West.* Albuquerque: University of New Mexico Press, 1996.

———. *Inventing the American Woman: An Inclusive History.* 2 vols. 4th ed. Wheeling, IL: Harlan Davidson, 2007.

———. *Women and Nature: Saving the "Wild" West.* Lincoln: University of Nebraska Press, 1999.

White, Richard. *"It's Your Misfortune and None of My Own": A New History of the American West.* Norman: University of Oklahoma Press, 1991.

INDEX